Wetlands

An Introduction to Ecology, the Law, and Permitting

Second Edition

THEDA BRADDOCK

With contributions from Lisa Berntsen

Government Institutes
An imprint of
THE SCARECROW PRESS, INC.
Lanham, Maryland • Toronto • Plymouth, UK
2007

 **Government Institutes**

Published in the United States of America
by Government Institutes, an imprint of The Scarecrow Press, Inc.
A wholly owned subsidiary of
The Rowman & Littlefield Publishing Group, Inc.
4501 Forbes Boulevard, Suite 200
Lanham, Maryland 20706
www.govinstpress.com/
Estover Road
Plymouth PL6 7PY
United Kingdom

British Library Cataloguing in Publication Information Available
Library of Congress Cataloging-in-Publication Data
Fowler, Theda Braddock.
  Wetlands : an introduction to ecology, the law, and permitting / Theda Braddock ; with contributions from Lisa
Berntsen. — 2nd ed.
      p. cm.
  Includes bibliographical references and index.
  ISBN-13: 978-0-86587-018-5 (pbk. : alk. paper)
  ISBN-10: 0-86587-018-7 (pbk. : alk. paper)
  1. Wetlands—Law and legislation—United States. 2. Wetland ecology—United States. I. Berntsen, Lisa. II. Title.
KF5624.B73 2007
346.7304'6918—dc22   2006100625

Dedicated to Jenny, Little Theda, and Edward

Contents

Table of Cases

CHAPTER ONE

Political Perspectives

The source of Congress's power to regulate wetlands is Article I, §8, Clause 3 of the United States Constitution, the "Commerce Clause," which requires that before the federal government can regulate an activity, it must have an effect on interstate commerce. The Commerce Clause is broadly construed because so many activities either have an actual immediate effect on interstate commerce or might have an effect. Indeed, the Commerce Clause was the original source of authority for such diverse federal laws as the original civil rights legislation, because racial segregation has an effect on interstate commerce. The federal authority under the Commerce Clause for the U.S. Army Corps of Engineers' assertion of jurisdiction over wetlands can be found in the words of §404 of the Clean Water Act[1] itself, in which the use, destruction, or degradation of wetlands "could affect interstate commerce."

It has been over ten years since the first edition of this book was published. Population pressure, particularly along the coastlines, continues to force developers to look toward less and less desirable land for development purposes. As a result, now more than ever, wetlands are in the crosshairs. And far from being the dark, odorous, disease-breeding miasmas once thought,[2] wetlands are now known to be an important, vital natural resource in their own right as well as a supplier to many other environmental systems.

The basic question becomes whether we should allow all wetlands to be filled in, as was the official government policy a century ago, or whether we should protect this dwindling resource at the expense of other important societal goals. Perhaps there will be less unproductive dissension if the real estate developer understands the real utility that wetlands provide to the natural landscape and if the scientist and the environmentalist understand the difficulties the courts have had in melding traditional concepts of the property rights of individual landowners with environmental science and the public good.

As we considered how to explain our position to two groups in traditional opposition to each other, we thought it might be helpful to explain the science and the law in terms that both sides could understand. Thus, we have opened the book with a chapter on basic wetland science, explaining what wetlands are, how they fit into the complex natural scheme, and the particular functions and values of wetlands themselves, followed by a chapter on the scientific classification of wetlands. In chapter 4 we describe how wetlands are delineated, which has been the source of much confusion and hard feeling between the two groups. Following that description, we added a chapter about §404 permits including a description of the permit requirement, the activities that require a permit, those activities that are exempt, and finally, a description of nationwide and general permits. Chapter 6 describes the permit

---

1. 33 U.S.C. §§ 1251 *et seq.* (originally entitled the Federal Water Pollution Control Act of 1972 but now popularly known as the "Clean Water Act").
2. Wetlands were even dubbed "nuisances." *Leovy v. United States*, 177 U.S. 621, 44 L.Ed. 914, 20 S.Ct. 797 (1900).

process itself and how the permits will be enforced through enforcement procedures and administrative penalties. Chapter 7 describes litigation and defenses under the Clean Water Act, especially the concept of regulatory takings. The final chapter returns to where this one begins—with the ongoing dispute over the extent of Congress's power to regulate wetlands. The controversy can only be resolved by a fuller understanding of the positions of landowners, wetland scientists, attorneys, and environmentalists on both sides of the fence.

Even though we have tried to give our readers a clear understanding of the Clean Water Act, it is equally important to recognize that wetlands are only part of the vast ecosystem and that the Clean Water Act is only a fairly recent expression of legal doctrines, some of which are thousands of years old and some of which are unique to recent American jurisprudence. Further, other federal statutes, especially the Endangered Species Act, frequently take over to protect wetlands as habitat for threatened and endangered species when the Clean Water Act fails.

For a society to call itself civilized in this modern era, however, it must address whether its practices are sustainable over the long term. The natural environment is not a depreciable asset to be discarded when its useful life has expired. Nor is the natural environment infinite in its capacity to absorb assaults on its functions. As we have learned especially in the past decade, all destruction of natural resources will have to be restored, perhaps many years from now, but restored nonetheless. It comes down to a moral and ethical question of how much destruction one generation should pass on to the next.

CHAPTER TWO

Appearance of Wetlands

The majority of people probably imagine a wetland as an area of open water fringed with wet or reedy plants. Indeed, that is one type of a wetland that is commonly encountered, but there are many other kinds of wetlands found throughout the world. Wetlands vary widely in appearance because they are located in many different types of environments. In fact, many wetlands do not even appear wet throughout the entire year.

Simply stated, a wetland is an area that has waterlogged soils for a portion of the year. Broadly defined, a wetland is a transitional zone between dry land and water. Within this zone, the level of water varies throughout the year, and this seasonal fluctuation of water level causes chemical reactions to occur in the soil. The interplay between water level and chemical reactions in the soil creates a unique environment where only certain plants can grow well. Therefore, the appearance a wetland presents depends on regional and local factors, including geography, topography, climate, the amount of water available, soil type, and vegetation (Briuer 1993).

Wetlands are found on every continent except Antarctica (Mitsch and Gosselink 1993) and are known by different names. In the far north regions where tundra is found, wetlands can be referred to as muskegs. Below the tundra region and in the lower forty-eight United States, wetlands fall into four basic descriptive types: marshes, swamps, bogs, and fens. Marshes are wetlands with soft-stemmed vegetation. Swamps have woody vegetation. Bogs are found in lakes that are slowly filling in with vegetation that often contains evergreen shrubs and trees and moss. Fens are peat-dominated wetlands where grasses, sedges, reeds, and wildflowers also grow (U.S. Army Corps of Engineers 1998). For descriptive purposes, wetlands can be placed within one of these four types. However, subsequent sections of this text will provide scientific information in order to make further distinctions among the types of wetlands.

Hydrology

Hydrology is the primary factor determining the existence of wetlands; in other words, without water there are no wetlands. This concept is simple, but the ways in which water moves through the landscape and interacts with the physical and biological environment make wetland hydrology an extremely complex subject. This complexity is due in part to wetlands' intermediate position between terrestrial and aquatic systems and to seasonal and longer-term climatic fluctuations.

Wetland hydrology largely controls the unique biological and geochemical processes characteristic of wetlands. Two methods of hydrologic input are the most significant, the hydroperiod (or seasonal hydrology) of the wetland and the water chemistry of the incoming water. Hydrology also strongly influences

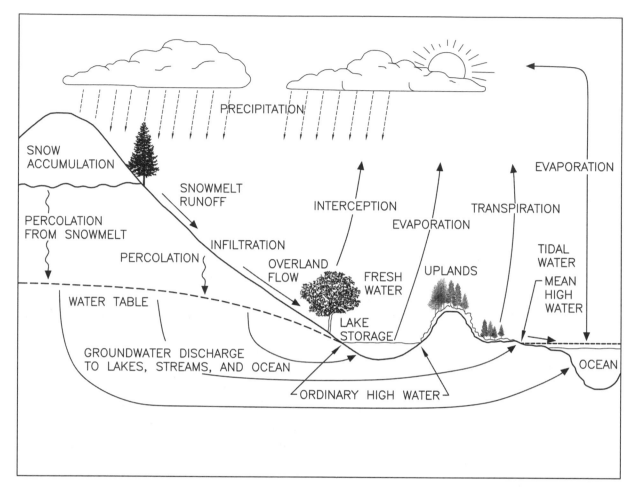

Figure 2.1.   Schematic Diagram of Hydrologic Cycle adapted from Dunne and Leopold (1978). Wetlands may occur throughout the terrestrial and intertidal portion of the diagram.

soil type and soil processes. Lastly, wetland hydrology is the primary determinant for the vegetation community that a given wetland supports. All of these factors determine the functions and values of a given wetland. Hence, wetland hydrology has long been the basis for wetland classification systems.

The manner in which water enters and leaves a wetland, which has been termed the hydrologic pathway, determines the hydrology of a given wetland (Mitsch and Gosselink 1993). Wetlands are components of the hydrologic cycle (figure 2.1).

The hydroperiod (i.e., the seasonal fluctuations of hydrology on an annual as well as a long-term basis) is another important aspect of the hydrologic pathway. Hydroperiod greatly influences the rates and types of processes taking place in a wetland during the course of a year. Hydroperiod and climate are also the prime determinants controlling the type of wetland plant species present in a given wetland.

Vegetation

Plants need oxygen for respiration. Nonwetland plants absorb oxygen through their root systems. Wetland plants, however, must adapt to the lack of oxygen in their environment. For example, sedges and reeds have hollow stems to allow quick transfer of oxygen up and down the plant; mangrove trees have much of their root systems above the water level; and cypress trees have "knees" of roots above the surface of the water. Plants that have adapted to growing in hydric (i.e., waterlogged for a portion of the year) soil are called hydrophytes.

The saturated conditions of wetlands, which affect biogeochemical conditions in wetland soils, also profoundly influence plants. Wetland or hydrophytic (water-loving) plants have evolved a range of adaptations to cope with wetland conditions. These adaptations, or hydrophytic characteristics, are most pronounced in species occupying continuously saturated soils, which are termed "obligate" wetland plants (see chapter 3). Hydrophytic characteristics are less pronounced in species that occupy seasonally saturated wetlands, and upland plants cannot survive in soils saturated for more than several weeks (Reed 1988; USDA National Resources Conservation Service 2005).

The primary factor affecting plants in wetland environments is the absence or low level of soil oxygen. Plant roots require oxygen for vital metabolic processes and without that oxygen suffer root anoxia. Wetland species have evolved specialized cell structures that permit diffusion of oxygen from the aerial portions of the plant down into the roots. These "aerenchymous" tissues are most pronounced in obligate wetland species. The biogeochemical transformations in wetland soils also affect other aspects of plant biology from nutrient uptake to reproduction. In addition, wetlands are subjected to regular or irregular periods of drying. Salts in marine and estuarine tidal waters are an additional stress that has required elaborate adaptations. These combined effects require both physiological and ecological adaptations for plant and animal life (Mitsch and Gosselink 1993). For a more detailed discussion the reader is referred to the cited reference.

Soils

As noted above, a wetland has waterlogged soil for a portion of the year. This hydric soil is an indicator of whether or not an area is a wetland. When the soil is wet or saturated, there is little free space between the soil particles for oxygen. Saturated soils often become anaerobic, a term to describe the absence of oxygen. Bacteria living in this oxygen-free environment cause the soil to exhibit the rotten-egg smell of hydrogen sulfide. In addition, chemical reactions occur in soils that are frequently or regularly saturated and manifest as different-colored mottles (patches of different-colored soil) depending on the dominant elements in the soil matrix.

In seasonally saturated wetland mineral soils, the soil column typically exhibits a gray matrix with interspersed reddish mottles. When found at or near the surface, this coloration is also a diagnostic feature of wetland mineral soils; the gray matrix results from the prevailing saturated conditions (reduced iron and manganese giving the color), and the red or orange mottles result from oxygen diffusion into the soil column during the dry season when the water table is lower. Other minerals turn parts of the soil black, brown, red, or even bluish gray. These color features are not present in all wetland soils. Organic (peaty) and sandy wetland soils do not exhibit these diagnostic color features.

The gleyed (or gray-colored) and mottled mineral soil color features are indicative of the range of reducing environments in wetlands and the type of chemical transformations that can occur in such environments. What are perhaps more important in terms of beneficial wetland functions are other associated anaerobic processes and their effects on other elements and compounds such as the nutrients (nitrogen and phosphorous) and carbon (Mitsch and Gosselink 1993). For a more detailed discussion, the reader is referred to the cited reference.

History of Wetlands in the United States

When settlers first began to populate the United States, it is estimated that the area comprising the current fifty states contained approximately 393 million acres of wetlands, of which about 220 million acres were located in the lower forty-eight states (Mitsch and Gosselink 1993). Prior to the mid-twentieth century a wetland was considered a bad, unhealthy environment. Wetlands were considered places that caused malaria, impediments to land and crop development, and even dwelling places for vile and scary creatures as exemplified by early Hollywood movies. *The Creature from the Black Lagoon* (1954) is a prime example of a film of this genre, where an unknown and mysterious thing, shaped like a human, caused havoc and death, and therefore needed to be destroyed. Of course, the origin of the creature was in a black, backwater swamp where people were afraid to venture.

In the nineteenth century Congress put forward the Swamp Land Acts, which granted states the authority to reclaim swamps to reduce destruction caused by flooding and to eliminate mosquito-breeding areas (Shaw and Fredine 1956). The willingness of the people to respond to governmental direction regarding wetland destruction resulted in a loss of approximately 53 percent of the original wetland area in the lower forty-eight states in about 200 years (Dahl 1990). The rate of wetland loss between the mid-1970s to mid-1980s slowed as an awareness of ecological, social, and economic benefits of wetlands began to emerge (Dahl and Johnson 1991). During this time period, wetlands came to be recognized as providing important benefits for waterfowl production; improving water quality; reducing flooding; and retaining sediments, nutrients, and metals (Clairain 2002).

Wetland Protection

In the 1970s the value of wetlands was being discussed in scientific circles and symposia (Helfgott et al. 1973). New positive public awareness increased the benefits of wetlands from the functional values identified above to also having societal value (USDA Natural Resources Conservation Service 2005). This shift is clearly shown in 1977 with Executive Order 11990, where wetland value was clearly changed to allow for wetland protection.

> By virtue of the authority vested in me by the Constitution and statutes of the United States of America, and as President of the United States of America, in furtherance of the National Environmental Policy Act of 1969, as amended (42 U.S.C. 4321 et seq.), in order to avoid to the extent possible the long and short term adverse impacts associated with the destruction or modification of wetlands and to avoid direct or indirect support of new construction in wetlands wherever there is a practicable alternative, it is hereby ordered as follows:
>
> Section 1. (a) Each agency shall provide leadership and shall take action to minimize the destruction, loss or degradation of wetlands, and to preserve and enhance the natural and beneficial values of wetlands in carrying out the agency's responsibilities for (1) acquiring, managing, and disposing of Federal lands and facilities; and (2) providing Federally undertaken, financed, or assisted construction and improvements; and (3) conducting Federal activities and programs affecting land use, including but not limited to, water and related land resources planning, regulating, and licensing activities.

In 1977, when announcing Executive Order 11990, President Jimmy Carter's statement regarding wetlands documented the shifting public perspective on wetlands.

The Nation's coastal and inland wetlands are vital natural resources of critical importance to the people of this country. Wetlands are areas of great natural productivity, hydrological utility, and environmental diversity, providing natural flood control, improved water quality, recharge of aquifers, flow stabilization of streams and rivers, and habitat for fish and wildlife resources. Wetlands contribute to the production of agricultural products and timber and provide recreational, scientific, and esthetic resources of national interest.

This Executive Order began the theme of "no net loss" of wetland acreage, function, and value at a national level. Over time, states, counties, and cities have enacted laws to regulate activities in wetlands and provide benefit for protection and preservation. Many national programs are in place to acquire wetlands to protect them and provide an avenue for public appreciation. Public education and wetland regulation have considerably slowed the rate of wetland loss. In the conterminous United States approximately 58,500 acres of wetlands were lost each year between 1986 and 1997 (USEPA n.d.). This rate, while large, is smaller than in the preceding decades.

The U.S. Fish and Wildlife Service operates an entire discipline whose mandate is to manage large wetland complexes for migratory waterfowl. Private and nonprofit entities are also participating in managing wetlands, either on their own or in partnership with the government.

In the 1990s the federal government and some states initiated wetland restoration programs to return a lost wetland or a degraded wetland to a normally functioning system (Institute for Wetland & Environmental Education & Research n.d.). These programs are growing and now play an active role in nationally increasing wetland acreage and the function and value of that wetland acreage (Institute for Wetland & Environmental Education & Research n.d).

Defining a Wetland

A wetland is a transition area between an aquatic and a terrestrial system where the water table is at or near the surface for part of the year. Multiple definitions of wetlands have been developed over the last forty years. The first definitions of a wetland had a scientific emphasis; later definitions included more of a legal foundation. Although the search for a clear definition has evolved over time, the main element considered in the definition of a wetland is the presence of water.

Developing a definition of a wetland that is all-inclusive is rather difficult. First of all, because a wetland is a transitional area between upland and aquatic environments, defining the boundary between these two environments is challenging. Second, defining many nontidal wetlands is complicated by seasonal variations as well as by hydrologic variables, such as precipitation patterns and other effects of climate, that can occur in cycles even longer than seasonal. Third, there is an enormous variation in wetlands between geographic areas as a result of differences in climate, geohydrology, and plant communities.

Consequently, wetland definitions often reflect the purpose for which they were developed. Earlier definitions were developed primarily for descriptive and/or classification purposes that could facilitate inventory and research. Soil scientists tended to define wetlands in terms of soil characteristics. Hydrologists would describe wetlands based on water levels and fluctuations in the groundwater table. Botanists, of course, would focus on plants (Lefor and Kennard 1977). In the last decade, the need for a legally binding and scientifically defensible definition has become critical as the battle over wetland protection and regulation has escalated.

The most common definition accepted by all areas of government in the United States, including government agencies at various regulatory levels, is a simple definition. It was initially developed by the

U.S. Army Corps of Engineers[1] and the U.S. Environmental Protection Agency (EPA).[2] Its text is as follows.

> Wetlands are those areas that are inundated or saturated by surface or ground water at a frequency and duration sufficient to support, and that under normal circumstances do support, a prevalence of vegetation typically adapted for life in saturated soil conditions.

Subsequent to the development of this definition, a distinction has been made between biological and regulated (or jurisdictional) wetlands. Biological wetlands meet the definition of a wetland as defined above. Regulated wetlands are biological wetlands that are also legally defined as wetlands.

There are over fifty different recognized wetland definitions and classification systems (U.S. Fish and Wildlife Service 1976). A history and sampling of differing international definitions includes those from the United States, Canada, and the international community.

CIRCULAR 39

An early wetland definition was developed by the U.S. Fish and Wildlife Service for the purposes of developing a wetland inventory in 1956. This publication, *Wetlands of the United States, Their Extent and Value for Waterfowl and Other Wildlife*, is better known by its government document designation, Circular 39 (Shaw and Fredine 1956). The definition of a wetland from Circular 39 follows.

> The term "wetlands" . . . refers to lowlands covered with shallow and sometimes temporary or intermittent waters. They are referred to by such names as marshes, swamps, bogs, wet meadows, potholes, sloughs, and river-overflow lands. Shallow lakes and ponds, usually with emergent vegetation as a conspicuous feature, are included in the definition, but the permanent waters of streams, reservoirs, and deep water lakes are not included. Neither are water areas that are so temporary as to have little or no effect on the development of moist soil vegetation.

The definition from Circular 39 clearly places wetlands between upland and aquatic environments. However, this system is biased toward waterfowl habitat and, therefore, toward the larger and wetter end of the wetland spectrum or continuum. Smaller, isolated, or topographically higher wetlands such as spring seeps or fens would not necessarily fit within the parameters of this definition. Nevertheless, this definition was effective for this early inventory of wetlands in the United States, and it has served as the primary basis for subsequent wetland definitions.

CANADIAN DEFINITION

The Canadian definition of a wetland was developed in 1979 also for the purposes of creating a wetland inventory. This definition is significant because of its emphasis on a range of hydrologic regimes, wetland or hydric soils, and the biogeochemical processes characteristic of wetlands (Tarnocai 1980).

---

1. 33 Federal Register 328.3 1982.
2. 40 Federal Register 230.3 1980.

Wetland is defined as land having the water table at, near, or above the land surface or which is saturated for a long enough period to promote wetland or aquatic processes as indicated by hydric soils, hydrophytic vegetation, and various kinds of biological activity which are adapted to the wet environment.

COWARDIN DEFINITION

In 1979, the U.S. Fish and Wildlife Service published a wetland definition in the Classification of Wetlands and Deepwater Habitats of the United States (Cowardin et al. 1979). This definition and classification system served as the basis for the National Wetland Inventory, which has been administered by the U.S. Fish and Wildlife Service. The wetland inventory is based on interpretation of colored infrared aerial photography at 1:60,000 scale. The Cowardin system definition was developed by an interdisciplinary team of biologists, ecologists, and geologists and is broad in scope.

> Wetlands are lands transitional between terrestrial and aquatic systems where the water table is usually at or near the surface or the land is covered by shallow water. . . . Wetlands must have one or more of the following three attributes: (1) at least periodically, the land supports predominantly hydrophytes, (2) the substrate is predominantly undrained hydric soil, and (3) the substrate is nonsoil and is saturated with water or covered by shallow water at some time during the growing season of each year.

The Cowardin definition is significant because it is very comprehensive. It includes areas that otherwise would have been considered aquatic habitats. In addition, although the Cowardin definition introduces a three-parameter approach to defining a wetland, it requires that only one of the three parameters be met in order for an area to be classified as a wetland. The Cowardin system is the most widely accepted descriptive system for wetlands in the United States. The system is discussed in more detail in chapter 3.

In 1995, the National Research Council developed yet another reference definition of a wetland.

> A wetland is an ecosystem that depends on constant or recurrent, shallow inundation or saturation at or near the surface of the substrate. The minimum essential characteristics of a wetland are recurrent, sustained inundation or saturation at or near the surface and the presence of physical, chemical, and biological features reflective of the recurrent, sustained inundation or saturation. Common diagnostic features of wetlands are hydric soils and hydrophytic vegetation. These features will be present except where specific physiochemical, biotic, or anthropogenic factors have removed them or prevented their development (National Research Council Committee on Characterization of Wetlands 1995).

While this definition was developed more recently than the Cowardin (1979) definition, the Cowardin system is still the most commonly used in the United States.

INTERNATIONAL WETLAND DEFINITIONS

A review of wetland definitions used internationally reveals that most countries use either the Cowardin definition noted above or a definition known as the Ramsar definition developed from the Convention on Wetlands held in Ramsar, Iran, in 1971. Resulting from this convention was an intergovernmental treaty signed to promote the conservation and wise use of wetlands and their resources. In 2002 this was solidified into a Mission Statement: "The Convention's mission is the conservation and wise use of all wetlands through local, regional and national actions and international cooperation, as a contribution toward achieving sustainable development throughout the world" (Ramsar Convention on Wetlands 2002). More on Ramsar and its international mission can be found at their website, www.ramsar.org. The following is the international definition of wetlands as defined by the Ramsar organization.

> Wetlands are areas of marsh, fen, peatland, or water, whether natural or artificial, permanent or temporary, with water that is static or flowing, fresh, brackish or salt, including areas of marine water the depth of which at low tide does not exceed six meters and may incorporate riparian and coastal zones adjacent to the wetlands, and islands or bodies of marine water deeper than six meters at low tide lying within the wetlands.

The Ramsar definition incorporates marine areas in deeper water than the conventional Cowardin definition of wetlands.

REGULATORY DEFINITION

The definitions discussed above have been primarily developed for purposes of inventorying wetlands, and, as such, they are not suitable for legally defining the boundaries of an individual wetland in the field for regulatory control. In order to regulate the dredge and fill permits allowed under §404 of the 1977 Clean Water Act, a more concise definition of a wetland was required.

The relatively simple definitions developed in 1980 by the EPA and in 1982 by the U.S. Army Corps of Engineers noted above served as a basis for the *1987 Corps of Engineers Wetland Delineation Manual.* This manual defines a wetland using a field investigative methodology that requires the presence of three wetland parameters: hydrology, hydric soils, and hydrophytic vegetation. The 1987 Manual draws a clear distinction between a technical guideline for wetland determination in the field and the Cowardin system for wetland classification. The 1987 Manual is also clearly more restrictive than the Cowardin system in that it requires all three of the parameters to be present whereas the Cowardin system requires only one. This definition and methodology are discussed in more detail in chapter 4, Wetland Delineation Methodology.

CHAPTER THREE

Types of Wetlands

In the United States published wetland classification systems date back to the beginning of the twentieth century (Mitsch and Gosselink 1993). Not surprisingly, the earlier efforts focused on northern peatlands and bogs, since these are the dominant wetland types in much of Europe. Most wetland classification systems are based on hydrology, which is the dominant factor controlling wetland location and type.

The first comprehensive effort in the U.S. that attempted to deal with all wetland types was Circular 39, published in 1956 by the U.S. Fish and Wildlife Service (described in chapter 2); it reflects the previously mentioned appreciation of wetlands in this country almost solely as waterfowl habitat. This classification system was developed in conjunction with a national inventory of wetlands. This descriptive system divided all wetlands into four types: inland freshwater, inland saline, coastal freshwater, and coastal saline. The second hierarchy in the system was based on hydroperiod (if seasonally inundated) or depth (if permanently inundated).

Cowardin Classification System

Circular 39 was the dominant wetland classification system until 1979 when the U.S. Fish and Wildlife Service published the Classification of Wetlands and Deepwater Habitats of the United States. This classification scheme, which is referred to as the Cowardin system after the lead author, is the predominant classification system used in the U.S. today. The document applies criteria and limits to defining where wetlands begin and end on the aquatic as well as upland boundary.

The Cowardin approach is a hierarchical classification that is based on five major hydrologic regimes or systems: marine, estuarine, palustrine, lacustrine, or riverine (Schot 1999). These major hierarchies are in turn subdivided into subsystems, classes, subclasses, and modifiers and submodifiers (figure 3.1). The subsystems further modify the hydrologic regime, while the classes describe the habitat type (e.g., rock bottom to forested in the palustrine system). This system was also devised for inventorying purposes, serving as the basis for the photointerpretive mapping of wetlands for the U.S. Fish and Wildlife Service's National Wetland Inventory. These maps, which are available for much of the United States using the U.S. Geological Survey topographic quadrangle, as base maps, generally serve as excellent guidelines for assessing wetland resources on a broad scale. As described in chapter 2, wetlands around the world have been characterized in many different ways over the years. The Cowardin (1979) system is in common use today both in the United States and throughout the world.

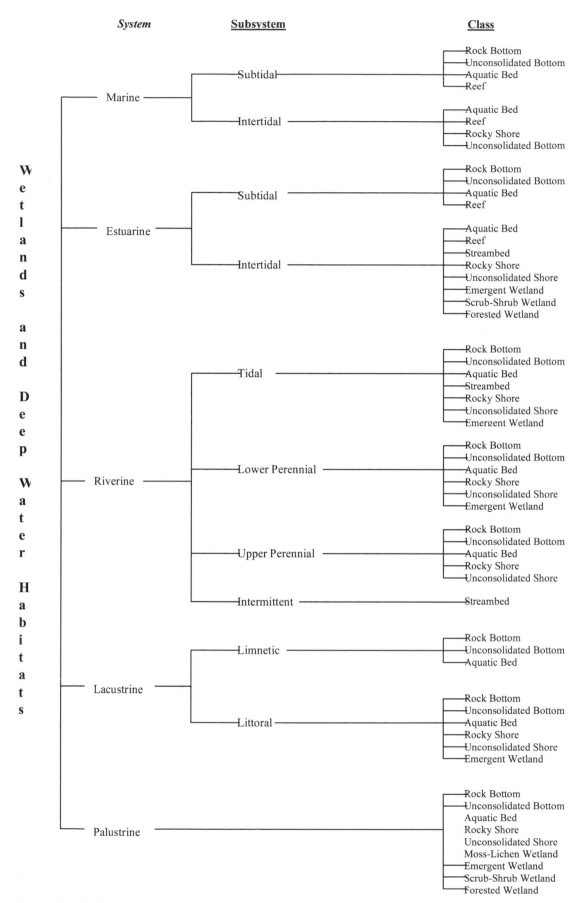

System	Subsystem	Class
Marine	Subtidal	Rock Bottom Unconsolidated Bottom Aquatic Bed Reef
	Intertidal	Aquatic Bed Reef Rocky Shore Unconsolidated Bottom
Estuarine	Subtidal	Rock Bottom Unconsolidated Bottom Aquatic Bed Reef
	Intertidal	Aquatic Bed Reef Streambed Rocky Shore Unconsolidated Shore Emergent Wetland Scrub-Shrub Wetland Forested Wetland
Riverine	Tidal	Rock Bottom Unconsolidated Bottom Aquatic Bed Streambed Rocky Shore Unconsolidated Shore Emergent Wetland
	Lower Perennial	Rock Bottom Unconsolidated Bottom Aquatic Bed Rocky Shore Unconsolidated Shore Emergent Wetland
	Upper Perennial	Rock Bottom Unconsolidated Bottom Aquatic Bed Rocky Shore Unconsolidated Shore
	Intermittent	Streambed
Lacustrine	Limnetic	Rock Bottom Unconsolidated Bottom Aquatic Bed
	Littoral	Rock Bottom Unconsolidated Bottom Aquatic Bed Rocky Shore Unconsolidated Shore Emergent Wetland
Palustrine		Rock Bottom Unconsolidated Bottom Aquatic Bed Rocky Shore Unconsolidated Shore Moss-Lichen Wetland Emergent Wetland Scrub-Shrub Wetland Forested Wetland

Figure 3.1. Wetland and Deepwater Classification Systems, Subsystems, and Classes (from Cowardin, et al., 1979).

Figure 3.2.   Marine Wetland

Marine wetlands are defined as saltwater areas along marine coasts. These wetlands are influenced by the daily tidal cycle and are affected by ocean currents, waves, and storms. The water in these wetlands is predominantly salty, at or near the percentage of salt in the open marine system adjoining these wetlands. The substrate in these wetlands can vary from unconsolidated deposits to bedrock. Vegetation in marine wetlands is either subtidal, which means that it is continually submerged, or intertidal, exposed at some point during the tidal cycle. Subtidal plants, often called algae, must have the ability to thrive in an environment with reduced light conditions. Intertidal plants have adapted to their environment with both short and long periods of drying, which may include long days of intense sunlight. Typical terms for this type of wetland include open ocean, continental shelf, rocky shores, shallow coral reefs, and lagoons.

Estuarine wetlands are described as coastal wetlands in which there is a mix of fresh and salt water. The interface of salt and fresh water forms a transitional area that shifts depending on the tidal cycle and the influence of fresh water from the uplands. The changes in salinity create a gradient that estuarine wetland plants must tolerate in order to survive. These salt-tolerant plants are called halophytes. Many examples of estuarine wetlands exist throughout the world: from mangrove swamps (where the mangrove trees look like they are standing on their prop roots) to bays to mudflats. Substrate in estuarine wetlands can vary from rocks to sand to fine silt.

Riverine wetlands are wet areas in and adjacent to channels of rivers and streams. Water flowing through riverine wetlands can be fast or slow, depending on the topography of the adjacent landscape.

Figure 3.3.   Estuarine Wetland

Figure 3.4.   Riverine Wetland

Figure 3.5.   Lacustrine Wetland

Riverine wetlands in steep ravines typically have a rocky bottom substrate. Riverine wetlands adjacent to flat floodplains have slow-moving water and thus typically have a muddy substrate. Wetland plants in up-gradient stream environments must be able to deal with a hydrologic cycle that shifts from very little water to an abundance of fast-moving water that may occur in a storm event. Wetlands located in river bottom areas are relatively more stable and plant species in these areas are more abundant and diverse.

Lacustrine wetlands are defined as wetlands located around lakes and reservoirs, and they typically exhibit characteristics that include a fringe of vegetation along the shore that disappears at depth. Substrate in lakes is typically muddy and rich in nutrients that allow a diversity of wetland plants to thrive.

Palustrine wetlands are the most difficult to describe, as they form the catchall of the remaining wetland types. They are smaller and shallower than lacustrine wetlands but can be forested, shrubby, grassy, or even unvegetated. Three main community types make up the palustrine wetland class: emergent, shrub/scrub, and forested. Emergent wetlands are wetlands with ground cover (grasses, sedges, rushes) but lack shrubs and trees. Shrub/scrub wetlands contain shrubs that are defined as woody plants less than twenty feet tall. Forested wetlands have a canopy of woody plants over twenty feet tall over 30 percent of the wetland area. Different terms for types of palustrine wetlands include playas, potholes, wet meadows, bogs, mires, and swamps. Substrate in palustrine wetlands can vary from rocky bottom to sands and silts.

Figure 3.6.   Palustrine Wetland

The five wetland types can be described to follow a hydrologic gradient from salty tidal areas to freshwater seasonally wet areas. The Cowardin system (1979) has been in place for over twenty-five years. Earlier, it was stated that wetland science is growing and evolving. Since the publication of the Cowardin system scientists have gone beyond the simple physical generalizations to describe wetlands to learn about the "why" and the "how" of wetlands. The Cowardin system is also not sufficient for determining the extent of wetland resources on a site or for delineation or determination of acreage of potential impacts.

For that reason, several other recent approaches to wetland classification are worthy of note. The U.S. Army Corps of Engineers Environmental Laboratory developed a hydrologic-based classification system for nontidal wetlands as a component of the *1987 Corps of Engineers Wetland Delineation Manual* (Environmental Laboratory 1987). This system divides nontidal wetlands into five different hydrologic regimes: (1) permanently inundated, (2) semipermanently to nearly permanently inundated, (3) regularly inundated or saturated, (4) seasonally inundated or saturated, and (5) irregularly inundated or saturated. This system is essentially an enhancement of the Circular 39 classification system for inland freshwater wetlands but does not incorporate a dominant vegetative community descriptor. It is a pure hydrologic regime system and can provide a first step for the functional description of a wetland for delineation or assessment purposes.

Hydrogeomorphic System

Currently there is a classification system in place that describes the geomorphic setting of the wetland. This newest classification system, called the hydrogeomorphic (HGM) system describes wetlands based

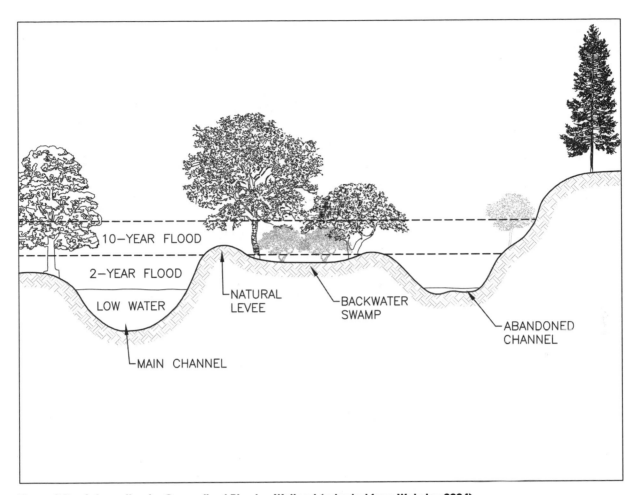

Figure 3.7. Schematic of a Generalized Riverine Wetland (adapted from Wakeley 2004)

upon where they are found in the landscape (Brinson 1993). Knowing the hydrogeomorphic setting of the wetland allows scientists to learn more about the functions and values of each wetland.

This system has been developed as the foundation for the U.S. Army Corps of Engineers' effort to develop a wetland functional assessment model. The HGM approach is based on the assumption that physical factors are the prime determinants of wetland function and that the wetland plant community cover type is likewise dependent on the same physical factors. The three parameters on which this system is based are: (1) hydrodynamics, (2) water source and water transport, and (3) geomorphic setting, or the wetland's position in the landscape. There are broad subdescriptors for each of these three parameters.

It is recognized that the three parameters are inherently interrelated. Geomorphic setting often determines hydrodynamics and water source and water transport; water source will often determine hydrodynamics. The system also recognizes that a given wetland may exhibit more than one type of water source. For example, a wetland in a floodplain may be both a depressional wetland supplied by shallow groundwater and runoff, as well as a riverine wetland that is seasonally or episodically inundated by flooding. The interrelatedness in this functional-based classification system reflects the various environmental gradients that control wetland occurrence and wetland type.

Five types of wetlands are described by the HGM system: estuarine, riverine, depressional, slope, or flats.

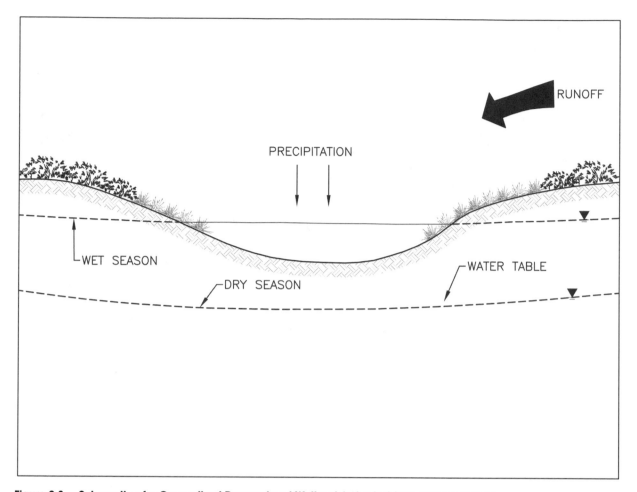

Figure 3.8.   Schematic of a Generalized Depressional Wetland (adapted from Wakeley 2004)

Estuarine wetlands have a two-way flow in the horizontal direction resulting from the tide coming in and out on a daily cycle.

Riverine wetlands by the HGM classification are those areas that have a channel with one-way flow. Thus, the source of hydrology to the wetland is via a flow channel.

Depressional wetlands are areas where the primary sources of water are groundwater or surface water runoff. The direction of water flow is vertical. Typically there is no surface water outflow unless the depression is "full" and groundwater recharge cannot keep up with surface water input. Overflow can happen at this point. One example of this type of wetland is a bog.

Slope wetlands are areas of groundwater discharge. Water flow is one way—out of the soil into the exposed wetland surface. Wetlands formed at seeps and springs are examples of slope wetlands.

Flats are a special type of wetland where precipitation is the primary source of hydrology. Examples include flat depressions in the arid west that seasonally fill with water. Many of these areas are vernal pools as they change vegetation type through the year reflecting the dominant hydrology at the time.

The HGM's method is being refined. In the beginning, the HGM attempted to encompass the entire country, where a landscape-level geomorphic factor would provide a more detailed context for wetland function and value assessment. The U.S. Army Corps of Engineers and others have recognized this limitation and are currently working on preparing guidance for a regional approach to address this is-

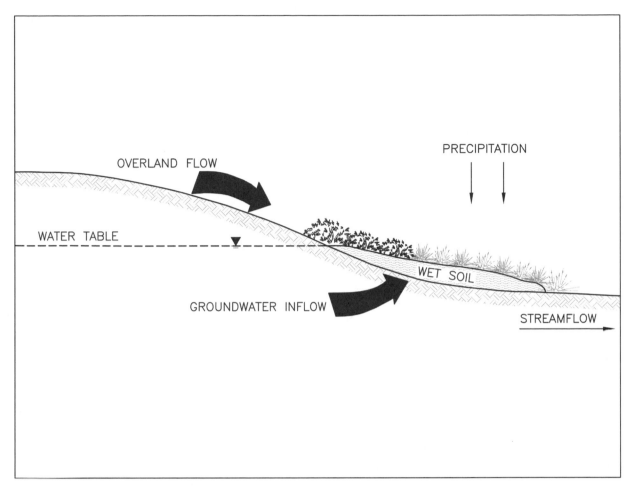

Figure 3.9.   Schematic of a Generalized Slope Wetland (adapted from Wakeley 2004)

sue. The first chapter of an eight-chapter series is called "Hydrogeomorphic Approach to Assessing Wetland Functions: Guidelines for Developing Regional Guidebooks" (Clairain 2002).

But the hydrogeomorphic system does provide an initial basis for a landscape-level, functional assessment for wetland management and decision making. It is relatively simple to apply in the field and can provide a valuable perspective on the functional values of an individual wetland, as well as on multiple wetlands within a drainage basin or landscape. However, since its focus is on the dominant physical factors affecting function, it does not include a cover-type modifier or vegetative community descriptor. Therefore, the HGM is most useful when used in conjunction with another system that addresses the vegetative or biotic component. The Cowardin system is the most sophisticated descriptive system. It was designed for, and is best suited for, large-scale mapping or analyzing wetland trends, such as loss of wetland area on a regional or larger scale. It also has the advantage of being the dominant descriptive system utilized by wetland scientists and regulators and provides an immediate reference base for discussion.

Using the HGM in combination with the Cowardin system can provide a thorough description of a wetland or wetland system. This combined approach allows experienced wetland scientists and regulators to accomplish many things. They can analyze potential impacts; assess cumulative impacts; assess the alternatives analysis; develop avoidance and minimization measures; and finally evaluate proposed mitigation measures during the design and engineering of projects that involve potential wetland impacts. The above step-wise analysis, after all, is the purpose of the Clean Water Act's §404 program as it is currently applied.

The HGM system is very good for rating the functions of the wetland. The next section describes various functions of wetlands.

Functions and Values of Wetlands

Wetlands have traditionally been valued for their attributes as protective habitat for fish and wildlife. Tidal wetlands and the adjacent tidewaters have long been productive fishing grounds for shellfish and finfish. Hunters have known for millennia that wetlands are the prime hunting grounds for waterfowl and many mammals. In fact, prior to the creation of the Clean Water Act, the majority of the wetlands protected in the United States during this century were purchased by the U.S. Fish and Wildlife Service or state fish and game agencies because of their importance as breeding, migratory, and/or wintering grounds for game species. Most of the U.S. Fish and Wildlife Refuge system is still managed primarily for game species, but these areas have also provided important refuge for numerous other nongame species as well. The management focus of the National Wildlife Refuge system is beginning to shift as public interest has grown in passive enjoyment of wildlife and natural areas, such as birding and environmental education (USDA Natural Resources Conservation Service 2005). But the hunting industry still supports a significant portion of the federal and state wildlife refuge programs and the wetlands they protect through the duck stamp/hunting permit program.

In recent decades, society has recognized that wetlands have values beyond providing habitat for fish and wildlife. These values are primarily related to the effects on water quality and water quantity resulting from the natural functions of many wetland systems. These functions and values have become standardized and somewhat institutionalized and are often attributed generically to all wetlands everywhere (Reppert et al. 1979). Wetlands, however, are extremely diverse and variable, and not all wetlands are created equal. No individual wetland is capable of providing all of the functions and values that can be attributed to wetlands. Furthermore, many of the functions that wetlands perform are complex and not that well understood. This is due not only to the great variety of wetlands and the relative youthfulness of wetland science, but also to the complex interactions of biological and geochemical processes at work in wetlands. Investigation of wetland functions requires an interdisciplinary scientific approach to unravel the interplay of natural processes at work.

The typical "functions and values" frequently attributed to wetlands are described below.

Water Quality: Wetlands are often described metaphorically as the "kidneys of the landscape" because many studies have demonstrated the capability of wetlands to cleanse water through transformation of various pollutants, particularly nutrients. Wetlands can also function as "sinks" that retain pollutants and sediments. However, research has also demonstrated that the beneficial water quality properties of wetlands are extremely complex and variable within and between individual wetlands and wetland systems and are dependent on environmental factors such as hydrology, season, position in the landscape, soils, and geology. Controlling temperature is another valuable component of the water quality function of a wetland. Some wetlands have been clearly shown to be net sinks for nutrients; others are net exporters of nutrients. Additionally, any given wetland may be a net sink during one season and a net exporter in another (Kent 1994; Mitsch and Gosselink 1993)

Many factors influence the effectiveness of a wetland in reducing the amount of nutrients, sediments, and other pollutants. Research has suggested that, in a given drainage basin, the topographic positions of individual wetlands may strongly influence cleansing functions (Whigham et al. 1988).

Sparsely vegetated wetlands and wetlands on slopes are not as effective at water-quality treatment. Small riparian wetlands adjacent to headwater streams have been shown to be more effective in removing nitrogen and coarse soil particles, and bottomland wetlands where there is prolonged contact between the vegetation and the water have been shown to be more effective in removing fine sediment particles and attached phosphorous.

Understanding how the water quality functions of wetlands operate has allowed environmental managers to create artificial wetland systems to treat storm water and wastewater. This understanding is also illustrated in a reciprocal example where waste water managers in South Carolina have determined that without the Congaree Bottomland Hardwood Swamp performing its natural water quality treatment function, a $5 million treatment plant would have to be constructed (USEPA n.d.).

Flood Attenuation and Stormwater Control: Wetlands are also described as sponges because they absorb water during rain or flooding and release it slowly after the storm subsides. Up to 1.5 million gallons of floodwater can be stored in an acre of wetland (USEPA n.d.). The function of flood attenuation is strongly influenced by the position of the wetland in the landscape. Riparian bottomland hardwood wetlands and floodplain wetlands probably have the greatest effect on flood attenuation, primarily due to the position in the landscape. They can store and attenuate floodwaters when streams or rivers overflow their banks. The economic value of protecting wetlands for floodwater storage can be quantified. Protecting wetlands around the Charles River in Massachusetts has saved $17 million in potential flood damage (USEPA n.d.).

Unaltered, natural floodplains provide the flood attenuation function with or without vegetation. But the presence of vegetation, and forests in particular, can enhance this function through the creation of roughness or friction that can slow floodwater velocities. To a lesser extent, flood attenuation is provided through transpiration, which during the growing season can release significant quantities of subsurface water through the trees and into the atmosphere.

Small wetlands in headwater drainage swales and streams can have the same effects on a smaller scale, as they slow down and dampen the delivery of upland runoff to downstream waters. Depressional wetlands can also store significant quantities of surface runoff during rain events, but this function is attributable to the existence of the depression, whether or not it contains a wetland.

Wetlands with a high through-flow component, such as emergent marshes that are dominated by herbaceous species and located in low-gradient rivers, may have very little impact on floodwaters. Isolated wetlands, by their position in the landscape, also have minimal effect on floodwater attenuation (U.S. Army Corps of Engineers 1998).

Ground Water Support: Wetlands often interface with ground water. They can function either as groundwater recharge or groundwater discharge depending on their position in the landscape. Often wetlands are generically credited with the ability to supply water to the shallow water table or to deeper aquifers. While certain wetlands have been shown to perform this function, it is probably not widespread and would most likely be dependent on site-specific conditions, which may be somewhat difficult to determine. Attributing this function to all wetlands is misleading. It is probably safe to say that there are more wetlands dependent on groundwater as a component of their water supply (groundwater discharge) than there are wetlands that result in a net recharge to an aquifer. However, protection of wetlands that do contribute to recharge of an aquifer is very important, as many people rely on well systems for their drinking water. Wetlands in depressions or flats have a greater potential for ground water recharge than those on slopes. Obviously, permeable soil is also a critical component (Mitsch and Gosselink 1993).

Fish and Wildlife Habitat: As noted previously, the fish and wildlife values of wetlands have long been recognized and served as the initial basis for wetland protection and preservation. As a general rule, large diverse wetlands contain a diversity of plants and animals. Comparatively, wetlands are among the most biologically productive areas in the world (Tiner 1989). Their productivity and diversity is similar to that of tropical rain forests and coral reefs (USEPA n.d.). Up to one-half of North American birds nest or feed in wetlands, and wetlands are home to 31 percent of the continent's plant species (USEPA n.d.).

Tidal wetlands are recognized as vital nursery grounds and foraging areas for shrimp, crabs, and other commercially valuable species of fish and shellfish. Tidal wetlands are a foundational building block, one of the basic components of the estuarine food web. In fact, about two-thirds of the major U.S. commercial fisheries depend on estuaries and salt marshes for nursery or spawning grounds (Institute for Wetland & Environmental Education & Research n.d.). In 1997, fish species that are dependent on wetlands generated almost $79 billion in revenue for the commercial fishing industry (USEPA n.d.).

Nontidal wetlands also provide vital habitat for many aquatic, terrestrial, and amphibious species including mammals, fish, amphibians, reptiles, and waterfowl and other birds. Nontidal wetlands encompass a wide variety of herbaceous and woody plant communities as cover and provide critical habitat for many rare, threatened, and endangered species.

Erosion and Shoreline Support: As dramatically illustrated in the devastating effects of Hurricane Katrina, wetlands and shorelines offer support and protection for upland environments. Wetland plants hold the soil in place. The energy of the waves and currents is dissipated by the roughness and complexity of the shoreline fringe.

Aesthetics: The aesthetic value of a wetland is difficult to quantify (Smardon 1988). The previously described attributes of wetlands are functions. This means that they are the natural processes of wetlands that will continue to exist (if not converted or filled) regardless of our perception of them. The perceived value that people place on an individual wetland's functions has a direct effect on whether or not it remains intact or is converted to an alternate use (National Audubon Society 1993). People enjoy the wetland environment through recreational activities such as picnicking, bird watching, fishing, boating, and hunting. More than half of U.S. adults participate in some of these recreational activities (USEPA n.d). According to the Environmental Protection Agency (EPA), wetland-related ecotourism activities added approximately $59 billion to the U.S. economy in 1991 (USEPA n.d.).

Landscape Perspective

Wetland scientists have increasingly recognized that the factors controlling the existence of a wetland as well as its functions and values are largely determined by landscape characteristics and the wetland's position in the landscape. Position in the landscape can be defined as topographic or spatial location relative to the drainage network of streams and rivers, other wetlands, topography, and other landscape features such as forests or agricultural fields. Landscape position in many cases determines wetland hydrology, throughflow, and the delivery and type of materials coming into a wetland. These physical factors dictate wetland function and ultimately wetland value. The landscape perspective provides for the evaluation of wetland impacts in the context of the larger system in which the wetland functions.

CHAPTER FOUR

Wetland Delineation Methodology

In chapters 2 and 3 the position of wetlands in the landscape as transitional or intermediate between upland and aquatic systems was discussed. The gradation between upland and aquatic features leads to a potential difficulty of determining the precise endpoint of a wetland. While some wetlands may end abruptly and therefore be readily delineated in the field, in many cases the wetland/upland or wetland/open water interface is a gradational zone, a part of the landscape transition from water to upland. In this zone, wetland characteristics decrease as upland or open water characteristics increase.

Determination of an exact and legally defensible wetland boundary in the field is the challenge of wetland delineation. And, as also mentioned in chapter 2, such a determination is impossible without a wetland definition based on detailed, discernable field parameters, and, perhaps more importantly, a prescribed methodology for determining wetland boundaries in the field.

The current methodology for the field determination of a wetland is the *1987 Corps of Engineers Wetland Delineation Manual* (the "1987 Manual" or "Corps Manual"). The 1987 Manual is very valuable for two reasons. It provides methodologies for identifying or determining an area as a wetland subject to federal jurisdiction and for determining the boundary of the wetland. This chapter will provide an overview of the methodology specified in this document. The reader should refer to the 1987 Manual and the U.S. Army Corps of Engineers' many Regulatory Guidance Letters for more detailed information and discussion.

In general, the process of delineating a wetland in the field involves the examination of plants, soils, and indicators of wetland hydrology. Wetland scientists begin a delineation process by first observing the landscape in the vicinity of the wetland. Specifically, they are looking for transitions and changes in elevations and plant communities. Region-specific, typical wetland plant assemblages indicate a place to start looking for the other wetland characteristics of hydric soil and hydrology. Soil pits are dug to see if they fill up with, or show indications of, water. Names and dominance of plant species in the immediate vicinity of the soil pit are recorded onto standardized data forms that will serve as documentation during the report-writing phase. The delineated boundary is the point where all three wetland criteria, hydric soils, hydrophytic vegetation, and wetland hydrology, are met. Finding this line is a repetitive process of digging multiple soil pits and taking numerous vegetation notes. Once found, the area is noted with flagging or stakes for future surveying. Sometimes the break between upland and wetland is abrupt. Most often, however, it is gradual, resulting in the actual delineated line being based on science and strongly tied to the experience and professional judgment of the wetland scientist.

The 1987 Manual was designed to identify and delineate wetlands on the basis of the three parameters in the current definition of wetlands: vegetation, soils, and hydrology. For field identification

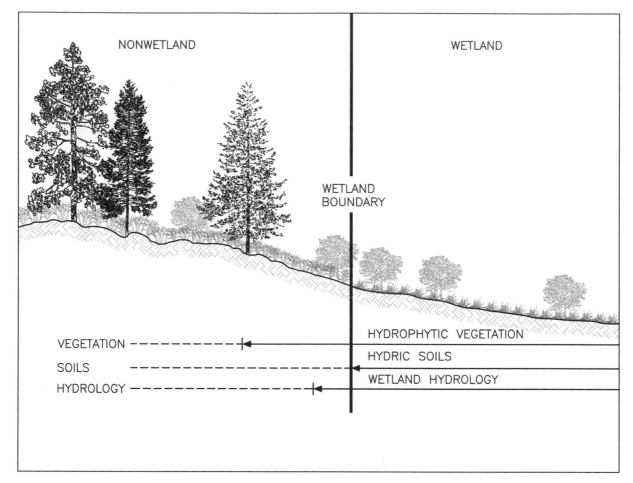

NONWETLAND   WETLAND

WETLAND
BOUNDARY

HYDROPHYTIC VEGETATION
VEGETATION
HYDRIC SOILS
SOILS
WETLAND HYDROLOGY
HYDROLOGY

Figure 4.1. Schematic of a Transition from an Upland to a Wetland

and delineation these three parameters must be defined in much greater detail than in the one-paragraph federal definition and in terms that can be measured, observed, or inferred in the field. Over one-quarter of the ninety-eight-page text of the 1987 Manual is devoted to technical guidelines for the identification and delineation of wetlands and characteristics and indicators of hydrophytic vegetation, hydric soils, and wetland hydrology.

The technical guidelines (table 4.1) provide straightforward diagnostic definitions of the environmental characteristics of wetlands, deepwater aquatic habitats, and nonwetlands on the basis of the three-parameter approach. These guidelines provide the methodology for determining if an area is a wetland versus an aquatic habitat or upland, which is the first step in the determination of an area as a wetland or not.

The three parameters are further defined and discussed in "Characteristics and Indicators of Hydrophytic Vegetation, Hydric Soils, and Wetland Hydrology." This section of the 1987 Manual provides essential, detailed information for the analysis of the three parameters in the field as well as conceptual support for the manual's working definition of wetlands. Below, the characteristics are given first, followed by the rules for indicator determination. A summary of the characteristics and indicator section follows.

Table 4.1.   Technical Guidelines for the Identification of Wetlands versus Deepwater Aquatic Habitats and Nonwetlands (Environmental Laboratory 1987, 13–15)

Wetlands

a. Definition—The Corps of Engineers (Federal Register 1982) and the EPA (Federal Register 1980) jointly define wetlands as: those areas that are inundated or saturated by surface or ground water at a frequency and duration sufficient to support, and that under normal circumstances do support, a prevalence of vegetation typically adapted for life in saturated soil conditions. Wetlands generally include swamps, marshes, bogs, and similar areas.

b. Diagnostic, general, environmental characteristics of wetlands:

    1. Vegetation—the prevalent vegetation consists of macrophytes that are typically adapted to areas having hydrologic and soil conditions as described above. Hydrophytic species, due to morphological, physiological, and/or reproductive adaptation(s), have the ability to grow, effectively compete, reproduce and/or persist in anaerobic soil conditions.

    2. Soil—soils are present and have been classified as hydric, or they possess characteristics that are associated with reducing soil conditions.

    3. Hydrology—the area is inundated either permanently or periodically at mean water depths 6.6 feet or less, or the soil is saturated to the surface at some time during the growing season of the prevalent vegetation.

c. Technical approach for the identification and delineation of wetlands—except in certain situations defined in this manual, evidence of a minimum of one positive wetland indicator from each parameter (hydrology, soil, and vegetation) must be found in order to make a positive wetland determination.

Deepwater Aquatic Habitats

a. Definition—Deepwater aquatic habitats are areas that are permanently inundated at mean annual water depths greater than 6.6 feet or permanently inundated areas less than or equal to 6.6 feet in depth that do not support rooted emergent or woody plant species.[1]

b. Diagnostic environmental characteristics:

    1. Vegetation—no rooted emergent or woody plant species are present in these permanently inundated areas.

    2. Soil—the substrate technically is not defined as a soil if the mean water depth is greater than 6.6 feet or if it will not support rooted emergent or woody plants.

    3. Hydrology—the area is permanently inundated at mean water depths greater than 6.6 feet.

Nonwetlands

a. Definition—Nonwetlands include uplands and lowland areas that are neither deepwater aquatic habitat, wetlands, nor other aquatic sites. They are seldom or never inundated, or frequently inundated, they have vegetated, they normally support a prevalence of vegetation typically adapted for life only in aerobic soil conditions.[2]

b. Diagnostic environmental characteristics:

    1. Vegetation—the prevalent vegetation consists of plant species that are typically adapted for life only in aerobic soils. These mesophytic and/or xerophytic macrophytes cannot persist in predominantly anaerobic soil conditions.

    2. Soil—soils, when present, are not classified as hydric, and possess characteristics associated with aerobic conditions.

    3. Hydrology—although the soil may be inundated or saturated by surface water or ground water periodically during the growing season of the prevalent vegetation, the average annual duration of inundation or soil saturation does not preclude the occurrence of plant species typically adapted for life in aerobic conditions.

c. Technical approach for the identification and delineation of nonwetlands—when any one of the diagnostic characteristics identified above is present, the area is a nonwetland.

---

[1] Areas less than or equal to 6.6 feet in mean annual depth that support only submergent aquatic plants (seaweeds, pondweeds, etc.) are vegetated shallows, not wetlands.

[2] Some species, due to their broad ecological tolerances, occur in both wetlands and nonwetlands (e.g., Red maple (Acer rubrum)).

Wetland Characteristics

HYDROPHYTIC VEGETATION

Hydrophytic vegetation is defined as

> the sum total of macrophytic plant life that occurs in areas where the frequency and duration of inundation or soil saturation produce permanently or periodically saturated soils of sufficient duration to exert a controlling influence on the plant species present.

Hydrophytic vegetation for the purposes of the 1987 Manual is also defined as macroscopic vegetation as opposed to microscopic vegetation. The authors of the 1987 Manual elected to adopt the "plant community" and "prevalence" approach versus an indicator species approach. This is a concept basic to plant ecology, which recognizes that plants rarely occur in monotypic stands in nature but rather in mixed groupings or associations of several to many species. Plant communities or associations, therefore, are best described on the basis of the dominant or prevalent species. Numerous sampling techniques have been developed to determine dominant species. Difficulties arise because of the diversity of plant community types and the necessity of different dominance determination methodologies for woody and herbaceous plant communities. What this means is that the presence of several typically upland species in an area dominated by hydrophytic vegetation would not preclude the area from being considered a wetland. Nor would the presence of several hydrophytic species confirm an area as a wetland.

The next key term in the definition, "typically adapted," is also clarified. Wetlands are characterized by soils saturated for at least part of the year, which creates anaerobic conditions. Wetland plants exhibit physiological adaptations for anaerobic conditions. If the dominant plants exhibit such adaptations, then the hydrophytic vegetation test is met. However, since there are virtually infinite degrees of wetness in the wetland universe, there is a vast assemblage of plant species that may occur in and across the boundaries of wetland types. Some species are wetland endemics, occurring almost always in wetland environments. And there are many species that may occur in both wetlands and uplands.

In order to reduce potential confusion, the Plant Indicator Status Categories were developed and applied to each species listed in the National List of Plant Species That Occur in Wetlands, which includes over 5,000 plants (Reed 1993; USDA National Resources Conservation Service 2006). The five categories and their respective estimated probability of occurrence are presented in table 4.2. The categories range from "obligate" wetland species, those that occur in wetlands 99 percent of the time, to obligate upland species, those that occur in uplands 99 percent of the time. The middle category, "facultative," includes plants that have an even chance of occurring in wetlands or uplands.

INDICATORS OF HYDROPHYTIC VEGETATION

The indicators for hydrophytic vegetation are presented in hierarchical order of "reliability" in the 1987 Manual as listed below:

1. Fifty percent or more of the *dominant* species have an obligate (OBL), facultative wet (FACW), or facultative (FAC) indicator status. [Methodologies for dominance determination are presented in the next section of field methods.]
2. Presence of plant species which, based on the delineator's knowledge and experience, typically grow in areas of prolonged inundation and/or saturated soils.

Table 4.2.   Plant Indicator Status Categories (Environmental Laboratory 1987, 18)

Indicator Category	Indicator Symbol	Definition
OBLIGATE WETLAND PLANTS	OBL	Plants that occur almost always (estimated probability >99%) in wetlands under natural conditions, but which may also occur rarely (estimated probability <1%) in nonwetlands. Examples: Salt marsh cordgrass (*Spartina alterniflora*), Bald cypress (*Taxodium distichum*)
FACULTATIVE WETLAND PLANTS	FACW	Plants that occur usually (estimated probability >67% to 99%) in wetlands, but also occur (estimated probability 1% to 33% in nonwetlands). Examples: Green ash (*Fraxinus pennsylvanica*), Red osier dogwood (*Cornus stolonifera*).
FACULTATIVE PLANTS	FAC	Plants with a similar likelihood (estimated probability 33% to 67%) of occurring in both wetlands and nonwetlands. Examples: Honey locust (*Gleditsia triecanthos*), Greenbriar (*Smilax rotundifolia*).
FACULTATIVE UPLAND PLANTS	FACU	Plants that occur sometimes (estimated probability 1% to <33%) in wetlands, but occur more often (estimated probability >67% to 99%) in nonwetlands. Examples: Northern red oak (*Quercus rubra*), Tall cinquefoil (*Potentilla arguta*).
OBLIGATE UPLAND PLANTS	UPL	Plants that rarely (estimated probability <1%) in wetlands, but occur almost always (estimated probability >99%) in nonwetlands under natural conditions. Examples: Short leaf pine (*Pinus echinata*), Soft chess (*Bromus mollis*).

3. Morphological adaptations for survival in areas of prolonged inundation and/or saturated soils. [A number of wetland plants exhibit macroscopic, morphological features developed for survival in wetland conditions; examples include "buttressed" trunks and shallow root systems. These features are discussed in detail in the appendixes to the 1987 Manual.]
4. Documentation of a species typical occurrence in wetlands in the technical literature.

The 1987 Manual clearly states that in the vast majority of cases only the first indicator should be used. The other three indicators are to be used as supporting evidence only. If one of the last three is the basis for the determination, then the decision should be second-guessed prior to finalizing the determination. The last three indicators, with the possible exception of the second, are essentially redundant since they are already incorporated in the national and regional listings of plant species likely to occur in wetlands. The second indicator recognizes that experienced wetland scientists and delineators may be aware of species that, in a region or subregion, typically occur in wetland environments yet are not listed or are incorrectly listed in the national or regional lists of plants typically occurring in wetlands.

Hydric Soils

HYDRIC SOILS CHARACTERISTICS

A hydric soil is defined as "a soil that is saturated, flooded, or ponded long enough during the growing season to develop anaerobic conditions that favor the growth and regeneration of hydrophytic vegetation" (USDA Soil Conservation Service 1985, as amended by the National Technical Committee for

Hydric Soils in December 1986). The National Technical Committee developed the following criteria for hydric soils using the Soil Conservation Service's soil nomenclature:

A. All histosols (organic soils such as peat) except folists;
B. Soils in Aquic suborders, Aquic subgroups, Albolls suborder, Salorthids great group, or Pell great groups of Vertisols that are:
    1. Somewhat poorly drained and have a water table less than 0.5 feet from the surface for a significant period (usually a week or more) during the growing season, or
    2. Poorly drained or very poorly drained and have either:
        (a) a water table at less than 1.0 foot from the surface for a significant period (usually a week or more) during the growing season if permeability is equal to or greater than 6.0 inches/hour in all layers within 20 inches; or
        (b) a water table at less than 1.5 feet from the surface for a significant period (usually a week or more) during the growing season; or
C. Soils that are ponded for a long or very long duration during the growing season; or
D. Soils that are frequently flooded for long duration or very long duration during the growing season.

Drained soils are discussed in some detail in the 1987 Manual. Drainage may result in a situation where the soil is technically a hydric soil but no longer has the hydrology to support hydrophytic plants; hence all areas with hydric soils are not necessarily wetlands. General background information on soils including a definition of soils, soil horizon descriptions, factors influencing soils and hydric soils in particular, and a very brief discussion of soil classification are also provided in the 1987 Manual. Soil colors have been standardized. Soil color chips, in the Munsell soil color chart are universally used to describe soil color (Kollmorgen Corporation 1988).

HYDRIC SOIL INDICATORS

This section is divided into nonsandy soils and sandy soils because of the very different nature of hydric characteristics in sandy soils. The indicators are listed in order of decreasing reliability, and confirmation of any one characteristic is indicative of a hydric soil. Indicator characteristics are listed below; for additional explanation and discussion, please refer to the 1987 Manual.

Nonsandy Soil Indicators:

A. Organic soils (histosols)
B. Histic epipedons
C. Sulfidic material
D. Aquic or peraquic moisture regime
E. Reducing soil conditions
F. Soil colors
    1. gleyed soils (gray colors)
    2. soils with bright mottles and/or low matrix chroma
G. Soils appearing on the hydric soil lists (based on the National List of Hydric Soils prepared by the National Technical Committee on Hydric Soils, which is included in an appendix in the manual;

hydric soil lists are also available for many states which may include soils not listed on the national list)

H. Iron and manganese concretions

Sandy Soil Indicators:

A. High organic matter content in surface horizon
B. Streaking of subsurface horizons by organic matter
C. Organic pans

Wetland Hydrology

WETLAND HYDROLOGY CHARACTERISTICS

The term "wetland hydrology" is defined as encompassing "all hydrologic characteristics of areas that are periodically inundated or have soils saturated to the surface at some time during the growing season." The 1987 Manual describes hydrology as "the least exact of the parameters" and emphasizes the potential difficulty of confirming hydrology in the field. Hydrology is easily confirmed on at least a daily basis in tidal wetlands, but in many nontidal wetlands, hydrology is visually evident only on a seasonal basis (e.g., spring high water table or floods) or sporadic basis (e.g., precipitation and/or runoff). If the site is visited during a drier period it may be difficult to document hydrology.

INDICATORS OF WETLAND HYDROLOGY

Indicators of wetland hydrology are numerous and are somewhat dependent on geographic location and climate (e.g., desert versus boreal environments) and position in the landscape (e.g., floodplain versus hill slope). The following list of indicators, presented in the 1987 Manual, is divided into recorded data and field (observational) data:

A. Recorded Data—Stream gage data, lake gage data, tidal gage data, flood predictions, and historical data may be available from the following sources:
1. Corps of Engineers District Offices
2. U.S. Geological Survey (USGS)
3. State, county, and local agencies
4. Soil Conservation Service Small Watershed Projects
5. Planning documents of developers

B. Field Data—The following field hydrologic indicators can be assessed quickly, and although some of them are not necessarily indicative of hydrologic events that occur only during the growing season, they do provide evidence that inundation and/or soil saturation has occurred:
1. Visual observation of inundation
2. Visual observation of soil saturation
3. Watermarks
4. Driftlines
5. Sediment deposits
6. Drainage patterns within wetlands

Wetland Delineation Field Methods

Part IV of the 1987 Manual describes the methodology(ies) for conducting wetland delineations in the field. There are five basic components: preliminary data gathering procedures, "routine determination" procedures, "comprehensive determination" procedures, "atypical situation" determination procedures, and "problem areas." All wetland delineations use either a routine or comprehensive approach initially, and are based on the positive or negative indicators of the three parameters. If one of the three parameters is absent due to recent alteration, then the atypical situation method is used to determine the status of the parameter. If one of the three parameters is absent due to "normal" seasonal or annual fluctuations, then the problem area method is applied for that parameter(s). Neither the atypical situation nor the problem area methods are intended to extend jurisdiction over areas that do not exhibit positive indicators of the three parameters.

The routine method is the most frequently used. It is a "qualitative" method in that the delineator investigates the three parameters to determine if wetlands are present, and if the answer is yes, then locates the wetland boundary on the basis of the three parameters in the field. The comprehensive method involves a more elaborate and labor-intensive sampling approach, where the vegetative parameter is quantitatively analyzed with sampling plots. This method is typically used in the larger and more complex or difficult field situations and/or when "rigid" documentation is required. The atypical situation procedure is used only when the routine or comprehensive methods have been applied and it has been determined that positive indicators of one or more of the three parameters had been obliterated due to recent human disturbance or natural events. The problem areas category exists for those natural wetland types and/or conditions where positive indication of one or more of the three parameters may be difficult or impossible for at least some period of the year. The five components are discussed in a little more detail below. For more extensive discussion, see the 1987 Manual.

PRELIMINARY DATA GATHERING

The preliminary data gathering section details sources for the type of information useful for making a wetland determination. This information is not necessarily required for making a determination, but analysis of such information will facilitate the determination and potentially save time and effort. Of course the level of information available will vary somewhat for different sites and regions of the country. The following typical information sources are listed and described in the 1987 Manual:

- USGS topographic quadrangle maps
- National Wetland Inventory (NWI) maps
- National List of Plants that Occur in Wetlands (appendix C in 1987 Manual)
- U.S. Department of Agriculture county soil surveys
- Stream and tidal gage data (USGS)
- Aerial photographs and remote sensing data illustrating land cover
- State, county, and local government information such as topographic maps, etc.
- Other studies, which may include wetland delineations on adjacent properties, environmental impact studies, etc.

- Local individuals and experts
- Applicant's survey plans and engineering designs

The most useful information sources for most applications are the soil surveys, recent aerial photographs, and topographic maps at scales of 1 inch to 200 feet or better.

The 1987 Manual goes on to list a detailed series of steps to follow for the analysis and synthesis of the information gathered prior to initiation of the field effort. This information is used, at least initially, for the selection of the appropriate method to make the determination.

ROUTINE DETERMINATIONS

As described above, the routine determination is the most frequently used method. The routine method is divided into three levels:

Level 1—onsite inspection unnecessary
Level 2—onsite inspection necessary
Level 3—combination of Levels 1 and 2

Detailed procedures for the application of all three levels are presented in the 1987 Manual, including the equipment required. Flow charts illustrating the steps in Levels 1 and 2 are given in figures 4.2 and 4.3, respectively. Level 2 is the most commonly applied method in nontidal wetland delineations. Level 2 is applied slightly differently for small sites and large sites. For sites less than or equal to five acres, the determination and delineation is conducted somewhat randomly through traverses of the site. For sites larger than five acres, a baseline parallel to the long axis of the site is set up with transects across the site perpendicular to the baseline. The delineator walks the transects to analyze the three parameters and make the wetland determination and delineation. However, this latter approach may not be practical on many large sites with nontidal wetlands occurring along or adjacent to small streams or creeks. The wetland delineator must often adapt the methodology to the site.

COMPREHENSIVE DETERMINATIONS

A flow chart illustrating the steps in the comprehensive method is presented in figure 4.4, on the following pages. The 1987 Manual describes the steps for comprehensive determinations in great detail, including the required equipment. This method is similar to the Level 2 routine method for sites greater than five acres in size. The difference is in the quantitative determination of dominance in the comprehensive method versus the estimated determination of dominance in the Level 2 routine method. The analysis of soil and hydrology is basically the same.

ATYPICAL SITUATIONS

This method is intended for use when the initial routine or comprehensive investigation determines that positive indicators of one or more of the three parameters are absent due to recent human activities

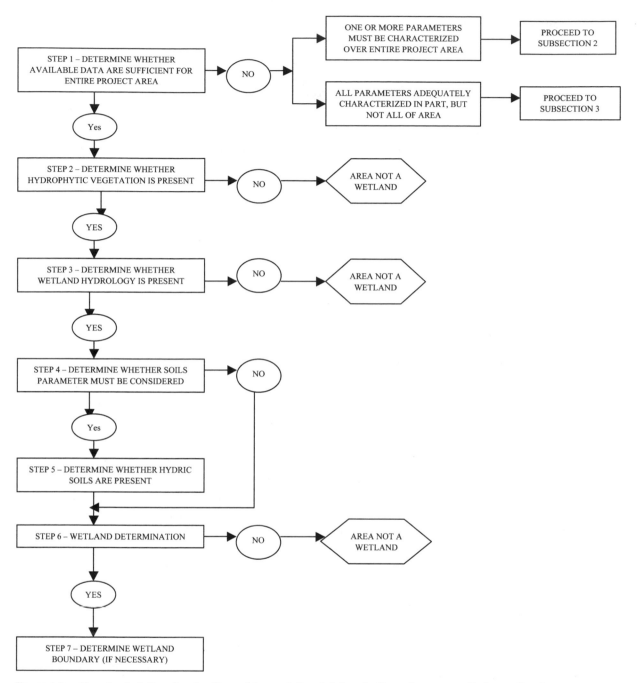

Figure 4.2. Flowchart of steps involved in making a wetland determination when an on-site inspection is unnecessary (from Corps of Engineers *Wetland Delineation Manual*, 1987)

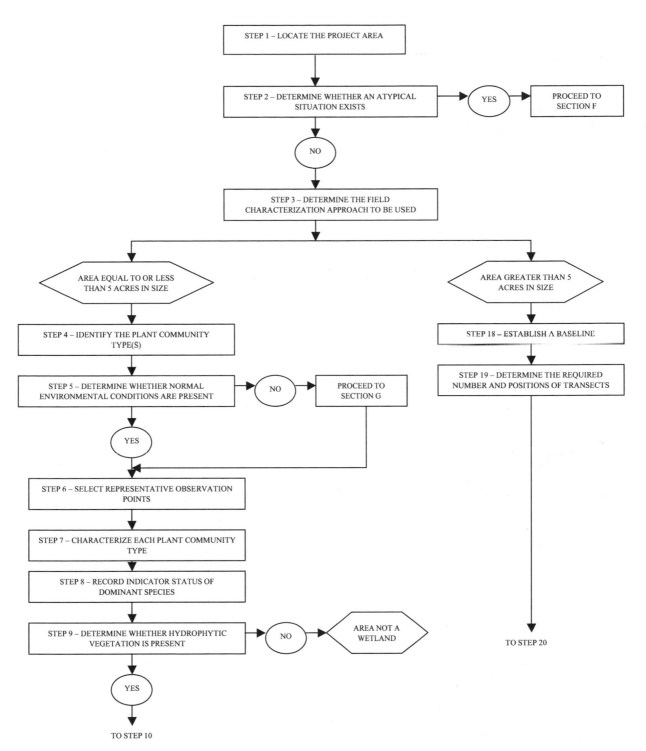

Figure 4.3.   Flowchart of steps involved in making a routine wetland delineation (from Corps of Engineers *Wetland Delineation Manual,* 1987)

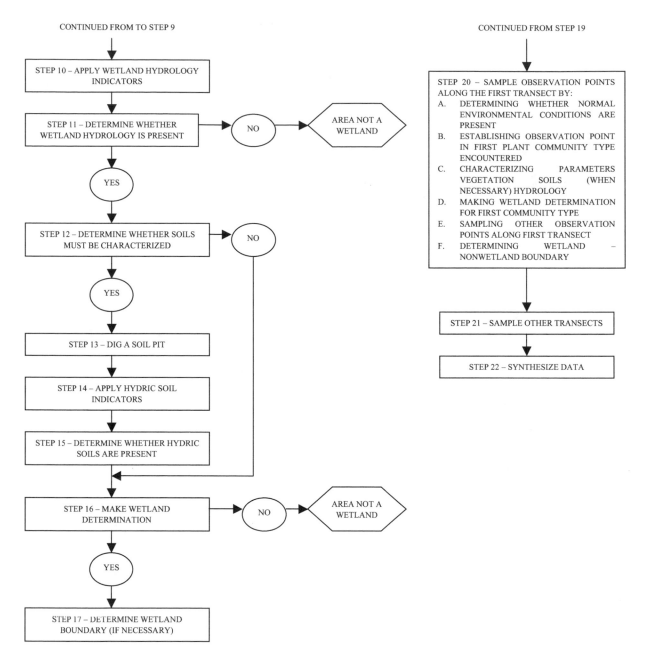

CONTINUED FROM TO STEP 9

STEP 10 – APPLY WETLAND HYDROLOGY INDICATORS

STEP 11 – DETERMINE WHETHER WETLAND HYDROLOGY IS PRESENT

NO → AREA NOT A WETLAND

YES

STEP 12 – DETERMINE WHETHER SOILS MUST BE CHARACTERIZED

NO

YES

STEP 13 – DIG A SOIL PIT

STEP 14 – APPLY HYDRIC SOIL INDICATORS

STEP 15 – DETERMINE WHETHER HYDRIC SOILS ARE PRESENT

STEP 16 – MAKE WETLAND DETERMINATION

NO → AREA NOT A WETLAND

YES

STEP 17 – DETERMINE WETLAND BOUNDARY (IF NECESSARY)

CONTINUED FROM STEP 19

STEP 20 – SAMPLE OBSERVATION POINTS ALONG THE FIRST TRANSECT BY:
A. DETERMINING WHETHER NORMAL ENVIRONMENTAL CONDITIONS ARE PRESENT
B. ESTABLISHING OBSERVATION POINT IN FIRST PLANT COMMUNITY TYPE ENCOUNTERED
C. CHARACTERIZING PARAMETERS VEGETATION SOILS (WHEN NECESSARY) HYDROLOGY
D. MAKING WETLAND DETERMINATION FOR FIRST COMMUNITY TYPE
E. SAMPLING OTHER OBSERVATION POINTS ALONG FIRST TRANSECT
F. DETERMINING WETLAND – NONWETLAND BOUNDARY

STEP 21 – SAMPLE OTHER TRANSECTS

STEP 22 – SYNTHESIZE DATA

Figure 4.3. *(Continued)*

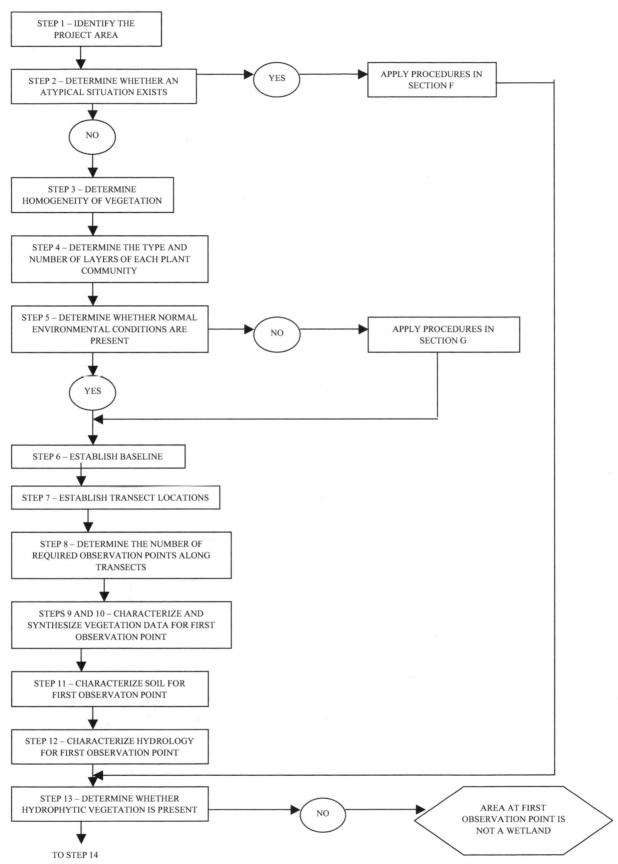

Figure 4.4.   Flowchart of steps involved in making a comprehensive wetlands determination (from Corps of Engineers *Wetland Delineation Manual*, 1987)

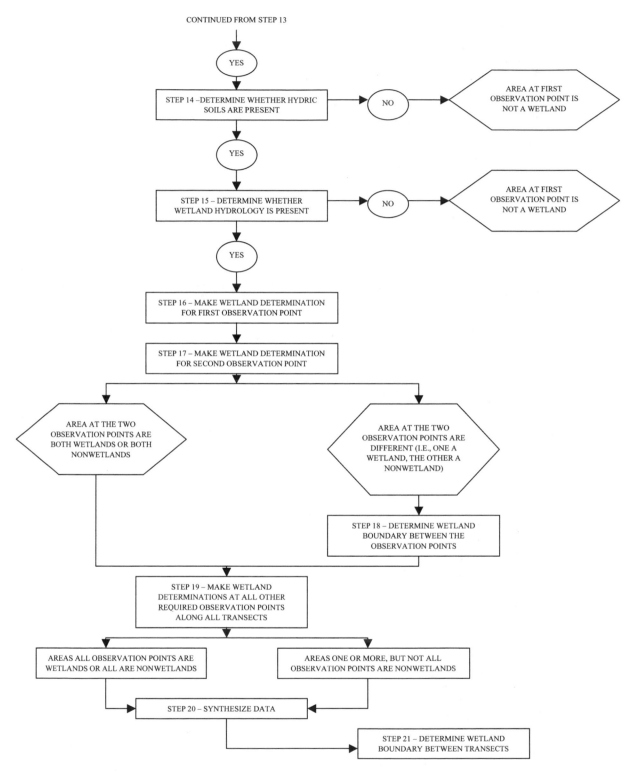

Figure 4.4. (*Continued*)

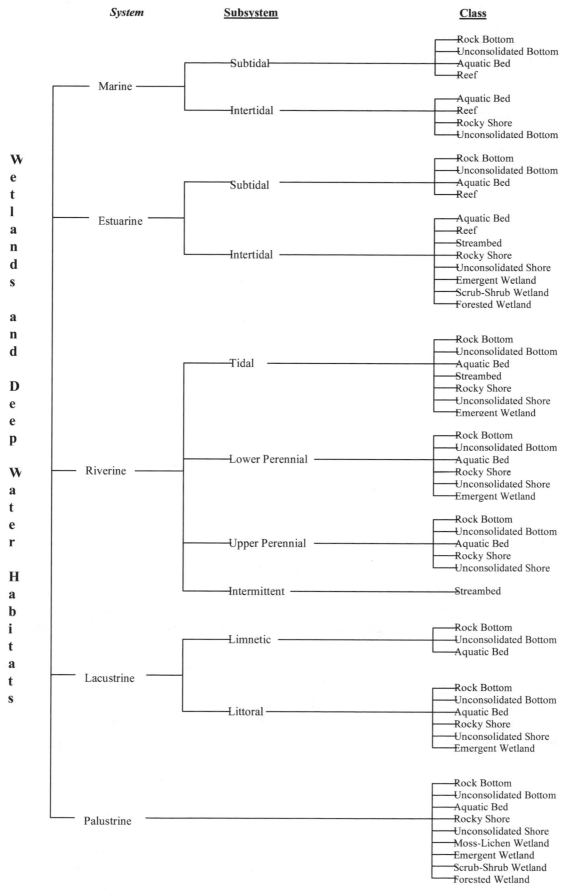

Figure 4.4. *(Continued)*

or natural events. Three specific situations are described in the manual in some detail and are paraphrased below:

unauthorized activities that have resulted in alterations of a wetland (i.e., removal of vegetation, filling of wetlands, or alteration of hydrology through construction of levees or drainage systems);
natural events that may result in the creation or alteration of wetlands, but where certain parameters such as hydric soil indicators have not had sufficient time to develop;
man-induced wetlands including those created intentionally or accidentally, and again, where there has been insufficient time for the development of indicators for the three parameters.

The atypical situation method takes a historical approach for determination in the first two cases, unauthorized activities and natural events. The decision is based on whether positive indicators of the three parameters existed prior to the alteration of the area. Acceptable data sources and procedures are described in a detailed step-by-step manner for the analysis of vegetation, soils, and hydrology. The procedure sends the investigator back to the appropriate point in the routine or comprehensive method after the historical analysis of the altered parameter(s) is finished.

The procedure for man-induced wetlands is discussed in a separate subsection. This method recognizes that the formation of hydric soil indicators (which may take hundreds of years) lags that of hydrology, which can occur immediately when a berm or levee is constructed, and vegetation, which can develop over the course of one or two growing seasons. This is the one case in the 1987 Manual where a wetland determination can be made on the basis of two parameters, vegetation and hydrology. However, the hydrology causing the presence of the hydrophytic vegetation must be very carefully analyzed prior to a positive determination. Irrigation for example, even if it has been taking place for a long period, does not constitute sufficient hydrology.

PROBLEM AREAS

The problem area procedures recognize that there are certain wetland types where positive indicators of all three parameters may be lacking even under normal circumstances due to regional climatic, geologic, or other conditions. Several representative examples of potential problem areas are listed and described in the 1987 Manual. These include: wetlands on drumlins; seasonal wetlands; prairie wetlands; and vegetated flats.

The first three examples represent different wetland types where hydrology may be very difficult to recognize during the drier months of the year. In the case of prairie potholes, during a dry year or cycle the hydrology may be so slight that farmers may actually farm wetlands that would potentially remove positive indicators of vegetation and soil. The vegetated flats example describes wetland communities where the vegetation consists of annual, obligate wetland plants that would not be present during the nongrowing season. A delineator operating during the nongrowing season could make an erroneous determination unless he or she was familiar with the ecology of the system.

The prescribed methodology in this section is not as clear as that in the proceeding sections because the approach is largely dependent on the type of system being investigated. Basic knowledge of the community type in question is listed as one of the three sources of evidence for determination. This may be provided by the delineator as well as local expertise from universities or other sources. Available information and field data are the others. The final decision rests on the conclusion that wetlands are or are not "normally present" during the growing season.

Regulatory Guidance Letters

The U.S. Army Corps of Engineers periodically issues Regulatory Guidance Letters (RGLs, or sometimes, "Regals"), which are published in the Federal Register. These letters, which range from clarifications of existing policy to statements of new policy in response to new developments within the wetland industry or as a result of court decisions, generally address permitting issues. Occasionally, Regulatory Guidance Letters are issued that pertain specifically to wetland delineation protocol and technique. Most Regulatory Guidance Letters list an effective date and an expiration date; however, they are normally in effect indefinitely regardless of the expiration date.

Two significant Regulatory Guidance Letters regarding wetland delineation were issued on August 14, 1990, and March 6, 1992. The August 14, 1990, letter established a specific time limitation for the validity of wetland delineations verified by the appropriate regulatory agency. The time standard established in this guidance letter was three years from the date of the official letter verifying the delineation. The March 6, 1992, letter provides "additional clarification and guidance" concerning the application for the 1987 Manual. This three-page memorandum simply embellishes specific procedural details for the assessment of vegetation, hydrology, and soil parameters during a delineation.

Although the Regulatory Guidance Letters generally address only small details or inconsistencies in the delineation techniques or other regulatory policies, it is important for wetland professionals specializing in delineation and permitting issues to stay abreast of these changes. This can be accomplished by reading the Federal Register or by contacting the U.S. Army Corps of Engineers in Washington, D.C., and requesting copies of the guidance letters (202-272-1782) or by going online to www.usace.army.mil/inet/functions/cw/cecwo/reg. The Corps publishes the text of all current guidance letters annually in the Federal Register.

Recent Supreme Court Cases

The Supreme Court has recently had the opportunity to dramatically affect how wetlands are regulated within the United States. A couple topics from a few of the more significant recent cases will be identified and discussed in the context of wetland science.

SOLID WASTE AGENCY OF NORTHERN COOK COUNTY (SWANCC) CASE

In 2001, with the decision of the SWANCC case, the Supreme Court began to limit the authority of the U.S. Army Corps of Engineers. To briefly summarize SWANCC, the Corps can continue to maintain jurisdiction over navigable waters, tributaries to navigable waters, and wetlands adjacent to navigable waters and their tributaries. The Corps is not to take jurisdiction over isolated intrastate nonnavigable waters, citing their importance in relationship to the Migratory Bird Rule.[1]

Key issues associated with this ruling include whether or not a wetland is isolated and what its relationship is to navigable waters. The navigable waters issue comes to the forefront in the Rapanos case (2006) discussed below. The determination of what constitutes an isolated wetland from both a physical and a regulatory perspective and, most important, whether the answer is the same from each of these perspectives is critical.

---

1. Solid Waste Agency of Northern Cook County v. U.S. Army Corps of Engineers, 531 U.S. 159 (2001).

There is quite a bit of information available to define and describe isolated wetlands. A typical definition of an isolated wetland is a wet area not connected by surface water to a river, lake, ocean, or other body of water. Isolated wetlands generally get their water from rain and snowmelt that is trapped in shallow depressions because of claylike soils that hold water (Tiner et al. 2002). The Corps defines isolated wetlands as wetlands that are not adjacent to or connected via surface water to a navigable water body such as a river, lake, or marine water.[2]

The Corps definition of isolated wetlands states that they are wetlands completely surrounded by upland (no outlet) and excludes wetlands with a groundwater connection to another water body. In reality, the term "isolated wetlands" is a relative one that can be defined from various perspectives: geographically, hydrologically, and ecologically. Geographic isolation is the easiest to determine since it describes the position of a wetland on the landscape similar to the Corps interpretation. From a landscape perspective the term "isolated wetland" takes on a much more restrictive definition and requires a more detailed examination of hydrologic interactions (surface and subsurface) and ecological relationships. Many wetlands that appear visually to be isolated are often connected to other waterways through subsurface water and from a landscape perspective are not isolated at all.

Tiner et al. (2002) states: "Isolated wetlands are defined by landscape position as 'wetlands with no apparent surface water connection to perennial rivers and streams, estuaries, or the ocean.'" These geographically isolated wetlands are surrounded by dry land. Streamside wetlands where the stream disappears underground or enters an isolated (no outflow) lake or pond are also classified as isolated. Although the latter wetland may appear to be separated from surface waters, many "isolated" wetlands are actually linked hydrologically to other wetlands or streams by subsurface flows.

Other researchers take a larger ecologic perspective on isolated wetlands by tying in biological and functional components. S. G. Leibowotz (2003) states that isolation needs to be considered with respect to specific processes and functions and suggests that isolation not be viewed discretely but be considered within an isolation-connectivity context. In addition, many of these "geographically isolated" wetlands are reported to contain a variety of rare and endangered species (Natureserve.org 2006), which may lose protection under the new interpretation of the Clean Water Act as defined by SWANCC.

In summary, the number of jurisdictionally isolated wetlands may be very small or very large depending on perspective and definition. But biologically, physically, and geographically there are likely very few truly isolated wetlands. The surface water connectivity topic will continue to be critical to the definition of isolation. The courts will ultimately define "hydrologically connected," which will directly affect the ability of the Corps to regulate isolated wetlands.

RAPANOS AND CARABELL CASES

The June 19, 2006, Supreme Court ruling on *Rapanos v. United States*, No. 04-1034, and *Carabell v. U.S. Army Corps of Engineers*, No. 04-1384 have further limited the federal jurisdiction over the Clean Water Act. While there is much in the ruling for legal council to consider, there are also elements that will require scientific explanation and research. A number of new terms will need to be fully defined and regulatory implications determined. In the referenced ruling, "significant nexus" is required connecting a wetland to a major water body, and it must have ecological (water quality) relevance to that water body for it to be jurisdictional. "Significant nexus," as forwarded by Justice Anthony M. Kennedy, will likely now become a test by which regulators determine whether or not they have jurisdiction over a wetland.

---

2. 33 CFR 328.3(a)(3).

The current legal thought is that Justice Kennedy's position is likely to be considered as the controlling opinion. Justice Kennedy believes that the Corps may rely on adjacency (bordering, contiguous, or neighboring) to establish jurisdiction, but also realizes that ecological factors such as flood control could create such a connection. Kennedy has said the "significant nexus test" requires true evidence of adequate flows in the adjacent water body and that the wetlands are not too far away from navigable waters and that the wetlands must "significantly affect the chemical, physical, and biological integrity" of nearby navigable waters to come under the Clean Water Act. Justice Kennedy provides some scientific elements that may be considered when determining whether a wetland has significant nexus or not. He cites three physical parameters—volume, flow, and distance evaluated in light of the purpose of the Clean Water Act—to restore and maintain the chemical, physical, and biological integrity of the nation's waters. He is clear in his argument that if the wetland has the physical nexus (volume, flow, and distance), that alone is not enough. The wetland also must have an effect on water quality of a downstream water body, and if this water quality connection is speculative or insubstantial, then the wetland is not regulated.

Furthermore, Justice Kennedy states that an aquatic feature simply containing an Ordinary High Water Mark is no longer good enough to prove hydrologic connectivity. This alone does not prove a measure of volume or a velocity of flow. For now, "the Corps must establish a significant nexus on a case-by-case basis when seeking to regulate wetlands based on adjacency to nonnavigable tributaries, in order to avoid unreasonable applications of the Act." Further details of evaluating nexus will certainly be developed in the upcoming months.

As an aside, Justice Antonin Scalia also proposed his own two-part test to determine whether or not a wetland was regulated. His test states that the wetland must have a continuous surface connection to nearby drains or tributaries and that the tributary be a "relatively permanent" body of water. It is unknown at this time whether or not the Scalia test will in some way blend in with the Kennedy triad test. The future will tell.

CHAPTER FIVE

The Permit Requirement

Jurisdictional Issues

Prior to the enactment of the Clean Water Act (CWA) in 1972, the Rivers and Harbors Act of 1899 was the only source of federal power to regulate dredging and filling in navigable waters[1] and to require a permit for the discharge of industrial pollution.[2] Gradually, the Corps's permitting function under the Rivers and Harbors Act of 1899 evolved by the enactment of new statutes and agreements with other federal departments to include the Corps's consideration of other impacts besides simple navigability. Ultimately, this authority included consideration of environmental impacts among other factors when the Corps was deciding whether to issue a Rivers and Harbors Act permit.[3] The evolutionary process led to the enactment of the Federal Water Pollution Control Act Amendments of 1972 (known popularly as the Clean Water Act), including §404,[4] which is used to regulate activities in wetlands because "pollutants" were specifically defined in the Clean Water Act to include "fill material."[5]

The stated goal of the Clean Water Act is "to restore and maintain the chemical, physical, and biological integrity of waters of the United States through the control of discharges of dredged or fill material."[6] To accomplish this halcyon goal, having determined that a geographical area is a "waters of the United States,"[7] the Clean Water Act thus prohibits discharging pollutants from a point source into "waters of the United States" without a permit, the purpose of the permit being to control pollution.[8] The Environmental Protection Agency (EPA) is empowered to grant pollutant discharge permits.[9] But, because of its historic role in dredging and fill activities under the Rivers and Harbors Act, the Corps

---

1. 33 U.S.C. §§403, 407.

2. *United States v. Republic Steel Corp.*, 362 U.S. 482, 4 L.Ed.2d 903, 80 S.Ct. 884, *reh'g. denied*, 363 U.S. 858, 4 L.Ed.2d 1739, 80 S.Ct. 1605 (1960), on remand, 286 F.2d 875 (7th Cir. Ill. 1961); *United States v. Standard Oil*, 384 U.S. 224, 16 L.Ed.2d 492, 86 S.Ct. 1427 (1966).

3. *Zabel v. Tabb*, 430 F.2d 199 (5th Cir. 1970), *cert. denied*, 401 U.S. 910, 27 L.Ed.2d 808, 91 S.Ct. 873 (1971).

4. 33 U.S.C §1344. The Clean Water Act has been amended twice since 1972, in 1977 and 1987, but no changes were made to §404.

5. "The term 'pollutant' means dredged spoil, solid waste, incinerator residue, sewage, garbage, sewage sludge, munitions, chemical wastes, biological materials, radioactive materials, heat, wrecked or discarded equipment, rock, sand, cellar dirt and industrial, municipal, and agricultural waste discharged into water." 33 U.S.C. §1362(6).

6. 40 CFR §230.1(a).

7. Wetlands are defined as "areas that are inundated or saturated by surface or groundwater at a frequency and duration sufficient to support, and that under normal circumstances do support, a prevalence of vegetation typically adapted for life in saturated soil conditions." 33 C.F.R. §328.3(b). *See also United States v. Mills*, 817 F.Supp. 1546 (N.D.Fla. 1993), *aff'd.* 36 F.3d 1052 (11th Cir. Fla. 1994). Whether an isolated wetland is a "water of the United States" is disputed. In a recent line of cases beginning with *Solid Waste Agency of Northern Cook County v. U.S.*, 531 U.S. 159, 148 L.Ed.2d 576, 121 S.Ct. 675 (2001), and, at this writing, ending with *Rapanos v. U.S.*, 126 S.Ct. 2208, 165 L.Ed.2d 159 (2006), the answer is far from clear.

8. 33 U.S.C. §1311.

9. 33 U.S.C. §1342. See also *Orange Environment, Inc. v. County of Orange*, 811 F.Supp. 926 (S.D.N.Y. 1993), *aff'd sub nom. Orange Env't. v. Orange County Legislature*, 2 F.3d 1235 (2d Cir. N.Y. 1993).

has been given a special duty under the Clean Water Act: the Corps is assigned the duty to grant the permits[10] to discharge "dredged and fill material into the navigable waters at specified disposal sites," wetlands among them.[11] Thus, if it is determined that the area in question is a wetland,[12] a permit to discharge dredged or fill material will be necessary unless one of the exempt activities is contemplated or the activity fits either a general or nationwide permit.

In addition, some assertions of jurisdiction over wetlands with less conspicuous connections either to navigable waters or interstate commerce have been upheld by the courts. In particular, so-called "artificially created wetlands," those which were not naturally present before but resulted from some manmade activity, are subject to Clean Water Act jurisdiction,[13] as are seasonal wetlands[14] and isolated wetlands.[15] On the other hand, "prior-converted" wetlands have been excluded from jurisdiction by regulation.[16]

Activities Requiring a Permit

While most activity occurring in a wetland, one which places solid matter in the wetland, will be subject to the permit requirement, it is important to remember that the §404 does not apply to prohibit all activities that may occur in a wetland, but only to the discharge of dredged and fill material from a "point source," even though these other activities may have an equally deleterious effect on wetlands, even to the point of destroying them. The definition of "point source" as

> any discernible, confined, and discrete conveyance, including but not limited to any pipe, ditch, channel, tunnel, conduit, well, discrete fissure, container, rolling stock, concentrated animal feeding operation, or vessel or other floating craft, from which pollutants may be discharged [but not agricultural stormwater discharges and return flows from irrigated agriculture][17]

---

10. Although the Corps actually grants the permits, the Environmental Protection Agency retains an oversight function and may, in certain circumstances, overrule the Corps's permit decision. See *Memorandum of Agreement Between the Department of the Army and the Environmental Protection Agency Concerning Determination of the Geographic Jurisdiction of the Section 404 Program and the Application of Exceptions Under Section 404(f) of the Clean Water Act* (January 19, 1989) (hereinafter the "Jurisdiction MOA").

11. 33 U.S.C. §1344(a). This statute is commonly known as, and will be hereinafter referred to as "§404." See also *United States v. Mills*, 817 F.Supp.1546 (N.D.Fla. 1993).

12. Even though the Clean Water Act never uses the word "wetlands," their inclusion in the regulatory scheme as "waters of the United States" is found in the regulations and case law. The Corps initially took the position that the extent of its permitting authority under the Clean Water Act was coterminous with its traditional authority under the Rivers and Harbors Act, namely navigable waters, including waters subject to the ebb and flow of the tides, waters which are or have been used to transport interstate commerce, tidal flats under navigable waters, and the natural meandering of rivers. A citizens suit forced the expansion of the Corps's regulatory definition of "waters of the United States" to include wetlands. *Natural Resources Defense Council v. Callaway*, 392 F.Supp. 685 (D.D.C. 1975). Now, the Corps's regulations are rife with references to wetlands. 33 C.F.R. §§ 328.3(a)(2), 328.3(a)(3), and 328.3(a)(7)33 C.F.R. §§ 328.3(a)(2), 328.3(a)(3), and 328.3(a)(7). These new regulations were specifically upheld in *United States v. Riverside Bayview Homes*, 474 U.S. 121, 88 L.Ed.2d 419, 106 S.Ct. 455 (1985). Usually the property owner conducts the wetland delineation, most likely using a consultant with specialized knowledge in this area. If the Corps or the Environmental Protection Agency determines that a wetland is present, there is not much chance that a court will overturn the decision, particularly if a permit is also issued, but, if they decide that a wetland is not present, judicial review is available. *Golden Gate Audubon Society v. U.S. Army Corps of Engineers*, 717 F.Supp. 1417 (N.D.Cal. 1988); *National Wildlife Federation v. Hanson*, 623 F.Supp. 1539 (E.D.N.C. 1985).

13. *Leslie Salt Co. v. United States*, 896 F.2d 354 (9th Cir. Cal. 1990), *cert. denied*, 498 U.S. 1126, 112 L.Ed.2d 1194, 111 S.Ct. 1089 (1991); *United States v. DeFelice*, 641 F.2d 1169 (5th Cir. La. 1981), *cert. denied*, 454 U.S. 940, 70 L.Ed.2d 247, 102 S.Ct. 474 (1981); *Swanson v. United States*, 789 F.2d 1368 (9th Cir. Idaho 1986); *United States v. Ft. Pierre*, 747 F.2d 464 (8th Cir. S.D. 1984); *Weiszmann v. District Engineer, U.S. Army Corps of Engineers*, 526 F.2d 1302 (5th Cir. Fla. 1976); *Track 12, Inc. v. District Engineer*, 618 F.Supp. 448 (D.Minn. 1985); *United States v. Bradshaw*, 541 F.Supp. 880 (D.Md. 1981).

14. *Quivira Mining Co. v. EPA*, 765 F.2d 126 (10th Cir. 1985), *cert. denied*, 474 U.S. 1055, 88 L.Ed.2d 769, 106 S.Ct. 791 (1986); *United States v. Phelps Dodge Corp.*, 391 F.Supp. 1181 (D.Ariz. 1975).

15. If the Corps asserts jurisdiction solely based upon an isolated wetlands' (defined at 33 C.F.R. §330.2(e)) potential use by migratory birds, there is no jurisdiction. *Solid Waste Agency of Northern Cook County v. U.S.*, 531 U.S. 159, 148 L.Ed.2d 576, 121 S.Ct. 675 (2001). There must be a "nexus" between the isolated wetland and navigable waters although what constitutes a sufficient "nexus" has not been fully developed by the courts. *Rapanos v. U.S.*, 126 S.Ct. 2208, 165 L.Ed.2d 159 (2006); *Northern California River Watch v. City of Healdsburg*, No. 04-15442, (9th Cir. 2006).

16. 33 C.F.R. §228.3(a)(8).

17. 33 U.S.C. §1362(14).

has evoked some controversy. Even the exclusion of agricultural stormwater discharges is subject to doubt, given new knowledge of the source of nitrates in confined lakes and bays.[18]

Such other unprohibited activities might include the dredging activity itself [19] (so long as there is no discharge of the excavated material), drainage activities,[20] vegetation destruction including land-clearing or mowing (so long as no mechanized equipment is used in wetlands),[21] and pile driving.[22]

Initially, there was some disagreement between the Corps and the Environmental Protection Agency over what constituted a discharge of "fill material" as defined in the Corps's Clean Water Act regulations at 33 C.F.R. §323.2(k). The Corps took the position that its jurisdiction extended over discharges of fill material that are intended to replace an aquatic area or change the bottom elevation of a waterbody. The Environmental Protection Agency took the position that all solid waste discharges, regardless of their intent or effect, were covered by §404. To resolve their conflict, the Corps and the Environmental Protection Agency entered into a "*Memorandum of Agreement . . . Concerning Regulation of Discharges of Solid Waste Under the Clean Water Act.*"[23] Now a discharge will be considered "fill material" under four circumstances, and thus subject to Corps jurisdiction, if

1. [t]he discharge has as its primary purpose or has as one principle purpose of multi-purposes to replace a portion of the waters of the United States with dry land or to raise the bottom elevation, or
2. [t]he discharge results from activities such as road construction or other activities where the material to be discharged is generally identified with construction-type activities, or
3. [a] principal effect of the discharge is physical loss or physical modification of waters of the United States, including smothering of aquatic life or habitat, or
4. [t]he discharge is heterogeneous in nature and of the type normally associated with sanitary landfill discharges.[24]

The Environmental Protection Agency retained jurisdiction over a discharge "in a liquid, semiliquid, or suspended form or if it is a discharge of solid material of a homogeneous nature normally associated with single industry wastes . . . including placer mining wastes, phosphate mining wastes, titanium mining wastes, sand and gravel wastes, fly ash, and drilling muds."[25]

18. Stormwater drainage has traditionally been considered a "non-point source," however, if fill material is placed in such a manner as to increase the likelihood that rainwater will carry the fill into a wetland, then jurisdiction has been asserted successfully. *Sierra Club v. Abston Construction Co.,* 620 F.2d 41 (5th Cir. Ala. 1980).

19. But see *Salt Pond Assocs. v. Army Corps of Engineers,* 815 F.Supp. 766 (D.Del. 1993).

20. *Save Our Community v. U.S. Environmental Protection Agency,* 971 F.2d 1155 (5th Cir. Tex. 1992); *Orleans Audubon Society v. Lee,* 742 F.2d 901 (5th Cir. La. 1984), *reh'g. denied en banc,* 750 F.2d 69 (5th Cir. La. 1984). A drained area may still be considered a wetland because of the "normal circumstances" provision of the definition, i.e. if the area under normal circumstances is a wetland, then any drainage will not destroy jurisdiction over it. A further caution remains that discharges of fill material into drained wetlands may require a §404 permit. The Corps will look to the effect on the wetland of the fill so as to exclude minor discharges as part of a dredging operation, which do not necessarily affect a wetland, and discharges, no matter how small, which do affect the wetland. The Corps has proposed a regulation on this subject to the question is still open as to how long an area must remain dry after drainage in order to avoid jurisdiction. See also "Recapture Provision," below. Prior converted croplands, so long as they are still in production, are not covered.

21. *Avoyelles Sportmen's League v. Marsh,* 715 F.2d 897 (5th Cir. La. 1983); *Save Our Wetlands, Inc. v. Sands,* 711 F.2d 634 (5th Cir. 1983). See also 52 ALR Fed. 788, Supp. §5; Regulatory Guidance Letter, No. 90-5, *Landclearing Activities Subject to Section 404 Jurisdiction,* July 18, 1990; *Salt Pond Association v. Army Corps of Engineers,* 815 F.Supp. 766 (D.Del. 1993) (Corps does *not* have jurisdiction to regulate dredging because Regulatory Guidance Letter 90-5 was not issued in accordance with the federal Administrative Procedure Act).

22. Pile driving can go too far. The Corps will assert §404 jurisdiction over pilings on a site-specific basis when they are placed so close together that they effectively replace "an aquatic area with dry land or [change] the bottom elevation of the waterbody. Pilings may have this function or effect when they are placed so as to facilitate sedimentation, or are placed so densely that they in effect displace a substantial percentage of the water in the project area." Regulatory Guidance Letter, *Applicability of Section 404 to Pilings, No. 90-8 (December 14, 1990).*

23. 51 Fed.Reg. 8871 (March 14, 1986).

24. *Id.*

25. *Id.*

General Permits

Section 404(e) of the Clean Water Act authorizes the Corps "after notice and opportunity for public hearing" to issue "general permits on a state, regional, or nationwide basis for any category of activities involving discharges of dredged or fill material if [the Corps] determines that such activities in such category are

1. similar in nature and similar in their impact on water quality and the aquatic environment;
2. will cause only minimal cumulative adverse effects when performed separately; and,
3. will have only minimal cumulative adverse effect on water quality and the aquatic environment."[26]

In the Corps's regulations the purpose of these "general permits," like "nationwide permits" discussed below, is "to allow certain activities to occur with little, if any, delay or paperwork."[27]

The purpose of the "general permit" program is to eliminate the need for a permit application if the activity is one covered by the general permit. In a *Section 404 Enforcement Memorandum of Agreement Procedures Regarding the Applicability of Previously-Issued Corps Permits*, the Corps and Environmental Protection Agency agreed that "the Corps will be responsible for determining whether an alleged illegal discharge of dredged or fill material is authorized under an individual or general permit."[28] When the Environmental Protection Agency becomes aware of an alleged illegal discharge, it has agreed to "contact the appropriate Corps district and request a determination as to whether the discharge is authorized by an individual or general permit."[29] A Corps determination, which must be made within either two or ten working days depending upon how much information the Environmental Protection Agency gives it, that the discharge is authorized or unauthorized is a final enforcement decision.[30] Nonetheless, if the Environmental Protection Agency either does not receive a timely Corps determination or "reasonably believes that such discharge is not authorized," the Environmental Protection Agency may take "immediate enforcement action against the discharger when necessary to minimize impacts to the environment."[31] The Environmental Protection Agency still has to contact the Corps in any event and, if the Corps finds that the discharge was authorized, that, too, is a "final determination."[32] In order to find out what kinds of activities in wetlands have been authorized in which states or regions, it is necessary to contact the local Corps division or district office directly. At this writing, only two states, New Jersey and Michigan, operate their wetland regulation program under a general permit.

Nationwide Permits

The Corps's regulations authorize it to issue, reissue, modify, suspend, revoke, in whole or for specific geographical areas, classes of activities, or classes of waters, or propose regional conditions to thirty-six "Nationwide Permits" (hereinafter "NWPs")[33] as long as thirteen general, and nine "Section 404 Only,"

---

26. 33 U.S.C. §1344(e)(1)33 U.S.C. §1344(e)(1). See also 40 C.F.R. §230.7(a), part of the *Guidelines*, and *Abenaki Nation of Mississquoi v. Hughes*, 805 F.Supp. 234 (D.Vt. 1992), *aff'd.*, 990 F.2d 729 (2d Cir. Vt. 1993), holding that a creation of compensatory wetlands as part of a project already authorized by a general permit is not itself a "discharge" requiring a permit.

27. 33 C.F.R. §320.1(a)(3);33 C.F.R. §330.1;33 C.F.R. §320.1(a)(3).

28. *Section 404 Enforcement Memorandum of Agreement Procedures Regarding the Applicability of Previously-Issued Corps Permits*, January 19, 1989.

29. *Id.* at ¶3.

30. *Id.* at ¶4 and 5.

31. *Id.* at ¶6. A "final determination" becomes important in issues regarding ripeness of a permit decision for judicial review. See chapter 9.

32. *Id.*

33. 33 C.F.R. §330.6.

conditions are met.[34] This program is so generous in its coverage that only thirteen of the thirty-six NWPs require a special notice procedure[35] before commencing the activity. The remainder of the NWPs are technically self-executing, though wisdom and practice teach that the Corps should be contacted whenever any activity will be conducted in a wetland just to make certain that an NWP applies.[36]

Coastal zone management consistency determinations[37] and state water quality certifications remain necessary, though that procedure may itself be eliminated by the applicability of the NWP in the individual state.[38] If the state issues a water quality certification with conditions on a statewide or regional basis, then under the Corps's regulations, the conditions will become part of the NWP in that particular state or region, unless the Corps determines that the conditions do not comply with other Corps regulations, in which case the water quality certification is deemed denied until the state issues a certification or waives its right to do so.[39]

NWPs frequently provide a safe harbor in violation cases since the Corps is authorized to terminate an enforcement proceeding with an after-the-fact NWP if all of the terms and conditions of the NWP have been satisfied either before or after the activity has been accomplished.[40] Nonetheless, the Corps retains discretionary authority,[41] even in cases in which an NWP would appear to apply, to suspend, modify, or revoke an NWP authorization if the Corps determines that the activity would have more than a minimal individual or cumulative net adverse effect on the environment, or that the activity is contrary to the public interest.[42] In these instances, the Corps must instruct the landowner to apply for either a general or individual permit. Another useful regulation is that two or more different NWPs may be applied to a single and complete project (but the same NWP may not be applied more than once to a single and complete project).[43] In addition, under certain conditions, an NWP may be applied to a portion of a larger project while the individual permit is being evaluated on a different portion.[44]

Some of the NWPs require a delineation. In these cases, if the Corps determines that the adverse effects are more than minimal, the Corps may either require an individual permit or allow the landowner to propose mitigation measures.[45] If the landowner bites the bullet and proposes mitigation along with the original notification, the Corps may consider the mitigation proposal at the same time it is deciding whether the adverse effects are minimal, thus enhancing the chances of permit issuance.[46] Nonetheless, the Corps is supposed to consider the availability of NWPs in reviewing all permit applications, and thus may contact a landowner that an activity could comply with an NWP after reasonable project modifications and/or activity-specific conditions.[47]

---

34. 33 C.F.R. §330.6 and appendix A.
35. *Id.*
36. 33 C.F.R. §330.6(a)(1) allows a landowner to request and receive a confirmation from the Corps that the proposed activity complies with an NWP.
37. 33 C.F.R. §330.4(d).
38. 33 C.F.R. §330.4(c).
39. 33 C.F.R. §§330.4(c)(2) and (3). Other federal statutes, such as the Endangered Species Act and the National Historic Preservation Act, remain applicable although there are provisions in 33 C.F.R. §§330.4(a), 330.4(d), 330.4(f) and appendix A to §330 Subpart C, "Nationwide Permits." See also *Vieux Carre Property Owners, Residents & Assocs. v. Brown*, 875 F.2d 453 (5th Cir. La. 1989), *cert. denied*, 493 U.S. 1020, 107 L.Ed.2d 739, 110 S.Ct. 720 (1990).
40. 33 C.F.R. §§330.1(c) and 330.6(e).
41. See also 33 C.F.R. §330.1(d).
42. 33 C.F.R. §§330.4 and 330.5.
43. 33 C.F.R. §330.6(c).
44. 33 C.F.R. §330.6(d).
45. 33 C.F.R. §330.1(e)(3)); appendix A to §330 subpart C, "Nationwide Permit Conditions," ¶13(f).
46. 33 C.F.R. §330.1(e).
47. 33 C.F.R. §330.1(f).

Effective as of March, 2002, are the following Nationwide Permits, excerpted from the *Federal Register*, vol. 67, no. 10 (January 15, 2002):

1. ***Aids to Navigation.*** The placement of aids to navigation and regulatory markers which are approved by and installed in accordance with the requirements of the U.S. Coast Guard (USCG) (see 33 CFR, chapter I, subchapter C, part 66). (Section 10)

2. ***Structures in Artificial Canals.*** Structures constructed in artificial canals within principally residential developments where the connection of the canal to navigable water of the U.S. has been previously authorized (see 33 CFR 322.5(g)). (Section 10)

3. ***Maintenance.*** Activities related to:
(i) The repair, rehabilitation, or replacement of any previously authorized, currently serviceable, structure, or fill, or of any currently serviceable structure or fill authorized by 33 CFR 330.3, provided that the structure or fill is not to be put to uses differing from those uses specified or contemplated for it in the original permit or the most recently authorized modification. Minor deviations in the structure's configuration or filled area including those due to changes in materials, construction techniques, or current construction codes or safety standards which are necessary to make repair, rehabilitation, or replacement are permitted, provided the adverse environmental effects resulting from such repair, rehabilitation, or replacement are minimal. Currently serviceable means useable as is or with some maintenance, but not so degraded as to essentially require reconstruction. This NWP authorizes the repair, rehabilitation, or replacement of those structures or fills destroyed or damaged by storms, floods, fire or other discrete events, provided the repair, rehabilitation, or replacement is commenced, or is under contract to commence, within two years of the date of their destruction or damage. In cases of catastrophic events, such as hurricanes or tornadoes, this two-year limit may be waived by the District Engineer, provided the permittee can demonstrate funding, contract, or other similar delays.
(ii) Discharges of dredged or fill material, including excavation, into all waters of the US to remove accumulated sediments and debris in the vicinity of, and within, existing structures (e.g., bridges, culverted road crossings, water intake structures, etc.) and the placement of new or additional riprap to protect the structure, provided the permittee notifies the District Engineer in accordance with General Condition 13. The removal of sediment is limited to the minimum necessary to restore the waterway in the immediate vicinity of the structure to the approximate dimensions that existed when the structure was built, but cannot extend further than 200 feet in any direction from the structure. The placement of riprap must be the minimum necessary to protect the structure or to ensure the safety of the structure. All excavated materials must be deposited and retained in an upland area unless otherwise specifically approved by the District Engineer under separate authorization. Any bank stabilization measures not directly associated with the structure will require a separate authorization from the District Engineer.
(iii) Discharges of dredged or fill material, including excavation, into all waters of the U.S. for activities associated with the restoration of upland areas damaged by a storm, flood, or other discrete event, including the construction, placement, or installation of upland protection structures and minor dredging to remove obstructions in a water of the U.S. (Uplands lost as a result of a storm, flood, or other discrete event can be replaced without a Section 404 permit provided the uplands are restored to their original pre-event location. This NWP is for the activities in waters of the U.S. associated with the replacement of the uplands.)

The permittee must notify the District Engineer, in accordance with General Condition 13, within 12 months of the date of the damage and the work must commence, or be under contract to commence, within two years of the date of the damage. The permittee should provide evidence, such as a recent topographic survey or photographs, to justify the extent of the proposed restoration. The restoration of the damaged areas cannot exceed the contours, or ordinary high water mark, that existed before the damage. The District Engineer retains the right to determine the extent of the pre-existing conditions and the extent of any restoration work authorized by this permit. Minor dredging to remove obstructions from the adjacent waterbody is limited to 50 cubic yards below the plane of the ordinary high water mark, and is limited to the amount necessary to restore the preexisting bottom contours of the waterbody. The dredging may not be done primarily to obtain fill for any restoration activities. The discharge of dredged or fill material and all related work needed to restore the upland must be part of a single and complete project. This permit cannot be used in conjunction with NWP 18 or NWP 19 to restore damaged upland areas. This permit cannot be used to reclaim historic lands lost, over an extended period, to normal erosion processes. This permit does not authorize maintenance dredging for the primary purpose of navigation and beach restoration. This permit does not authorize new stream channelization or stream relocation projects. Any work authorized by this permit must not cause more than minimal degradation of water quality, more than minimal changes to the flow characteristics of the stream, or increase flooding (see General Conditions 9 and 21). (Sections 10 and 404)

Note: This NWP authorizes the repair, rehabilitation, or replacement of any previously authorized structure or fill that does not qualify for the Section 404(f) exemption for maintenance.

4. *Fish and Wildlife Harvesting, Enhancement, and Attraction Devices and Activities.* Fish and wildlife harvesting devices and activities such as pound nets, crab traps, crab dredging, eel pots, lobster traps, duck blinds, clam and oyster digging; and small fish attraction devices such as open water fish concentrators (sea kites, etc.). This NWP authorizes shellfish seeding provided this activity does not occur in wetlands or sites that support submerged aquatic vegetation (including sites where submerged aquatic vegetation is documented to exist, but may not be present in a given year.). This NWP does not authorize artificial reefs or impoundments and semi-impoundments of waters of the U.S. for the culture or holding of motile species such as lobster or the use of covered oyster trays or clam racks. (Sections 10 and 404)

5. *Scientific Measurement Devices.* Devices, whose purpose is to measure and record scientific data such as staff gages, tide gages, water recording devices, water quality testing and improvement devices and similar structures. Small weirs and flumes constructed primarily to record water quantity and velocity are also authorized provided the discharge is limited to 25 cubic yards and further for discharges of 10 to 25 cubic yards provided the permittee notifies the District Engineer in accordance with the "Notification" General Condition. (Sections 10 and 404)

6. *Survey Activities.* Survey activities including core sampling, seismic exploratory operations, plugging of seismic shot holes and other exploratory-type bore holes, soil survey, sampling, and historic resources surveys. Discharges and structures associated with the recovery of historic resources are not authorized by this NWP. Drilling and the discharge of excavated material from test wells for oil and gas exploration is not authorized by this NWP; the plugging of such wells is authorized. Fill placed for roads, pads and other similar activities is not authorized by this NWP. The NWP does not authorize any permanent

structures. The discharge of drilling mud and cuttings may require a permit under section 402 of the CWA. (Sections 10 and 404)

7. *Outfall Structures and Maintenance.* Activities related to:

(i) Construction of outfall structures and associated intake structures where the effluent from the outfall is authorized, conditionally authorized, or specifically exempted, or are otherwise in compliance with regulations issued under the National Pollutant Discharge Elimination System Program (Section 402 of the CWA), and

(ii) Maintenance excavation, including dredging, to remove accumulated sediments blocking or restricting outfall and intake structures, accumulated sediments from small impoundments associated with outfall and intake structures, and accumulated sediments from canals associated with outfall and intake structures, provided that the activity meets all of the following criteria:

  a. The permittee notifies the District Engineer in accordance with General Condition 13;

  b. The amount of excavated or dredged material must be the minimum necessary to restore the outfalls, intakes, small impoundments, and canals to original design capacities and design configurations (i.e., depth and width);

  c. The excavated or dredged material is deposited and retained at an upland site, unless otherwise approved by the District Engineer under separate authorization; and

  d. Proper soil erosion and sediment control measures are used to minimize reentry of sediments into waters of the U.S.

The construction of intake structures is not authorized by this NWP, unless they are directly associated with an authorized outfall structure. For maintenance excavation and dredging to remove accumulated sediments, the notification must include information regarding the original design capacities and configurations of the facility and the presence of special aquatic sites (e.g., vegetated shallows) in the vicinity of the proposed work. (Sections 10 and 404)

8. *Oil and Gas Structures.* Structures for the exploration, production, and transportation of oil, gas, and minerals on the outer continental shelf within areas leased for such purposes by the DOI [Department of the Interior], Minerals Management Service (MMS). Such structures shall not be placed within the limits of any designated shipping safety fairway or traffic separation scheme, except temporary anchors that comply with the fairway regulations in 33 CFR 322.5(l). (Where such limits have not been designated, or where changes are anticipated, District Engineers will consider asserting discretionary authority in accordance with 33 CFR 330.4(e) and will also review such proposals to ensure they comply with the provisions of the fairway regulations in 33 CFR 322.5(l). Any Corps review under this permit will be limited to the effects on navigation and national security in accordance with 33 CFR 322.5(f)). Such structures will not be placed in established danger zones or restricted areas as designated in 33 CFR part 334, nor will such structures be permitted in EPA or Corps designated dredged material disposal areas. (Section 10)

9. *Structures in Fleeting and Anchorage Areas.* Structures, buoys, floats and other devices placed within anchorage or fleeting areas to facilitate moorage of vessels where the USCG [U.S. Coast Guard] has established such areas for that purpose. (Section 10)

10. *Mooring Buoys.* Non-commercial, single-boat, mooring buoys. (Section 10)

11. *Temporary Recreational Structures.* Temporary buoys, markers, small floating docks, and similar structures placed for recreational use during specific events such as water skiing competitions and boat

races or seasonal use provided that such structures are removed within 30 days after use has been discontinued. At Corps of Engineers reservoirs, the reservoir manager must approve each buoy or marker individually. (Section 10)

12. ***Utility Line Activities***. Activities required for the construction, maintenance and repair of utility lines and associated facilities in waters of the U.S. as follows:

(i) Utility lines: The construction, maintenance, or repair of utility lines, including outfall and intake structures and the associated excavation, backfill, or bedding for the utility lines, in all waters of the U.S., provided there is no change in preconstruction contours. A "utility line" is defined as any pipe or pipeline for the transportation of any gaseous, liquid, liquescent, or slurry substance, for any purpose, and any cable, line, or wire for the transmission for any purpose of electrical energy, telephone, and telegraph messages, and radio and television communication (see Note 1, p. 52). Material resulting from trench excavation may be temporarily sidecast (up to three months) into waters of the U.S., provided that the material is not placed in such a manner that it is dispersed by currents or other forces. The District Engineer may extend the period of temporary side casting not to exceed a total of 180 days, where appropriate. In wetlands, the top 6" to 12" of the trench should normally be backfilled with topsoil from the trench. Furthermore, the trench cannot be constructed in such a manner as to drain waters of the U.S. (e.g., backfilling with extensive gravel layers, creating a french drain effect). For example, utility line trenches can be backfilled with clay blocks to ensure that the trench does not drain the waters of the U.S. through which the utility line is installed. Any exposed slopes and stream banks must be stabilized immediately upon completion of the utility line crossing of each waterbody.

(ii) Utility line substations: The construction, maintenance, or expansion of a substation facility associated with a power line or utility line in non-tidal waters of the U.S., excluding non-tidal wetlands adjacent to tidal waters, provided the activity does not result in the loss of greater than 12-acre of non-tidal waters of the U.S.

(iii) Foundations for overhead utility line towers, poles, and anchors: The construction or maintenance of foundations for overhead utility line towers, poles, and anchors in all waters of the U.S., provided the foundations are the minimum size necessary and separate footings for each tower leg (rather than a larger single pad) are used where feasible.

(iv) Access roads: The construction of access roads for the construction and maintenance of utility lines, including overhead power lines and utility line substations, in non-tidal waters of the U.S., excluding non-tidal wetlands adjacent to tidal waters, provided the discharges do not cause the loss of greater than 12-acre of non-tidal waters of the U.S. Access roads shall be the minimum width necessary (see Note 2, p. 52). Access roads must be constructed so that the length of the road minimizes the adverse effects on waters of the U.S. and as near as possible to preconstruction contours and elevations (e.g., at grade corduroy roads or geotextile/gravel roads). Access roads constructed above preconstruction contours and elevations in waters of the U.S. must be properly bridged or culverted to maintain surface flows. The term "utility line" does not include activities which drain a water of the U.S., such as drainage tile, or french drains; however, it does apply to pipes conveying drainage from another area. For the purposes of this NWP, the loss of waters of the U.S. includes the filled area plus waters of the U.S. that are adversely affected by flooding, excavation, or drainage as a result of the project.

Activities authorized by paragraph (i) through (iv) may not exceed a total of 12-acre loss of waters of the U.S. Waters of the U.S. temporarily affected by filling, flooding, excavation, or drainage, where the project area is restored to preconstruction contours and elevation, is not included in the calculation of permanent loss of waters of the U.S. This includes temporary construction mats (e.g., timber, steel, geotextile) used during construction and removed upon completion of the work. Where certain functions and values of waters of the U.S. are permanently adversely affected, such as the conversion of a forested wetland to a herbaceous wetland in the permanently maintained utility line right-of-way, mitigation will be required to reduce the adverse effects of the project to the minimal level. Mechanized land clearing necessary for the construction, maintenance, or repair of utility lines and the construction, maintenance and expansion of utility line substations, foundations for overhead utility lines, and access roads is authorized, provided the cleared area is kept to the minimum necessary and preconstruction contours are maintained as near as possible. The area of waters of the U.S. that is filled, excavated, or flooded must be limited to the minimum necessary to construct the utility line, substations, foundations, and access roads. Excess material must be removed to upland areas immediately upon completion of construction. This NWP may authorize utility lines in or affecting navigable waters of the U.S. even if there is no associated discharge of dredged or fill material (see 33 CFR part 322).

Notification: The permittee must notify the District Engineer in accordance with General Condition 13, if any of the following criteria are met:
(a) Mechanized land clearing in a forested wetland for the utility line right-of-way;
(b) A Section 10 permit is required;
(c) The utility line in waters of the U.S., excluding overhead lines, exceeds 500 feet;
(d) The utility line is placed within a jurisdictional area (i.e., water of the U.S.), and it runs parallel to a stream bed that is within that jurisdictional area;
(e) Discharges associated with the construction of utility line substations that result in the loss of greater than 110-acre of waters of the U.S.;
(f) Permanent access roads constructed above grade in waters of the US for a distance of more than 500 feet; or
(g) Permanent access roads constructed in waters of the U.S. with impervious materials. (Sections 10 and 404)

Note 1: Overhead utility lines constructed over Section 10 waters and utility lines that are routed in or under Section 10 waters without a discharge of dredged or fill material require a Section 10 permit; except for pipes or pipelines used to transport gaseous, liquid, liquescent, or slurry substances over navigable waters of the U.S., which are considered to be bridges, not utility lines, and may require a permit from the USCG pursuant to section 9 of the Rivers and Harbors Act of 1899. However, any discharges of dredged or fill material associated with such pipelines will require a Corps permit under Section 404.

Note 2: Access roads used for both construction and maintenance may be authorized, provided they meet the terms and conditions of this NWP. Access roads used solely for construction of the utility line must be removed upon completion of the work and the area restored to preconstruction contours, elevations, and wetland conditions. Temporary access roads for construction may be authorized by NWP 33.

Note 3: Where the proposed utility line is constructed or installed in navigable waters of the U.S. (i.e., Section 10 waters), copies of the PCN and NWP verification will be sent by the Corps to the National Oceanic and Atmospheric Administration (NOAA), National Ocean Service (NOS), for charting the utility line to protect navigation.

13. *Bank Stabilization.* Bank stabilization activities necessary for erosion prevention provided the activity meets all of the following criteria:
a. No material is placed more than the minimum needed for erosion protection;
b. The bank stabilization activity is less than 500 feet in length;

c. The activity will not exceed an average of one cubic yard per running foot placed along the bank below the plane of the ordinary high water mark or the high tide line;

d. No material is placed in any special aquatic site, including wetlands;

e. No material is of the type, or is placed in any location, or in any manner, to impair surface water flow into or out of any wetland area;

f. No material is placed in a manner that will be eroded by normal or expected high flows (properly anchored trees and treetops may be used in low energy areas); and,

g. The activity is part of a single and complete project. Bank stabilization activities in excess of 500 feet in length or greater than an average of one cubic yard per running foot may be authorized if the permittee notifies the District Engineer in accordance with the *"Notification"* General Condition 13 and the District Engineer determines the activity complies with the other terms and conditions of the NWP and the adverse environmental effects are minimal both individually and cumulatively. This NWP may not be used for the channelization of waters of the U.S. (Sections 10 and 404)

14. *Linear Transportation Projects.* Activities required for the construction, expansion, modification, or improvement of linear transportation crossings (e.g., highways, railways, trails, airport runways, and taxiways) in waters of the U.S., including wetlands, if the activity meets the following criteria:

a. This NWP is subject to the following acreage limits:

(1) For linear transportation projects in non-tidal waters, provided the discharge does not cause the loss of greater than 12-acre of waters of the U.S.;

(2) For linear transportation projects in tidal waters, provided the discharge does not cause the loss of greater than 13-acre of waters of the U.S.

b. The permittee must notify the District Engineer in accordance with General Condition 13 if any of the following criteria are met:

(1) The discharge causes the loss of greater than 110-acre of waters of the U.S.; or

(2) There is a discharge in a special aquatic site, including wetlands;

c. The *notification* must include a compensatory mitigation proposal to offset permanent losses of waters of the U.S. to ensure that those losses result only in minimal adverse effects to the aquatic environment and a statement describing how temporary losses will be minimized to the maximum extent practicable;

d. For discharges in special aquatic sites, including wetlands, and stream riffle and pool complexes, the *notification* must include a delineation of the affected special aquatic sites;

e. The width of the fill is limited to the minimum necessary for the crossing;

f. This permit does not authorize stream channelization, and the authorized activities must not cause more than minimal changes to the hydraulic flow characteristics of the stream, increase flooding, or cause more than minimal degradation of water quality of any stream (see General Conditions 9 and 21);

g. This permit cannot be used to authorize non-linear features commonly associated with transportation projects, such as vehicle maintenance or storage buildings, parking lots, train stations, or aircraft hangars; and

h. The crossing is a single and complete project for crossing waters of the U.S. Where a road segment (i.e., the shortest segment of a road with independent utility that is part of a larger project) has multiple crossings of streams (several single and complete projects) the Corps will consider whether it should use its discretionary authority to require an Individual Permit. (Sections 10 and 404)

Note: Some discharges for the construction of farm roads, forest roads, or temporary roads for moving mining equipment may be eligible for an exemption from the need for a Section 404 permit (see 33 CFR 323.4).

15. ***U.S. Coast Guard Approved Bridges.*** Discharges of dredged or fill material incidental to the construction of bridges across navigable waters of the US, including cofferdams, abutments, foundation seals, piers, and temporary construction and access fills provided such discharges have been authorized by the USCG as part of the bridge permit. Causeways and approach fills are not included in this NWP and will require an individual or regional Section 404 permit. (Section 404)

16. ***Return Water From Upland Contained Disposal Areas.*** Return water from upland, contained dredged material disposal area. The dredging itself may require a Section 404 permit (33 CFR 323.2(d)), but will require a Section 10 permit if located in navigable waters of the U.S. The return water from a contained disposal area is administratively defined as a discharge of dredged material by 33 CFR 323.2(d), even though the disposal itself occurs on the upland and does not require a Section 404 permit. This NWP satisfies the technical requirement for a Section 404 permit for the return water where the quality of the return water is controlled by the state through the Section 401 certification procedures. (Section 404)

17. ***Hydropower Projects.*** Discharges of dredged or fill material associated with (a) small hydropower projects at existing reservoirs where the project, which includes the fill, are licensed by the Federal Energy Regulatory Commission (FERC) under the Federal Power Act of 1920, as amended; and has a total generating capacity of not more than 5000 kW; and the permittee notifies the District Engineer in accordance with the "Notification" General Condition; or (b) hydropower projects for which the FERC has granted an exemption from licensing pursuant to section 408 of the Energy Security Act of 1980 (16 U.S.C. 2705 and 2708) and section 30 of the Federal Power Act, as amended; provided the permittee notifies the District Engineer in accordance with the "Notification" General Condition. (Section 404)

18. ***Minor Discharges.*** Minor discharges of dredged or fill material into all waters of the U.S. if the activity meets all of the following criteria:
a. The quantity of discharged material and the volume of area excavated do not exceed 25 cubic yards below the plane of the ordinary high water mark or the high tide line;
b. The discharge, including any excavated area, will not cause the loss of more than 110-acre of a special aquatic site, including wetlands. For the purposes of this NWP, the acreage limitation includes the filled area and excavated area plus special aquatic sites that are adversely affected by flooding and special aquatic sites that are drained so that they would no longer be a water of the U.S. as a result of the project;
c. If the discharge, including any excavated area, exceeds 10 cubic yards below the plane of the ordinary high water mark or the high tide line or if the discharge is in a special aquatic site, including wetlands, the permittee notifies the District Engineer in accordance with the "Notification" General Condition. For discharges in special aquatic sites, including wetlands, the notification must also include a delineation of affected special aquatic sites, including wetlands (also see 33 CFR 330.1(e)); and
d. The discharge, including all attendant features, both temporary and permanent, is part of a single and complete project and is not placed for the purpose of a stream diversion. (Sections 10 and 404)

19. ***Minor Dredging.*** Dredging of no more than 25 cubic yards below the plane of the ordinary high water mark or the mean high water mark from navigable waters of the U.S. (i.e., Section 10 waters) as part of a single and complete project. This NWP does not authorize the dredging or degradation through siltation of coral reefs, sites that support submerged aquatic vegetation (including sites where submerged aquatic vegetation is documented to exist, but may not be present in a given year), anadro-

mous fish spawning areas, or wetlands, or the connection of canals or other artificial waterways to navigable waters of the U.S. (see 33 CFR 322.5(g)). (Sections 10 and 404)

20. ***Oil Spill Cleanup.*** Activities required for the containment and cleanup of oil and hazardous substances which are subject to the National Oil and Hazardous Substances Pollution Contingency Plan (40 CFR part 300) provided that the work is done in accordance with the Spill Control and Countermeasure Plan required by 40 CFR 112.3 and any existing state contingency plan and provided that the Regional Response Team (if one exists in the area) concurs with the proposed containment and cleanup action. (Sections 10 and 404)

21. ***Surface Coal Mining Activities.*** Discharges of dredged or fill material into waters of the U.S. associated with surface coal mining and reclamation operations provided the coal mining activities are authorized by the DOI, Office of Surface Mining (OSM), or by states with approved programs under Title V of the Surface Mining Control and Reclamation Act of 1977 and provided the permittee notifies the District Engineer in accordance with the "Notification" General Condition. In addition, to be authorized by this NWP, the District Engineer must determine that the activity complies with the terms and conditions of the NWP and that the adverse environmental effects are minimal both individually and cumulatively and must notify the project sponsor of this determination in writing. The Corps, at the discretion of the District Engineer, may require a bond to ensure success of the mitigation, if no other Federal or state agency has required one. For discharges in special aquatic sites, including wetlands, and stream riffle and pool complexes, the notification must also include a delineation of affected special aquatic sites, including wetlands (also, see 33 CFR 330.1(e)).

Mitigation: In determining the need for as well as the level and type of mitigation, the District Engineer will ensure no more than minimal adverse effects to the aquatic environment occur. As such, District Engineers will determine on a case-by-case basis the requirement for adequate mitigation to ensure the effects to aquatic systems are minimal. In cases where OSM or the state has required mitigation for the loss of aquatic habitat, the Corps may consider this in determining appropriate mitigation under Section 404. (Sections 10 and 404)

22. ***Removal of Vessels.*** Temporary structures or minor discharges of dredged or fill material required for the removal of wrecked, abandoned, or disabled vessels, or the removal of man-made obstructions to navigation. This NWP does not authorize the removal of vessels listed or determined eligible for listing on the National Register of Historic Places unless the District Engineer is notified and indicates that there is compliance with the "Historic Properties" General Condition. This NWP does not authorize maintenance dredging, shoal removal, or riverbank snagging. Vessel disposal in waters of the U.S. may need a permit from EPA (see 40 CFR 229.3). (Sections 10 and 404)

23. ***Approved Categorical Exclusions.*** Activities undertaken, assisted, authorized, regulated, funded, or financed, in whole or in part, by another Federal agency or department where that agency or department has determined, pursuant to the Council on Environmental Quality Regulation for Implementing the Procedural Provisions of the National Environmental Policy Act (NEPA) (40 CFR part 1500 *et seq.*), that the activity, work, or discharge is categorically excluded from environmental documentation, because it is included within a category of actions which neither individually nor cumulatively have a significant effect on the human environment, and the Office of the Chief of Engineers (ATTN: CEC-WOR) has been furnished notice of the agency's or department's application for the categorical exclusion

and concurs with that determination. Before approval for purposes of this NWP of any agency's categorical exclusions, the Chief of Engineers will solicit public comment. In addressing these comments, the Chief of Engineers may require certain conditions for authorization of an agency's categorical exclusions under this NWP. (Sections 10 and 404)

24. *State Administered Section 404 Program.* Any activity permitted by a state administering its own Section 404 permit program pursuant to 33 U.S.C. 1344(g)–(l) is permitted pursuant to Section 10 of the Rivers and Harbors Act of 1899. Those activities that do not involve a Section 404 state permit are not included in this NWP, but certain structures will be exempted by Section 154 of Pub. L. 94–587, 90 Stat. 2917 (33 U.S.C. 591) (see 33 CFR 322.3(a)(2)). (Section 10)

25. *Structural Discharges.* Discharges of material such as concrete, sand, rock, etc., into tightly sealed forms or cells where the material will be used as a structural member for standard pile supported structures, such as bridges, transmission line footings, and walkways or for general navigation, such as mooring cells, including the excavation of bottom material from within the form prior to the discharge of concrete, sand, rock, etc. This NWP does not authorize filled structural members that would support buildings, building pads, homes, house pads, parking areas, storage areas and other such structures. The structure itself may require a Section 10 permit if located in navigable waters of the U.S. (Section 404)

26. [Reserved]

27. *Stream and Wetland Restoration Activities.* Activities in waters of the U.S. associated with the restoration of former waters, the enhancement of degraded tidal and non-tidal wetlands and riparian areas, the creation of tidal and non-tidal wetlands and riparian areas, and the restoration and enhancement of non-tidal streams and non-tidal open water areas as follows:
(a) *The activity is conducted on:*
    (1) Non-Federal public lands and private lands, in accordance with the terms and conditions of a binding wetland enhancement, restoration, or creation agreement between the landowner and the U.S. Fish and Wildlife Service (FWS) or the Natural Resources Conservation Service (NRCS), the National Marine Fisheries Service, the National Ocean Service, or voluntary wetland restoration, enhancement, and creation actions documented by the NRCS pursuant to NRCS regulations; or
    (2) Reclaimed surface coal mine lands, in accordance with a Surface Mining Control and Reclamation Act permit issued by the OSM or the applicable state agency (the future reversion does not apply to streams or wetlands created, restored, or enhanced as mitigation for the mining impacts, nor naturally due to hydrologic or topographic features, nor for a mitigation bank); or
    (3) Any other public, private or tribal lands;
(b) *Notification:* For activities on any public or private land that are not described by paragraphs (a)(1) or (a)(2) above, the permittee must notify the District Engineer in accordance with General Condition 13; and
(c) Planting of only native species should occur on the site.
    Activities authorized by this NWP include, to the extent that a Corps permit is required, but are not limited to: the removal of accumulated sediments; the installation, removal, and maintenance of small water control structures, dikes, and berms; the installation of current deflectors; the enhancement, restoration, or creation of riffle and pool stream structure; the placement of in-stream habitat structures; modifications of the stream bed and/or banks to restore or create stream meanders; the backfilling of artificial channels and drainage ditches; the removal of existing drainage structures; the construction of

small nesting islands; the construction of open water areas; the construction of oyster habitat over unvegetated bottom in tidal waters; activities needed to reestablish vegetation, including plowing or discing for seed bed preparation and the planting of appropriate wetland species; mechanized land clearing to remove non-native invasive, exotic or nuisance vegetation; and other related activities. This NWP does not authorize the conversion of a stream to another aquatic use, such as the creation of an impoundment for waterfowl habitat. This NWP does not authorize stream channelization. This NWP does not authorize the conversion of natural wetlands to another aquatic use, such as creation of waterfowl impoundments where a forested wetland previously existed. However, this NWP authorizes the relocation of non-tidal waters, including non-tidal wetlands, on the project site provided there are net gains in aquatic resource functions and values. For example, this NWP may authorize the creation of an open water impoundment in a non-tidal emergent wetland, provided the non-tidal emergent wetland is replaced by creating that wetland type on the project site. This NWP does not authorize the relocation of tidal waters or the conversion of tidal waters, including tidal wetlands, to other aquatic uses, such as the conversion of tidal wetlands into open water impoundments.

Reversion. For enhancement, restoration, and creation projects conducted under paragraphs (a)(3), this NWP does not authorize any future discharge of dredged or fill material associated with the reversion of the area to its prior condition. In such cases a separate permit would be required for any reversion. For restoration, enhancement, and creation projects conducted under paragraphs (a)(1) and (a)(2), this NWP also authorizes any future discharge of dredged or fill material associated with the reversion of the area to its documented prior condition and use (i.e., prior to the restoration, enhancement, or creation activities). The reversion must occur within five years after expiration of a limited term wetland restoration or creation agreement or permit, even if the discharge occurs after this NWP expires. This NWP also authorizes the reversion of wetlands that were restored, enhanced, or created on prior-converted cropland that has not been abandoned, in accordance with a binding agreement between the landowner and NRCS or FWS (even though the restoration, enhancement, or creation activity did not require a Section 404 permit). The five-year reversion limit does not apply to agreements without time limits reached under paragraph (a)(1). The prior condition will be documented in the original agreement or permit, and the determination of return to prior conditions will be made by the Federal agency or appropriate state agency executing the agreement or permit. Before any reversion activity the permittee or the appropriate Federal or state agency must notify the District Engineer and include the documentation of the prior condition. Once an area has reverted to its prior physical condition, it will be subject to whatever the Corps Regulatory requirements will be at that future date. (Sections 10 and 404)

Note: Compensatory mitigation is not required for activities authorized by this NWP, provided the authorized work results in a net increase in aquatic resource functions and values in the project area. This NWP can be used to authorize compensatory mitigation projects, including mitigation banks, provided the permittee notifies the District Engineer in accordance with General Condition 13, and the project includes compensatory mitigation for impacts to waters of the US caused by the authorized work. However, this NWP does not authorize the reversion of an area used for a compensatory mitigation project to its prior condition. NWP 27 can be used to authorize impacts at a mitigation bank, but only in circumstances where it has been approved under the Interagency Federal Mitigation Bank Guidelines.

28. *Modifications of Existing Marinas.* Reconfiguration of existing docking facilities within an authorized marina area. No dredging, additional slips, dock spaces, or expansion of any kind within waters of the US is authorized by this NWP. (Section 10)

29. ***Single-family Housing.*** Discharges of dredged or fill material into non-tidal waters of the U.S., including non-tidal wetlands for the construction or expansion of a single-family home and attendant features (such as a garage, driveway, storage shed, and/or septic field) for an Individual Permittee provided that the activity meets all of the following criteria:

a. The discharge does not cause the loss of more than 14-acre of non-tidal waters of the U.S., including non-tidal wetlands;

b. The permittee notifies the District Engineer in accordance with the "Notification" General Condition;

c. The permittee has taken all practicable actions to minimize the on-site and off-site impacts of the discharge. For example, the location of the home may need to be adjusted onsite to avoid flooding of adjacent property owners;

d. The discharge is part of a single and complete project; furthermore, that for any subdivision created on or after November 22, 1991, the discharges authorized under this NWP may not exceed an aggregate total loss of waters of the U.S. of 14-acre for the entire subdivision;

e. An individual may use this NWP only for a single-family home for a personal residence;

f. This NWP may be used only once per parcel;

g. This NWP may not be used in conjunction with NWP 14 or NWP 18, for any parcel; and,

h. Sufficient vegetated buffers must be maintained adjacent to all open water bodies, streams, etc., to preclude water quality degradation due to erosion and sedimentation.

For the purposes of this NWP, the acreage of loss of waters of the U.S. includes the filled area previously permitted, the proposed filled area, and any other waters of the U.S. that are adversely affected by flooding, excavation, or drainage as a result of the project. This NWP authorizes activities only by individuals; for this purpose, the term "individual" refers to a natural person and/or a married couple, but does not include a corporation, partnership, or similar entity. For the purposes of this NWP, a parcel of land is defined as "the entire contiguous quantity of land in possession of, recorded as property of, or owned (in any form of ownership, including land owned as a partner, corporation, joint tenant, etc.) by the same individual (and/or that individual's spouse), and comprises not only the area of wetlands sought to be filled, but also all land contiguous to those wetlands, owned by the individual (and/or that individual's spouse) in any form of ownership." (Sections 10 and 404)

30. ***Moist Soil Management for Wildlife.*** Discharges of dredged or fill material and maintenance activities that are associated with moist soil management for wildlife performed on non-tidal Federally-owned or managed, state-owned or managed property, and local government agency-owned or managed property, for the purpose of continuing ongoing, site-specific, wildlife management activities where soil manipulation is used to manage habitat and feeding areas for wildlife. Such activities include, but are not limited to: The repair, maintenance or replacement of existing water control structures; the repair or maintenance of dikes; and plowing or discing to impede succession, prepare seed beds, or establish fire breaks. Sufficient vegetated buffers must be maintained adjacent to all open water bodies, streams, etc., to preclude water quality degradation due to erosion and sedimentation. This NWP does not authorize the construction of new dikes, roads, water control structures, etc., associated with the management areas. This NWP does not authorize converting wetlands to uplands, impoundments or other open water bodies. (Section 404)

31. ***Maintenance of Existing Flood Control Facilities.*** Discharge of dredge or fill material resulting from activities associated with the maintenance of existing flood control facilities, including debris basins, retention/detention basins, and channels that

(i) were previously authorized by the Corps by Individual Permit, General Permit, by 33 CFR 330.3, or did not require a permit at the time it was constructed, or

(ii) were constructed by the Corps and transferred to a non-Federal sponsor for operation and maintenance. Activities authorized by this NWP are limited to those resulting from maintenance activities that are conducted within the "maintenance baseline," as described in the definition below. Activities including the discharges of dredged or fill materials, associated with maintenance activities in flood control facilities in any watercourse that has previously been determined to be within the maintenance baseline, are authorized under this NWP. The NWP does not authorize the removal of sediment and associated vegetation from the natural water courses except to the extent that these have been included in the maintenance baseline. All dredged material must be placed in an upland site or an authorized disposal site in waters of the US, and proper siltation controls must be used. (Activities of any kind that result in only incidental fallback, or only the cutting and removing of vegetation above the ground, e.g., mowing, rotary cutting, and chainsawing, where the activity neither substantially disturbs the root system nor involves mechanized pushing, dragging, or other similar activities that redeposit excavated soil material, do not require a Section 404 permit in accordance with 33 CFR 323.2(d)(2)).

Notification: After the maintenance baseline is established, and before any maintenance work is conducted, the permittee must notify the District Engineer in accordance with the "Notification" General Condition. The notification may be for activity-specific maintenance or for maintenance of the entire flood control facility by submitting a five-year (or less) maintenance plan.

Maintenance Baseline: The maintenance baseline is a description of the physical characteristics (e.g., depth, width, length, location, configuration, or design flood capacity, etc.) of a flood-control project within which maintenance activities are normally authorized by NWP 31, subject to any case-specific conditions required by the District Engineer. The District Engineer will approve the maintenance baseline based on the approved or constructed capacity of the flood-control facility, whichever is smaller, including any areas where there are no constructed channels, but which are part of the facility. If no evidence of the constructed capacity exists, the approved constructed capacity will be used. The prospective permittee will provide documentation of the physical characteristics of the flood-control facility (which will normally consist of as-built or approved drawings) and documentation of the design capacities of the flood-control facility. The documentation will also include BMPs [Best Management Plans] to ensure that the impacts to the aquatic environment are minimal, especially in maintenance areas where there are no constructed channels. (The Corps may request maintenance records in areas where there has not been recent maintenance.) Revocation or modification of the final determination of the maintenance baseline can only be done in accordance with 33 CFR 330.5. Except in emergencies as described below, this NWP can not be used until the District Engineer approves the maintenance baseline and determines the need for mitigation and any regional or activity-specific conditions. Once determined, the maintenance baseline will remain valid for any subsequent reissuance of this NWP. This permit does not authorize maintenance of a flood control facility that has been abandoned. A flood control facility will be considered abandoned if it has operated at a significantly reduced capacity without needed maintenance being accomplished in a timely manner.

Mitigation: The District Engineer will determine any required mitigation one time only for impacts associated with maintenance work at the same time that the maintenance baseline is approved. Such one-time mitigation will be required when necessary to ensure that adverse environmental impacts are no more than minimal, both individually and cumulatively. Such mitigation will only be required once for any specific reach of a flood control project. However, if one-time mitigation is required for impacts associated with maintenance activities, the District Engineer will not delay needed maintenance, provided the District Engineer and the permittee establish a schedule for identification, approval, development, construction and completion of any such required mitigation. Once the one-time mitigation described above has been completed, or a determination made that mitigation is not required, no further mitigation will be required for maintenance activities within the maintenance baseline. In determining appropriate mitigation, the District Engineer will give special consideration to natural water courses that have been included in the maintenance baseline and require compensatory mitigation and/or BMPs as appropriate.

Emergency Situations: In emergency situations, this NWP may be used to authorize maintenance activities in flood control facilities for which no maintenance baseline has been approved. Emergency situations are those which would result in an unacceptable hazard to life, a significant loss of property, or an immediate, unforeseen, and significant economic hardship if action is not taken before a maintenance baseline can be approved. In such situations, the determination of mitigation requirements, if any, may be deferred until the emergency has been resolved. Once the emergency has ended, a maintenance baseline must be established expeditiously, and mitigation, including mitigation for maintenance conducted during the emergency, must be required as appropriate. (Sections 10 and 404)

32. *Completed Enforcement Actions.* Any structure, work or discharge of dredged or fill material, remaining in place, or undertaken for mitigation, restoration, or environmental benefit in compliance with either:
(i) The terms of a final written Corps non-judicial settlement agreement resolving a violation of section 404 of the CWA and/or section 10 of the Rivers and Harbors Act of 1899; or the terms of an EPA 309(a) order on consent resolving a violation of section 404 of the CWA, provided that:
  a. The unauthorized activity affected no more than 5 acres of non-tidal wetlands or 1 acre of tidal wetlands;
  b. The settlement agreement provides for environmental benefits, to an equal or greater degree, than the environmental detriments caused by the unauthorized activity that is authorized by this NWP; and
  c. The District Engineer issues a verification letter authorizing the activity subject to the terms and conditions of this NWP and the settlement agreement, including a specified completion date; or
(ii) The terms of a final Federal court decision, consent decree, or settlement agreement resulting from an enforcement action brought by the U.S. under section 404 of the CWA and/or section 10 of the Rivers and Harbors Act of 1899; or
(iii) The terms of a final court decision, consent decree, settlement agreement, or non-judicial settlement agreement resulting from a natural resource damage claim brought by a trustee or trustees for natural resources (as defined by the National Contingency Plan at 40 CFR subpart G) under section 311 of the Clean Water Act (CWA), section 107 of the Comprehensive Environmental Response, Compensation and Liability Act (CERCLA or Superfund), section 312 of the National Marine Sanctuaries Act (NMSA), section 1002 of the Oil Pollution Act of 1990 (OPA), or the Park System Resource Protection Act at 16 U.S.C. §19jj, to the extent that a Corps permit is required.

  For either (i), (ii), or (iii) above, compliance is a condition of the NWP itself. Any authorization under this NWP is automatically revoked if the permittee does not comply with the terms of this NWP or the terms of the court decision, consent decree, or judicial/non-judicial settlement agreement or fails to complete the work by the specified completion date. This NWP does not apply to any activities occurring after the date of the decision, decree, or agreement that are not for the purpose of mitigation, restoration, or environmental benefit. Before reaching any settlement agreement, the Corps will ensure compliance with the provisions of 33 CFR part 326 and 33 CFR 330.6 (d)(2) and (e). (Sections 10 and 404)

33. *Temporary Construction, Access and Dewatering.* Temporary structures, work and discharges, including cofferdams, necessary for construction activities or access fills or dewatering of construction sites; provided that the associated primary activity is authorized by the Corps of Engineers or the USCG, or for other construction activities not subject to the Corps or USCG regulations. Appropriate measures must be taken to maintain near normal downstream flows and to minimize flooding. Fill must be of materials, and placed in a manner, that will not be eroded by expected high flows. The use of dredged material may be allowed if it is determined by the District Engineer that it will not cause more than minimal adverse effects on aquatic resources. Temporary fill must be entirely removed to upland areas, or dredged material returned to its original location, following completion of the construction activity, and the affected areas must be restored to the pre-project conditions. Cofferdams cannot be used to dewater wetlands or other aquatic areas to change their use. Structures left in place after cofferdams are removed require a Section 10 permit if located in navigable waters of the U.S. (see 33 CFR part 322). The permittee must notify the District Engineer in accordance with the "Notification" General Condition. The notification must also include a restoration plan of reasonable measures to avoid and minimize adverse effects to aquatic resources. The District Engineer will add Special Conditions, where necessary, to ensure environmental adverse effects are minimal. Such conditions may include: limiting the temporary work to the minimum necessary; requiring seasonal restrictions; modifying the restoration plan; and requiring alternative construction methods (e.g., construction mats in wetlands where practicable). (Sections 10 and 404)

34. *Cranberry Production Activities.* Discharges of dredged or fill material for dikes, berms, pumps, water control structures or leveling of cranberry beds associated with expansion, enhancement, or modification activities at existing cranberry production operations provided that the activity meets all of the following criteria:
a. The cumulative total acreage of disturbance per cranberry production operation, including but not limited to, filling, flooding, ditching, or clearing, does not exceed 10 acres of waters of the U.S., including wetlands;
b. The permittee notifies the District Engineer in accordance with the "Notification" General Condition. The notification must include a delineation of affected special aquatic sites, including wetlands; and,
c. The activity does not result in a net loss of wetland acreage. This NWP does not authorize any discharge of dredged or fill material related to other cranberry production activities such as warehouses, processing facilities, or parking areas. For the purposes of this NWP, the cumulative total of 10 acres will be measured over the period that this NWP is valid. (Section 404)

35. *Maintenance Dredging of Existing Basins.* Excavation and removal of accumulated sediment for maintenance of existing marina basins, access channels to marinas or boat slips, and boat slips to previously authorized depths or controlling depths for ingress/egress, whichever is less, provided the dredged material is disposed of at an upland site and proper siltation controls are used. (Section 10)

36. *Boat Ramps.* Activities required for the construction of boat ramps provided:
a. The discharge into waters of the U.S. does not exceed 50 cubic yards of concrete, rock, crushed stone or gravel into forms, or placement of pre-cast concrete planks or slabs. (Unsuitable material that causes unacceptable chemical pollution or is structurally unstable is not authorized);

b. The boat ramp does not exceed 20 feet in width;

c. The base material is crushed stone, gravel or other suitable material;

d. The excavation is limited to the area necessary for site preparation and all excavated material is removed to the upland; and,

e. No material is placed in special aquatic sites, including wetlands. Another NWP, Regional General Permit, or Individual Permit may authorize dredging to provide access to the boat ramp after obtaining a Section 10 if located in navigable waters of the U.S. (Sections 10 and 404)

37. *Emergency Watershed Protection and Rehabilitation*. Work done by or funded by:

a. The NRCS which is a situation requiring immediate action under its emergency Watershed Protection Program (7 CFR part 624); or

b. The USFS under its Burned-Area Emergency Rehabilitation Handbook (FSH 509.13); or

c. The DOI for wildland fire management burned area emergency stabilization and rehabilitation (DOI Manual part 620, ch. 3). For all of the above provisions, the District Engineer must be notified in accordance with the General Condition 13 (also, see 33 CFR 330.1(e)). (Sections 10 and 404)

38. *Cleanup of Hazardous and Toxic Waste*. Specific activities required to effect the containment, stabilization, or removal of hazardous or toxic waste materials that are performed, ordered, or sponsored by a government agency with established legal or regulatory authority provided the permittee notifies the District Engineer in accordance with the "Notification" General Condition. For discharges in special aquatic sites, including wetlands, the notification must also include a delineation of affected special aquatic sites, including wetlands. Court ordered remedial action plans or related settlements are also authorized by this NWP. This NWP does not authorize the establishment of new disposal sites or the expansion of existing sites used for the disposal of hazardous or toxic waste. Activities undertaken entirely on a Comprehensive Environmental Response, Compensation, and Liability Act (CERCLA) site by authority of CERCLA as approved or required by EPA, are not required to obtain permits under section 404 of the CWA or section 10 of the Rivers and Harbors Act. (Sections 10 and 404)

39. *Residential, Commercial, and Institutional Developments*. Discharges of dredged or fill material into non-tidal waters of the U.S., excluding non-tidal wetlands adjacent to tidal waters, for the construction or expansion of residential, commercial, and institutional building foundations and building pads and attendant features that are necessary for the use and maintenance of the structures. Attendant features may include, but are not limited to, roads, parking lots, garages, yards, utility lines, stormwater management facilities, and recreation facilities such as playgrounds, playing fields, and golf courses (provided the golf course is an integral part of the residential development). The construction of new ski areas or oil and gas wells is not authorized by this NWP. Residential developments include multiple and single unit developments. Examples of commercial developments include retail stores, industrial facilities, restaurants, business parks, and shopping centers. Examples of institutional developments include schools, fire stations, government office buildings, judicial buildings, public works buildings, libraries, hospitals, and places of worship. The activities listed above are authorized, provided the activities meet all of the following criteria:

a. The discharge does not cause the loss of greater than 12-acre of non-tidal waters of the U.S., excluding non-tidal wetlands adjacent to tidal waters;

b. The discharge does not cause the loss of greater than 300 linear-feet of a stream bed, unless for intermittent stream beds this criterion is waived in writing pursuant to a determination by the District Engineer, as specified below, that the project complies with all terms and conditions of this NWP and that any adverse impacts of the project on the aquatic environment are minimal, both individually and cumulatively;

c. The permittee must notify the District Engineer in accordance with General Condition 13, if any of the following criteria are met:

(1) The discharge causes the loss of greater than 110-acre of non-tidal waters of the U.S., excluding non-tidal wetlands adjacent to tidal waters; or

(2) The discharge causes the loss of any open waters, including perennial or intermittent streams, below the ordinary high water mark (see Note, below); or

(3) The discharge causes the loss of greater than 300 linear feet of intermittent stream bed. In such case, to be authorized the District Engineer must determine that the activity complies with the other terms and conditions of the NWP, determine adverse environmental effects are minimal both individually and cumulatively, and waive the limitation on stream impacts in writing before the permittee may proceed;

d. For discharges in special aquatic sites, including wetlands, the notification must include a delineation of affected special aquatic sites;

e. The discharge is part of a single and complete project;

f. The permittee must avoid and minimize discharges into waters of the U.S. at the project site to the maximum extent practicable. The notification, when required, must include a written statement explaining how avoidance and minimization of losses of waters of the U.S. were achieved on the project site. Compensatory mitigation will normally be required to offset the losses of waters of the U.S. (See General Condition 19.) The notification must also include a compensatory mitigation proposal for offsetting unavoidable losses of waters of the U.S. If an applicant asserts that the adverse effects of the project are minimal without mitigation, then the applicant may submit justification explaining why compensatory mitigation should not be required for the District Engineer's consideration;

g. When this NWP is used in conjunction with any other NWP, any combined total permanent loss of waters of the US exceeding 110-acre requires that the permittee notify the District Engineer in accordance with General Condition 13;

h. Any work authorized by this NWP must not cause more than minimal degradation of water quality or more than minimal changes to the flow characteristics of any stream (see General Conditions 9 and 21);

i. For discharges causing the loss of 110-acre or less of waters of the U.S., the permittee must submit a report, within 30 days of completion of the work, to the District Engineer that contains the following information: (1) the name, address, and telephone number of the permittee; (2) the location of the work; (3) a description of the work; (4) the type and acreage of the loss of waters of the U.S. (e.g., 112-acre of emergent wetlands); and (5) the type and acreage of any compensatory mitigation used to offset the loss of waters of the U.S. (e.g., 112-acre of emergent wetlands created on-site);

j. If there are any open waters or streams within the project area, the permittee will establish and maintain, to the maximum extent practicable, wetland or upland vegetated buffers next to those open waters or streams consistent with General Condition 19. Deed restrictions, conservation easements, protective covenants, or other means of land conservation and preservation are required to protect and maintain the vegetated buffers established on the project site. Only residential, commercial, and institutional activities with structures on the foundation(s) or building pad(s), as well as the attendant features, are authorized by this NWP. The compensatory mitigation proposal that is required in paragraph (e) of this NWP may be either conceptual or detailed. The wetland or upland vegetated buffer required in paragraph (i) of this NWP will be determined on a case-by-case basis by the District Engineer for addressing water quality concerns. The required wetland or upland vegetated buffer is part of the overall compensatory mitigation requirement for this NWP. If the project site was previously used for agricultural purposes and the farm owner/operator used NWP 40 to authorize activities in waters of the U.S. to increase production or construct farm buildings, NWP 39 cannot be used by the developer to authorize additional activities. This is more than the acreage limit for NWP 39 impacts to waters of the U.S. (i.e., the combined acreage loss authorized under NWPs 39 and 40 cannot exceed 12-acre, see General Condition 15).

Subdivisions: For residential subdivisions, the aggregate total loss of waters of U.S. authorized by NWP 39 can not exceed 12-acre. This includes any loss of waters associated with development of individual subdivision lots. (Sections 10 and 404)

Note: Areas where wetland vegetation is not present should be determined by the presence or absence of an ordinary high water mark or bed and bank. Areas that are waters of the U.S. based on this criterion would require a PCN although water is infrequently present in the stream channel (except for ephemeral waters, which do not require PCNs).

40. ***Agricultural Activities.*** Discharges of dredged or fill material into non-tidal waters of the U.S., excluding non-tidal wetlands adjacent to tidal waters, for improving agricultural production and the construction of building pads for farm buildings. Authorized activities include the installation, placement, or construction of drainage tiles, ditches, or levees; mechanized land clearing; land leveling; the relocation of existing serviceable drainage ditches constructed in waters of the U.S.; and similar activities, provided the permittee complies with the following terms and conditions:

a. For discharges into non-tidal wetlands to improve agricultural production, the following criteria must be met if the permittee is a United States Department of Agriculture (USDA) Program participant:

(1) The permittee must obtain a categorical minimal effects exemption, minimal effect exemption, or mitigation exemption from NRCS in accordance with the provisions of the Food Security Act of 1985, as amended (16 U.S.C. 3801 et seq.);

(2) The discharge into non-tidal wetlands does not result in the loss of greater than 12-acre of non-tidal wetlands on a farm tract;

(3) The permittee must have NRCS certified wetland delineation;

(4) The permittee must implement an NRCS-approved compensatory mitigation plan that fully offsets wetland losses, if required; and

(5) The permittee must submit a report, within 30 days of completion of the authorized work, to the District Engineer that contains the following information: (a) the name, address, and telephone number of the permittee; (b) the location of the work; (c) a description of the work; (d) the type and acreage (or square feet) of the loss of wetlands (e.g., 13-acre of emergent wetlands); and (e) the type, acreage (or square feet), and location of compensatory mitigation (e.g., 13-acre of emergent wetland on a farm tract; credits purchased from a mitigation bank); or

b. For discharges into non-tidal wetlands to improve agricultural production, the following criteria must be met if the permittee is not a USDA Program participant (or a USDA Program participant for which the proposed work does not qualify for authorization under paragraph (a) of this NWP):

(1) The discharge into non-tidal wetlands does not result in the loss of greater than 12-acre of non-tidal wetlands on a farm tract;

(2) The permittee must notify the District Engineer in accordance with General Condition 13, if the discharge results in the loss of greater than 110-acre of non-tidal wetlands;

(3) The notification must include a delineation of affected wetlands; and

(4) The notification must include a compensatory mitigation proposal to offset losses of waters of the US; or

c. For the construction of building pads for farm buildings, the discharge does not cause the loss of greater than 12-acre of non-tidal wetlands that were in agricultural production prior to December 23, 1985 (i.e., farmed wetlands), and the permittee must notify the District Engineer in accordance with General Condition 13; and

d. Any activity in other waters of the U.S. is limited to the relocation of existing serviceable drainage ditches constructed in non-tidal streams. This NWP does not authorize the relocation of greater than 300 linear feet of existing serviceable drainage ditches constructed in non-tidal streams unless, for drainage ditches constructed in intermittent nontidal streams, the District Engineer waives this criterion in writing, and the District Engineer has determined that the project complies with all terms and conditions of this NWP, and that any adverse impacts of the project on the aquatic environment are minimal, both individually and cumulatively. For impacts exceeding 300 linear feet of impacts to existing serviceable ditches constructed in intermittent non-tidal streams, the permittee must notify the District Engineer in accordance with the "Notification" General Condition 13; and

e. The term "farm tract" refers to a parcel of land identified by the Farm Service Agency. The Corps will identify other waters of the U.S. on the farm tract. NRCS will determine if a proposed agricultural activity meets the terms and conditions of paragraph a of this NWP, except as provided below. For those activities that require notification, the District Engineer will determine if a proposed agricultural activity is authorized by paragraphs b, c, and/or d of this NWP. USDA Program participants requesting authorization for discharges of dredged or fill material into waters of the U.S. authorized by paragraphs c or d of this NWP, in addition to paragraph a, must notify the District Engineer in accordance with General Condition 13 and the District Engineer will determine if the entire single and complete project is authorized by this NWP. Discharges of dredged or fill material into waters of the U.S. associated with completing required compensatory mitigation are authorized by this NWP. However, total impacts, including other authorized impacts under this NWP, may not exceed the 12-acre limit of this NWP. This NWP does not affect, or otherwise regulate, discharges associated with agricultural activities when the discharge qualifies for an exemption under section 404(f) of the CWA, even though a categorical minimal effects exemption, minimal effect exemption, or mitigation exemption from NRCS pursuant to the Food Security Act of 1985, as amended, may be required. Activities authorized by paragraphs a through d may not exceed a total of 12-acre on a single farm tract. If the site was used for agricultural purposes and the farm owner/operator used either paragraphs a, b, or c of this NWP to authorize activities in waters of the U.S. to increase agricultural production or construct farm buildings, and the current landowner wants to use NWP 39 to authorize residential, commercial, or industrial development activities in waters of the U.S. on the site, the combined acreage loss authorized by NWPs 39 and 40 cannot exceed 12-acre (see General Condition 15). (Section 404)

41. *Reshaping Existing Drainage Ditches.* Discharges of dredged or fill material into non-tidal waters of the U.S., excluding non-tidal wetlands adjacent to tidal waters, to modify the cross-sectional configuration of currently serviceable drainage ditches constructed in waters of the U.S. The reshaping of the ditch cannot increase drainage capacity beyond the original design capacity. Nor can it expand the area drained by the ditch as originally designed (i.e., the capacity of the ditch must be the same as originally designed and it cannot drain additional wetlands or other waters of the U.S.). Compensatory mitigation is not required because the work is designed to improve water quality (e.g., by regrading the drainage ditch with gentler slopes, which can reduce erosion, increase growth of vegetation, increase uptake of nutrients and other substances by vegetation, etc.).

Notification: The permittee must notify the District Engineer in accordance with General Condition 13 if greater than 500 linear feet of drainage ditch will be reshaped. Material resulting from excavation may not be permanently sidecast into waters but may be temporarily sidecast (up to three months) into waters of the U.S., provided the material is not placed in such a manner that it is dispersed by currents or other forces. The District Engineer may extend the period of temporary sidecasting not to exceed a total of 180 days, where appropriate. In general, this NWP does not apply to reshaping drainage ditches constructed in uplands, since these areas are generally not waters of the U.S., and thus no permit from the Corps is required, or to the maintenance of existing drainage ditches to their original dimensions and configuration, which does not require a Section 404 permit (see 33 CFR 323.4(a)(3)). This NWP does not authorize the relocation of drainage ditches constructed in waters of the U.S.; the location of the centerline of the reshaped drainage ditch must be approximately the same as the location of the centerline of the original drainage ditch. This NWP does not authorize stream channelization or stream relocation projects. (Section 404)

42. *Recreational Facilities.* Discharges of dredged or fill material into non-tidal waters of the U.S., excluding non-tidal wetlands adjacent to tidal waters, for the construction or expansion of recreational facilities, provided the activity meets all of the following criteria:
a. The discharge does not cause the loss of greater than 12-acre of non-tidal waters of the U.S., excluding non-tidal wetlands adjacent to tidal waters;
b. The discharge does not cause the loss of greater than 300 linear feet of a stream bed, unless for intermittent stream beds this criterion is waived in writing pursuant to a determination by the District Engineer, as specified below, that the project complies with all terms and conditions of this NWP and that any adverse impacts of the project on the aquatic environment are minimal, both individually and cumulatively;
c. The permittee notifies the District Engineer in accordance with the "Notification" General Condition 13 for discharges exceeding 300 linear feet of impact of intermittent stream beds. In such cases, to be authorized the District Engineer must determine that the activity complies with the other terms and conditions of the NWP, determine the adverse environmental effects are minimal both individually and cumulatively, and waive this limitation in writing before the permittee may proceed;
d. For discharges causing the loss of greater than 110-acre of non-tidal waters of the U.S., the permittee notifies the District Engineer in accordance with General Condition 13;
e. For discharges in special aquatic sites, including wetlands, the notification must include a delineation of affected special aquatic sites;
f. The discharge is part of a single and complete project; and
g. Compensatory mitigation will normally be required to offset the losses of waters of the U.S. The notification must also include a compensatory mitigation proposal to offset authorized losses of waters of the U.S. For the purposes of this NWP, the term "recreational facility" is defined as a recreational activity that is integrated into the natural landscape and does not substantially change preconstruction grades or deviate from natural landscape contours. For the purpose of this permit, the primary function of recreational facilities does not include the use of motor vehicles, buildings, or impervious surfaces. Examples of recreational facilities that may be authorized by this NWP include hiking trails, bike paths, horse paths, nature centers, and campgrounds (excluding trailer parks). This NWP may authorize the construction or expansion of golf courses and the expansion of ski areas, provided the golf course or ski area does not substantially deviate from natural landscape contours. Additionally, these activities are designed to minimize adverse effects to waters of the U.S. and riparian areas through the use of such practices as integrated pest management, adequate stormwater management facilities, vegetated buffers, re-

duced fertilizer use, etc. The facility must have an adequate water quality management plan in accordance with General Condition 9, such as a stormwater management facility, to ensure that the recreational facility results in no substantial adverse effects to water quality. This NWP also authorizes the construction or expansion of small support facilities, such as maintenance and storage buildings and stables that are directly related to the recreational activity. This NWP does not authorize other buildings, such as hotels, restaurants, etc. The construction or expansion of playing fields (e.g., baseball, soccer, or football fields), basketball and tennis courts, racetracks, stadiums, arenas, and the construction of new ski areas are not authorized by this NWP. (Section 404)

43. *Stormwater Management Facilities.* Discharges of dredged or fill material into non-tidal waters of the U.S., excluding non-tidal wetlands adjacent to tidal waters, for the construction and maintenance of stormwater management facilities, including activities for the excavation of stormwater ponds/facilities, detention basins, and retention basins; the installation and maintenance of water control structures, outfall structures and emergency spillways; and the maintenance dredging of existing stormwater management ponds/facilities and detention and retention basins, provided the activity meets all of the following criteria:
a. The discharge for the construction of new stormwater management facilities does not cause the loss of greater than 12-acre of non-tidal waters of the U.S., excluding non-tidal wetlands adjacent to tidal waters;
b. The discharge does not cause the loss of greater than 300 linear feet of a stream bed, unless for intermittent stream beds this criterion is waived in writing pursuant to a determination by the District Engineer, as specified below, that the project complies with all terms and conditions of this NWP and that any adverse impacts of the project on the aquatic environment are minimal, both individually and cumulatively;
c. For discharges causing the loss of greater than 300 linear feet of intermittent stream beds, the permittee notifies the District Engineer in accordance with the "Notification" General Condition 13. In such cases, to be authorized the District Engineer must determine that the activity complies with the other terms and conditions of the NWP, determine the adverse environmental effects are minimal both individually and cumulatively, and waive this limitation in writing before the permittee may proceed;
d. The discharges of dredged or fill material for the construction of new stormwater management facilities in perennial streams is not authorized;
e. For discharges or excavation for the construction of new stormwater management facilities or for the maintenance of existing stormwater management facilities causing the loss of greater than 110-acre of non-tidal waters, excluding non-tidal wetlands adjacent to tidal waters, provided the permittee notifies the District Engineer in accordance with the "Notification" General Condition 13. In addition, the notification must include:
   (1) A maintenance plan. The maintenance plan should be in accordance with state and local requirements, if any such requirements exist;
   (2) For discharges in special aquatic sites, including wetlands and submerged aquatic vegetation, the notification must include a delineation of affected areas; and
   (3) A compensatory mitigation proposal that offsets the loss of waters of the U.S. Maintenance in constructed areas will not require mitigation provided such maintenance is accomplished in designated maintenance areas and not within compensatory mitigation areas (i.e., District Engineers may designate nonmaintenance areas, normally at the downstream end of the stormwater management facility, in existing stormwater management facilities). (No mitigation will be required for activities that are exempt from Section 404 permit requirements.)

f. The permittee must avoid and minimize discharges into waters of the U.S. at the project site to the maximum extent practicable, and the notification must include a written statement to the District Engineer detailing compliance with this condition (i.e., why the discharge must occur in waters of the U.S. and why additional minimization cannot be achieved);

g. The stormwater management facility must comply with General Condition 21 and be designed using BMPs and watershed protection techniques. Examples may include forebays (deeper areas at the upstream end of the stormwater management facility that would be maintained through excavation), vegetated buffers, and siting considerations to minimize adverse effects to aquatic resources. Another example of a BMP would be bioengineering methods incorporated into the facility design to benefit water quality and minimize adverse effects to aquatic resources from storm flows, especially downstream of the facility, that provide, to the maximum extent practicable, for long term aquatic resource protection and enhancement;

h. Maintenance excavation will be in accordance with an approved maintenance plan and will not exceed the original contours of the facility as approved and constructed; and

i. The discharge is part of a single and complete project. (Section 404)

44. *Mining Activities.* Discharges of dredged or fill material into:

(i) Isolated waters; streams where the annual average flow is one cubic foot per second or less, and non-tidal wetlands adjacent to headwater streams, for aggregate mining (i.e., sand, gravel, and crushed and broken stone) and associated support activities;

(ii) Lower perennial streams, excluding wetlands adjacent to lower perennial streams, for aggregate mining activities (support activities in lower perennial streams or adjacent wetlands are not authorized by this NWP); and/or

(iii) Isolated waters and non-tidal wetlands adjacent to headwater streams, for hard rock/mineral mining activities (i.e., extraction of metalliferous ores from subsurface locations) and associated support activities, provided the discharge meets the following criteria:

a. The mined area within waters of the U.S., plus the acreage loss of waters of the U.S. resulting from support activities, cannot exceed 12-acre;

b. The permittee must avoid and minimize discharges into waters of the US at the project site to the maximum extent practicable, and the notification must include a written statement detailing compliance with this condition (i.e., why the discharge must occur in waters of the US and why additional minimization cannot be achieved);

c. In addition to General Conditions 17 and 20, activities authorized by this permit must not substantially alter the sediment characteristics of areas of concentrated shellfish beds or fish spawning areas. Normally, the mandated water quality management plan should address these impacts;

d. The permittee must implement necessary measures to prevent increases in stream gradient and water velocities and to prevent adverse effects (e.g., head cutting, bank erosion) to upstream and downstream channel conditions;

e. Activities authorized by this permit must not result in adverse effects on the course, capacity, or condition of navigable waters of the U.S.;

f. The permittee must use measures to minimize downstream turbidity;

g. Wetland impacts must be compensated through mitigation approved by the Corps;

h. Beneficiation and mineral processing for hard rock/mineral mining activities may not occur within 200 feet of the ordinary high water mark of any open waterbody. Although the Corps does not regulate discharges from these activities, a CWA section 402 permit may be required;

i. All activities authorized must comply with General Conditions 9 and 21. Further, the District Engineer may require modifications to the required water quality management plan to ensure that the authorized work results in minimal adverse effects to water quality;

j. Except for aggregate mining activities in lower perennial streams, no aggregate mining can occur within stream beds where the average annual flow is greater than one cubic foot per second or in waters of the U.S. within 100 feet of the ordinary high water mark of headwater stream segments where the average annual flow of the stream is greater than one cubic foot per second (aggregate mining can occur in areas immediately adjacent to the ordinary high water mark of a stream where the average annual flow is one cubic foot per second or less);

k. Single and complete project: The discharge must be for a single and complete project, including support activities. Discharges of dredged or fill material into waters of the U.S. for multiple mining activities on several designated parcels of a single and complete mining operation can be authorized by this NWP provided the 12-acre limit is not exceeded; and

Notification: The permittee must notify the District Engineer in accordance with General Condition 13. The notification must include: (1) a description of waters of the US adversely affected by the project; (2) a written statement to the District Engineer detailing compliance with paragraph b, above (i.e., why the discharge must occur in waters of the U.S. and why additional minimization cannot be achieved); (3) a description of measures taken to ensure that the proposed work complies with paragraphs c through f, above; and (4) a reclamation plan (for aggregate mining in isolated waters and nontidal wetlands adjacent to headwaters and hard rock/mineral mining only). This NWP does not authorize hard rock/mineral mining, including placer mining, in streams. No hard rock/mineral mining can occur in waters of the U.S. within 100 feet of the ordinary high water mark of headwater streams. The terms "headwaters" and "isolated waters" are defined at 33 CFR 330.2(d) and (e), respectively. For the purposes of this NWP, the term "lower perennial stream" is defined as follows: "A stream in which the gradient is low and water velocity is slow, there is no tidal influence, some water flows throughout the year, and the substrate consists mainly of sand and mud." (Sections 10 and 404)

Nationwide Permit General Conditions

The following General Conditions must be followed in order for any authorization by an NWP to be valid:

1. *Navigation.* No activity may cause more than a minimal adverse effect on navigation.

2. *Proper Maintenance.* Any structure or fill authorized shall be properly maintained, including maintenance to ensure public safety.

3. *Soil Erosion and Sediment Controls.* Appropriate soil erosion and sediment controls must be used and maintained in effective operating condition during construction, and all exposed soil and other fills, as well as any work below the ordinary high water mark or high tide line, must be permanently stabilized at the earliest practicable date. Permittees are encouraged to perform work within waters of the United States during periods of low-flow or no-flow.

4. *Aquatic Life Movements.* No activity may substantially disrupt the necessary life-cycle movements of those species of aquatic life indigenous to the waterbody, including those species that normally migrate through the area, unless the activity's primary purpose is to impound water. Culverts placed in streams must be installed to maintain low flow conditions.

5. ***Equipment***. Heavy equipment working in wetlands must be placed on mats, or other measures must be taken to minimize soil disturbance.

6. ***Regional and Case-By-Case Conditions***. The activity must comply with any regional conditions that may have been added by the Division Engineer (see 33 CFR 330.4(e)). Additionally, any case specific conditions added by the Corps or by the state or tribe in its Section 401 Water Quality Certification and Coastal Zone Management Act consistency determination.

7. ***Wild and Scenic Rivers***. No activity may occur in a component of the National Wild and Scenic River System, or in a river officially designated by Congress as a "study river" for possible inclusion in the system, while the river is in an official study status, unless the appropriate Federal agency, with direct management responsibility for such river, has determined in writing that the proposed activity will not adversely affect the Wild and Scenic River designation, or study status. Information on Wild and Scenic Rivers may be obtained from the appropriate Federal land management agency in the area (e.g., National Park Service, U.S. Forest Service, Bureau of Land Management, U.S. Fish and Wildlife Service).

8. ***Tribal Rights***. No activity or its operation may impair reserved tribal rights, including, but not limited to, reserved water rights and treaty fishing and hunting rights.

9. ***Water Quality***.
(a) In certain states and tribal lands an individual 401 Water Quality Certification must be obtained or waived (See 33 CFR 330.4(c)).
(b) For NWPs 12, 14, 17, 18, 32, 39, 40, 42, 43, and 44, where the state or tribal 401 certification (either generically or individually) does not require or approve water quality management measures, the permittee must provide water quality management measures that will ensure that the authorized work does not result in more than minimal degradation of water quality (or the Corps determines that compliance with state or local standards, where applicable, will ensure no more than minimal adverse effect on water quality). An important component of water quality management includes stormwater management that minimizes degradation of the downstream aquatic system, including water quality (refer to General Condition 21 for stormwater management requirements). Another important component of water quality management is the establishment and maintenance of vegetated buffers next to open waters, including streams (refer to General Condition 19 for vegetated buffer requirements for the NWPs). This condition is only applicable to projects that have the potential to affect water quality. While appropriate measures must be taken, in most cases it is not necessary to conduct detailed studies to identify such measures or to require monitoring.

10. ***Coastal Zone Management***. In certain states, an individual state coastal zone management consistency concurrence must be obtained or waived (see Section 30.4(d)).

11. ***Endangered Species***.
(a) No activity is authorized under any NWP which is likely to jeopardize the continued existence of a threatened or endangered species or a species proposed for such designation, as identified under the Federal Endangered Species Act (ESA), or which will destroy or adversely modify the critical habitat of such species. Non-federal permittees shall notify the District Engineer if any listed species or designated critical habitat might be affected or is in the vicinity of the project, or is located in the designated crit-

ical habitat and shall not begin work on the activity until notified by the District Engineer that the requirements of the ESA have been satisfied and that the activity is authorized. For activities that may affect Federally-listed endangered or threatened species or designated critical habitat, the notification must include the name(s) of the endangered or threatened species that may be affected by the proposed work or that utilize the designated critical habitat that may be affected by the proposed work. As a result of formal or informal consultation with the FWS or NMFS the District Engineer may add species-specific regional endangered species conditions to the NWPs.

(b) Authorization of an activity by a NWP does not authorize the "take" of a threatened or endangered species as defined under the ESA. In the absence of separate authorization (e.g., an ESA Section 10 Permit, a Biological Opinion with "incidental take" provisions, etc.) from the USFWS or the NMFS, both lethal and non-lethal "takes" of protected species are in violation of the ESA. Information on the location of threatened and endangered species and their critical habitat can be obtained directly from the offices of the USFWS and NMFS or their world wide web pages at *www.fws.gov/r9endspp/endspp.html* and *www.nfms.gov/prot_res/esahome.html* respectively.

12. *Historic Properties*. No activity which may affect historic properties listed, or eligible for listing, in the National Register of Historic Places is authorized, until the District Engineer has complied with the provisions of 33 CFR part 325, appendix C. The prospective permittee must notify the District Engineer if the authorized activity may affect any historic properties listed, determined to be eligible, or which the prospective permittee has reason to believe may be eligible for listing on the National Register of Historic Places, and shall not begin the activity until notified by the District Engineer that the requirements of the National Historic Preservation Act have been satisfied and that the activity is authorized. Information on the location and existence of historic resources can be obtained from the State Historic Preservation Office and the National Register of Historic Places (see 33 CFR 330.4(g)). For activities that may affect historic properties listed in, or eligible for listing in, the National Register of Historic Places, the notification must state which historic property may be affected by the proposed work or include a vicinity map indicating the location of the historic property.

13. *Notification*.

(a) *Timing:* Where required by the terms of the NWP, the prospective permittee must notify the District Engineer with a preconstruction notification (PCN) as early as possible. The District Engineer must determine if the notification is complete within 30 days of the date of receipt and can request additional information necessary to make the PCN complete only once. However, if the prospective permittee does not provide all of the requested information, then the District Engineer will notify the prospective permittee that the notification is still incomplete and the PCN review process will not commence until all of the requested information has been received by the District Engineer. The prospective permittee shall not begin the activity:

(1) Until notified in writing by the District Engineer that the activity may proceed under the NWP with any special conditions imposed by the District or Division Engineer; or

(2) If notified in writing by the District or Division Engineer that an Individual Permit is required; or

(3) Unless 45 days have passed from the District Engineer's receipt of the complete notification and the prospective permittee has not received written notice from the District or Division Engineer. Subsequently, the permittee's right to proceed under the NWP may be modified, suspended, or revoked only in accordance with the procedure set forth in 33 CFR 330.5(d)(2).

(b) ***Contents of Notification:*** The notification must be in writing and include the following information:

(1) Name, address and telephone numbers of the prospective permittee;

(2) Location of the proposed project;

(3) Brief description of the proposed project; the project's purpose; direct and indirect adverse environmental effects the project would cause; any other NWP(s), Regional General Permit(s), or Individual Permit(s) used or intended to be used to authorize any part of the proposed project or any related activity. Sketches should be provided when necessary to show that the activity complies with the terms of the NWP (sketches usually clarify the project and when provided result in a quicker decision);

(4) For NWPs 7, 12, 14, 18, 21, 34, 38, 39, 41, 42, and 43, the PCN must also include a delineation of affected special aquatic sites, including wetlands, vegetated shallows (e.g., submerged aquatic vegetation, seagrass beds), and riffle and pool complexes (see paragraph 13(f));

(5) For NWP 7 (Outfall Structures and Maintenance), the PCN must include information regarding the original design capacities and configurations of those areas of the facility where maintenance dredging or excavation is proposed;

(6) For NWP 14 (Linear Transportation Crossings), the PCN must include a compensatory mitigation proposal to offset permanent losses of waters of the U.S. and a statement describing how temporary losses of waters of the U.S. will be minimized to the maximum extent practicable;

(7) For NWP 21 (Surface Coal Mining Activities), the PCN must include an Office of Surface Mining (OSM) or state approved mitigation plan, if applicable. To be authorized by this NWP, the District Engineer must determine that the activity complies with the terms and conditions of the NWP and that the adverse environmental effects are minimal both individually and cumulatively and must notify the project sponsor of this determination in writing;

(8) For NWP 27 (Stream and Wetland Restoration), the PCN must include documentation of the prior condition of the site that will be reverted by the permittee;

(9) For NWP 29 (Single-Family Housing), the PCN must also include:

　(i) Any past use of this NWP by the Individual Permittee and/or the permittee's spouse;

　(ii) A statement that the single-family housing activity is for a personal residence of the permittee;

　(iii) A description of the entire parcel, including its size, and a delineation of wetlands. For the purpose of this NWP, parcels of land measuring 14-acre or less will not require a formal on-site delineation. However, the applicant shall provide an indication of where the wetlands are and the amount of wetlands that exists on the property. For parcels greater than 14-acre in size, formal wetland delineation must be prepared in accordance with the current method required by the Corps (see paragraph 13(f));

　(iv) A written description of all land (including, if available, legal descriptions) owned by the prospective permittee and/or the prospective permittee's spouse, within a one-mile radius of the parcel, in any form of ownership (including any land owned as a partner, corporation, joint tenant, co-tenant, or as a tenant-by-the-entirety) and any land on which a purchase and sale agreement or other contract for sale or purchase has been executed;

(10) For NWP 31 (Maintenance of Existing Flood Control Projects), the prospective permittee must either notify the District Engineer with a PCN prior to each maintenance activity or submit a five-year (or less) maintenance plan. In addition, the PCN must include all of the following:

　(i) Sufficient baseline information identifying the approved channel depths and configurations and existing facilities. Minor deviations are authorized, provided the approved flood control protection or drainage is not increased;

　(ii) A delineation of any affected special aquatic sites, including wetlands; and,

　(iii) Location of the dredged material disposal site;

(11) For NWP 33 (Temporary Construction, Access, and Dewatering), the PCN must also include a restoration plan of reasonable measures to avoid and minimize adverse effects to aquatic resources;

(12) For NWPs 39, 43 and 44, the PCN must also include a written statement to the District Engineer explaining how avoidance and minimization for losses of waters of the U.S. were achieved on the project site;

(13) For NWP 39 and NWP 42, the PCN must include a compensatory mitigation proposal to offset losses of waters of the U.S. or justification explaining why compensatory mitigation should not be required. For discharges that cause the loss of greater than 300 linear feet of an intermittent stream bed to be authorized, the District Engineer must determine that the activity complies with the other terms and conditions of the NWP, determine adverse environmental effects are minimal both individually and cumulatively, and waive the limitation on stream impacts in writing before the permittee may proceed;

(14) For NWP 40 (Agricultural Activities), the PCN must include a compensatory mitigation proposal to offset losses of waters of the U.S. This NWP does not authorize the relocation of greater than 300 linear feet of existing serviceable drainage ditches constructed in non-tidal streams unless, for drainage ditches constructed in intermittent nontidal streams, the District Engineer waives this criterion in writing, and the District Engineer has determined that the project complies with all terms and conditions of this NWP, and that any adverse impacts of the project on the aquatic environment are minimal, both individually and cumulatively;

(15) For NWP 43 (Stormwater Management Facilities), the PCN must include, for the construction of new stormwater management facilities, a maintenance plan (in accordance with state and local requirements, if applicable) and a compensatory mitigation proposal to offset losses of waters of the U.S. For discharges that cause the loss of greater than 300 linear feet of an intermittent stream bed, to be authorized, the District Engineer must determine that the activity complies with the other terms and conditions of the NWP, determine adverse environmental effects are minimal both individually and cumulatively, and waive the limitation on stream impacts in writing before the permittee may proceed;

(16) For NWP 44 (Mining Activities), the PCN must include a description of all waters of the U.S. adversely affected by the project, a description of measures taken to minimize adverse effects to waters of the U.S., a description of measures taken to comply with the criteria of the NWP, and a reclamation plan (for all aggregate mining activities in isolated waters and non-tidal wetlands adjacent to headwaters and any hard rock/mineral mining activities);

(17) For activities that may adversely affect Federally-listed endangered or threatened species, the PCN must include the name(s) of those endangered or threatened species that may be affected by the proposed work or utilize the designated critical habitat that may be affected by the proposed work; and

(18) For activities that may affect historic properties listed in, or eligible for listing in, the National Register of Historic Places, the PCN must state which historic property may be affected by the proposed work or include a vicinity map indicating the location of the historic property.

(c) *Form of Notification:* The standard Individual Permit application form (Form ENG 4345) may be used as the notification but must clearly indicate that it is a PCN and must include all of the information required in (b) (1)–(18) of General Condition 13. A letter containing the requisite information may also be used.

(d) *District Engineer's Decision:* In reviewing the PCN for the proposed activity, the District Engineer will determine whether the activity authorized by the NWP will result in more than minimal individual or cumulative adverse environmental effects or may be contrary to the public interest. The prospective permittee may submit a proposed mitigation plan with the PCN to expedite the process. The District Engineer will consider any proposed compensatory mitigation the applicant has included in the proposal in determining whether the net adverse environmental effects to the aquatic environment of the proposed work are minimal. If the District Engineer determines that the activity complies with the terms and conditions of the NWP and that the adverse effects on the aquatic environment are minimal, after considering mitigation, the District Engineer will notify the permittee and include any conditions the District Engineer deems necessary. The District Engineer must approve any compensatory mitigation proposal before the permittee commences work. If the prospective permittee is required to submit a compensatory mitigation proposal with the PCN, the proposal may be either conceptual or detailed. If the prospective permittee elects to submit a compensatory mitigation plan with the PCN, the District Engineer will expeditiously review the proposed compensatory mitigation plan. The District Engineer must review the plan within 45 days of receiving a complete PCN and determine whether the conceptual or specific proposed mitigation would ensure no more than minimal adverse effects on the aquatic environment. If the net adverse effects of the project on the aquatic environment (after consideration of the compensatory mitigation proposal) are determined by the District Engineer to be minimal, the District Engineer will provide a timely written response to the applicant. The response will state that the project can proceed under the terms and conditions of the NWP. If the District Engineer determines that the adverse effects of the proposed work are more than minimal, then the District Engineer will notify the applicant either: (1) that the project does not qualify for authorization under the NWP and instruct the applicant on the procedures to seek authorization under an Individual Permit; (2) that the project is authorized under the NWP subject to the applicant's submission of a mitigation proposal that would reduce the adverse effects on the aquatic environment to the minimal level; or (3) that the project is authorized under the NWP with specific modifications or conditions. Where the District Engineer determines that mitigation is required to ensure no more than minimal adverse effects occur to the aquatic environment, the activity will be authorized within the 45-day PCN period. The authorization will include the necessary conceptual or specific mitigation or a requirement that the applicant submit a mitigation proposal that would reduce the adverse effects on the aquatic environment to the minimal level. When conceptual mitigation is included, or a mitigation plan is required under item (2) above, no work in waters of the U.S. will occur until the District Engineer has approved a specific mitigation plan.

(e) *Agency Coordination:* The District Engineer will consider any comments from Federal and state agencies concerning the proposed activity's compliance with the terms and conditions of the NWPs and the need for mitigation to reduce the project's adverse environmental effects to a minimal level. For activities requiring notification to the District Engineer that result in the loss of greater than 12-acre of waters of the U.S., the District Engineer will provide immediately (e.g., via facsimile transmission, overnight mail, or other expeditious manner) copy to the appropriate Federal or state offices (USFWS, state natural resource or water quality agency, EPA, State Historic Preservation Officer [SHPO], and, if appropriate, the NMFS). With the exception of NWP 37, these agencies will then have 10 calendar days from the date the material is transmitted to telephone or fax the District Engineer notice that they intend to provide substantive, site-specific comments. If so contacted by an agency, the District Engineer will wait an additional 15 calendar days before making a decision on the notification. The District Engineer will fully consider agency comments received within the specified time frame, but will provide no response to the resource agency, except as provided below. The District Engineer will indicate in the administrative record associated with each notification that the resource agencies' concerns were considered. As required by section 305(b)(4)(B) of the Magnuson-Stevens Fishery Conservation and

Management Act, the District Engineer will provide a response to NMFS within 30 days of receipt of any Essential Fish Habitat conservation recommendations. Applicants are encouraged to provide the Corps multiple copies of notifications to expedite agency notification.

(f) *Wetland Delineations:* Wetland delineations must be prepared in accordance with the current method required by the Corps (For NWP 29 see paragraph (b)(9)(iii) for parcels less than 14-acre in size). The permittee may ask the Corps to delineate the special aquatic site. There may be some delay if the Corps does the delineation. Furthermore, the 45-day period will not start until the wetland delineation has been completed and submitted to the Corps, where appropriate.

14. *Compliance Certification.* Every permittee who has received NWP verification from the Corps will submit a signed certification regarding the completed work and any required mitigation. The certification will be forwarded by the Corps with the authorization letter and will include:
(a) a statement that the authorized work was done in accordance with the Corps authorization, including any general or specific conditions;
(b) a statement that any required mitigation was completed in accordance with the permit conditions; and
(c) the signature of the permittee certifying the completion of the work and mitigation.

15. *Use of Multiple Nationwide Permits.* The use of more than one NWP for a single and complete project is prohibited, except when the acreage loss of waters of the U.S. authorized by the NWPs does not exceed the acreage limit of the NWP with the highest specified acreage limit (e.g., if a road crossing over tidal waters is constructed under NWP 14, with associated bank stabilization authorized by NWP 13, the maximum acreage loss of waters of the U.S. for the total project cannot exceed 13-acre).

16. *Water Supply Intakes.* No activity, including structures and work in navigable waters of the U.S. or discharges of dredged or fill material, may occur in the proximity of a public water supply intake except where the activity is for repair of the public water supply intake structures or adjacent bank stabilization.

17. *Shellfish Beds.* No activity, including structures and work in navigable waters of the U.S. or discharges of dredged or fill material, may occur in areas of concentrated shellfish populations, unless the activity is directly related to a shellfish harvesting activity authorized by NWP 4.

18. *Suitable Material.* No activity, including structures and work in navigable waters of the U.S. or discharges of dredged or fill material, may consist of unsuitable material (e.g., trash, debris, car bodies, asphalt, etc.) and material used for construction or discharged must be free from toxic pollutants in toxic amounts (see section 307 of the CWA).

19. *Mitigation.* The District Engineer will consider the factors discussed below when determining the acceptability of appropriate and practicable mitigation necessary to offset adverse effects on the aquatic environment that are more than minimal.
(a) The project must be designed and constructed to avoid and minimize adverse effects to waters of the U.S. to the maximum extent practicable at the project site (i.e., on site).
(b) Mitigation in all its forms (avoiding, minimizing, rectifying, reducing or compensating) will be required to the extent necessary to ensure that the adverse effects to the aquatic environment are minimal.

(c) Compensatory mitigation at a minimum one-for-one ratio will be required for all wetland impacts requiring a PCN, unless the District Engineer determines in writing that some other form of mitigation would be more environmentally appropriate and provides a project-specific waiver of this requirement. Consistent with National policy, the District Engineer will establish a preference for restoration of wetlands as compensatory mitigation, with reservation used only in exceptional circumstances.

(d) Compensatory mitigation (i.e., replacement or substitution of aquatic resources for those impacted) will not be used to increase the acreage losses allowed by the acreage limits of some of the NWPs. For example, 14-acre of wetlands cannot be created to change a 34-acre loss of wetlands to a 12-acre loss associated with NWP 39 verification. However, 12-acre of created wetlands can be used to reduce the impacts of a 12-acre loss of wetlands to the minimum impact level in order to meet the minimal impact requirement associated with NWPs.

(e) To be practicable, the mitigation must be available and capable of being done considering costs, existing technology, and logistics in light of the overall project purposes. Examples of mitigation that may be appropriate and practicable include, but are not limited to: reducing the size of the project; establishing and maintaining wetland or upland vegetated buffers to protect open waters such as streams; and replacing losses of aquatic resource functions and values by creating, restoring, enhancing, or preserving similar functions and values, preferably in the same watershed.

(f) Compensatory mitigation plans for projects in or near streams or other open waters will normally include a requirement for the establishment, maintenance, and legal protection (e.g., easements, deed restrictions) of vegetated buffers to open waters. In many cases, vegetated buffers will be the only compensatory mitigation required. Vegetated buffers should consist of native species. The width of the vegetated buffers required will address documented water quality or aquatic habitat loss concerns. Normally, the vegetated buffer will be 25 to 50 feet wide on each side of the stream, but the District Engineers may require slightly wider vegetated buffers to address documented water quality or habitat loss concerns. Where both wetlands and open waters exist on the project site, the Corps will determine the appropriate compensatory mitigation (e.g., stream buffers or wetlands compensation) based on what is best for the aquatic environment on a watershed basis. In cases where vegetated buffers are determined to be the most appropriate form of compensatory mitigation, the District Engineer may waive or reduce the requirement to provide wetland compensatory mitigation for wetland impacts.

(g) Compensatory mitigation proposals submitted with the "notification" may be either conceptual or detailed. If conceptual plans are approved under the verification, then the Corps will condition the verification to require detailed plans be submitted and approved by the Corps prior to construction of the authorized activity in waters of the U.S.

(h) Permittees may propose the use of mitigation banks, in-lieu fee arrangements or separate activity-specific compensatory mitigation. In all cases that require compensatory mitigation, the mitigation provisions will specify the party responsible for accomplishing and/or complying with the mitigation plan.

20. *Spawning Areas.* Activities, including structures and work in navigable waters of the U.S. or discharges of dredged or fill material, in spawning areas during spawning seasons must be avoided to the maximum extent practicable. Activities that result in the physical destruction (e.g., excavate, fill, or smother downstream by substantial turbidity) of an important spawning area are not authorized.

21. *Management of Water Flows.* To the maximum extent practicable, the activity must be designed to maintain preconstruction downstream flow conditions (e.g., location, capacity, and flow rates). Furthermore, the activity must not permanently restrict or impede the passage of normal or expected high

flows (unless the primary purpose of the fill is to impound waters) and the structure or discharge of dredged or fill material must withstand expected high flows. The activity must, to the maximum extent practicable, provide for retaining excess flows from the site, provide for maintaining surface flow rates from the site similar to preconstruction conditions, and provide for not increasing water flows from the project site, relocating water, or redirecting water flow beyond preconstruction conditions. Stream channelizing will be reduced to the minimal amount necessary, and the activity must, to the maximum extent practicable, reduce adverse effects such as flooding or erosion downstream and upstream of the project site, unless the activity is part of a larger system designed to manage water flows. In most cases, it will not be a requirement to conduct detailed studies and monitoring of water flow. This condition is only applicable to projects that have the potential to affect waterflows. While appropriate measures must be taken, it is not necessary to conduct detailed studies to identify such measures or require monitoring to ensure their effectiveness. Normally, the Corps will defer to state and local authorities regarding management of water flow.

22. ***Adverse Effects From Impoundments.*** If the activity creates an impoundment of water, adverse effects to the aquatic system due to the acceleration of the passage of water and/or the restricting of its flow shall be minimized to the maximum extent practicable. This includes structures and work in navigable waters of the U.S., or discharges of dredged or fill material.

23. ***Waterfowl Breeding Areas.*** Activities, including structures and work in navigable waters of the U.S. or discharges of dredged or fill material, into breeding areas for migratory waterfowl must be avoided to the maximum extent practicable.

24. ***Removal of Temporary Fills.*** Any temporary fills must be removed in their entirety and the affected areas returned to their preexisting elevation.

25. ***Designated Critical Resource Waters.*** Critical resource waters include NOAA-designated marine sanctuaries, National Estuarine Research Reserves, National Wild and Scenic Rivers, critical habitat for Federally listed threatened and endangered species, coral reefs, state natural heritage sites, and outstanding national resource waters or other waters officially designated by a state as having particular environmental or ecological significance and identified by the District Engineer after notice and opportunity for public comment. The District Engineer may also designate additional critical resource waters after notice and opportunity for comment.

(a) Except as noted below, discharges of dredged or fill material into waters of the US are not authorized by NWPs 7, 12, 14, 16, 17, 21, 29, 31, 35, 39, 40, 42, 43, and 44 for any activity within, or directly affecting, critical resource waters, including wetlands adjacent to such waters. Discharges of dredged or fill materials into waters of the US may be authorized by the above NWPs in National Wild and Scenic Rivers if the activity complies with General Condition 7. Further, such discharges may be authorized in designated critical habitat for Federally listed threatened or endangered species if the activity complies with General Condition 11 and the USFWS or the NMFS has concurred in a determination of compliance with this condition.

(b) For NWPs 3, 8, 10, 13, 15, 18, 19, 22, 23, 25, 27, 28, 30, 33, 34, 36, 37, and 38, notification is required in accordance with General Condition 13, for any activity proposed in the designated critical resource waters including wetlands adjacent to those waters. The District Engineer may authorize activities under these NWPs only after it is determined that the impacts to the critical resource waters will be no more than minimal.

26. *Fills Within 100-Year Floodplains.* For purposes of this General Condition, 100-year floodplains will be identified through the existing Federal Emergency Management Agency's (FEMA) Flood Insurance Rate Maps or FEMA-approved local floodplain maps.

(a) *Discharges in Floodplain; Below Headwaters.* Discharges of dredged or fill material into waters of the U.S. within the mapped 100-year floodplain, below headwaters (i.e., five cfs), resulting in permanent above-grade fills, are not authorized by NWPs 39, 40, 42, 43, and 44.

(b) *Discharges in Floodway; Above Headwaters.* Discharges of dredged or fill material into waters of the US within the FEMA or locally mapped floodway, resulting in permanent above-grade fills, are not authorized by NWPs 39, 40, 42, and 44.

(c) The permittee must comply with any applicable FEMA-approved state or local floodplain management requirements.

27. *Construction Period.* For activities that have not been verified by the Corps and the project was commenced or under contract to commence by the expiration date of the NWP (or modification or revocation date), the work must be completed within 12 months after such date (including any modification that affects the project). For activities that have been verified and the project was commenced or under contract to commence within the verification period, the work must be completed by the date determined by the Corps. For projects that have been verified by the Corps, an extension of a Corps-approved completion date maybe requested. This request must be submitted at least one month before the previously approved completion date.

Further Information

1. District Engineers have authority to determine if an activity complies with the terms and conditions of an NWP.

2. NWPs do not obviate the need to obtain other Federal, state, or local permits, approvals, or authorizations required by law.

3. NWPs do not grant any property rights or exclusive privileges.

4. NWPs do not authorize any injury to the property or rights of others.

5. NWPs do not authorize interference with any existing or proposed Federal project.

Definitions:

Best Management Practices (BMPs): BMPs are policies, practices, procedures, or structures implemented to mitigate the adverse environmental effects on surface water quality resulting from development. BMPs are categorized as structural or nonstructural. A BMP policy may affect the limits on a development.

Compensatory Mitigation: For purposes of Section 10/404, compensatory mitigation is the restoration, creation, enhancement, or in exceptional circumstances, preservation of wetlands and/or other aquatic resources for the purpose of compensating for unavoidable adverse impacts which remain after all appropriate and practicable avoidance and minimization has been achieved.

Creation: The establishment of a wetland or other aquatic resource where one did not formerly exist.

Enhancement: Activities conducted in existing wetlands or other aquatic resources that increase one or more aquatic functions.

Ephemeral Stream: An ephemeral stream has flowing water only during and for a short duration after, precipitation events in a typical year. Ephemeral stream beds are located above the water table year-round. Groundwater is not a source of water for the stream. Runoff from rainfall is the primary source of water for stream flow.

Farm Tract: A unit of contiguous land under one ownership that is operated as a farm or part of a farm.

Flood Fringe: That portion of the 100-year floodplain outside of the floodway (often referred to as "floodway fringe").

Floodway: The area regulated by Federal, state, or local requirements to provide for the discharge of the base flood so the cumulative increase in water surface elevation is no more than a designated amount (not to exceed one foot as set by the National Flood Insurance Program) within the 100-year floodplain.

Independent Utility: A test to determine what constitutes a single and complete project in the Corps regulatory program. A project is considered to have independent utility if it would be constructed absent the construction of other projects in the project area. Portions of a multi-phase project that depend upon other phases of the project do not have independent utility. Phases of a project that would be constructed even if the other phases were not built can be considered as separate single and complete projects with independent utility.

Intermittent Stream: An intermittent stream has flowing water during certain times of the year, when groundwater provides water for stream flow. During dry periods, intermittent streams may not have flowing water. Runoff from rainfall is a supplemental source of water for stream flow.

Loss of Waters of the U.S.: Waters of the US that include the filled area and other waters that are permanently adversely affected by flooding, excavation, or drainage because of the regulated activity. Permanent adverse effects include permanent above-grade, at-grade, or below-grade fills that change an aquatic area to dry land, increase the bottom elevation of a waterbody, or change the use of a waterbody. The acreage of loss of waters of the U.S. is the threshold measurement of the impact to existing waters for determining whether a project may qualify for an NWP; it is not a net threshold that is calculated after considering compensatory mitigation that may be used to offset losses of aquatic functions and values. The loss of stream bed includes the linear feet of stream bed that is filled or excavated. Waters of the U.S. temporarily filled, flooded, excavated, or drained, but restored to preconstruction contours and elevations after construction, are not included in the measurement of loss of waters of the U.S. Impacts to ephemeral waters are only not included in the acreage or linear foot measurements of loss of waters of the U.S. or loss of stream bed, for the purpose of determining compliance with the threshold limits of the NWPs.

Non-tidal Wetland: A non-tidal wetland is a wetland (i.e., a water of the U.S.) that is not subject to the ebb and flow of tidal waters. The definition of a wetland can be found at 33 CFR 328.3(b). Non-tidal wetlands contiguous to tidal waters are located landward of the high tide line (i.e., spring high tide line).

Open Water: An area that, during a year with normal patterns of precipitation, has standing or flowing water for sufficient duration to establish an ordinary high water mark. Aquatic vegetation within the area of standing or flowing water is either non-emergent, sparse, or absent. Vegetated shallows are considered to be open waters. The term "open water" includes rivers, streams, lakes, and ponds. For the purposes of the NWPs, this term does not include ephemeral waters.

Perennial Stream: A perennial stream has flowing water year-round during a typical year. The water table is located above the stream bed for most of the year. Groundwater is the primary source of water for stream flow. Runoff from rainfall is a supplemental source of water for stream flow.

Permanent Above-grade Fill: A discharge of dredged or fill material into waters of the U.S., including wetlands, that results in a substantial increase in ground elevation and permanently converts part or all of the waterbody to dry land. Structural fills authorized by NWPs 3, 25, 36, etc., are not included.

Preservation: The protection of ecologically important wetlands or other aquatic resources in perpetuity through the implementation of appropriate legal and physical mechanisms. Preservation may include protection of upland areas adjacent to wetlands as necessary to ensure protection and/or enhancement of the overall aquatic ecosystem.

Restoration: Re-establishment of wetland and/or other aquatic resource characteristics and function(s) at a site where they have ceased to exist, or exist in a substantially degraded state.

Riffle and Pool Complex: Riffle and pool complexes are special aquatic sites under the 404(b)(1) Guidelines. Riffle and pool complexes sometimes characterize steep gradient sections of streams. Such stream sections are recognizable by their hydraulic characteristics. The rapid movement of water over a course substrate in riffles results in a rough flow, a turbulent surface, and high dissolved oxygen levels in the water. Pools are deeper areas associated with riffles. A slower stream velocity, a streaming flow, a smooth surface, and a finer substrate characterize pools.

Single and Complete Project: The term "single and complete project" is defined at 33 CFR 330.2(i) as the total project proposed or accomplished by one owner/developer or partnership or other association of owners/developers (see definition of independent utility). For linear projects, the "single and complete project" (i.e., a single and complete crossing) will apply to each crossing of a separate water of the U.S. (i.e., a single waterbody) at that location. An exception is for linear projects crossing a single waterbody several times at separate and distant locations: each crossing is considered a single and complete project. However, individual channels in a braided stream or river, or individual arms of a large, irregularly shaped wetland or lake, etc., are not separate waterbodies.

Stormwater Management: Stormwater management is the mechanism for controlling stormwater runoff for the purposes of reducing downstream erosion, water quality degradation, and flooding and mitigating the adverse effects of changes in land use on the aquatic environment.

Stormwater Management Facilities: Stormwater management facilities are those facilities, including but not limited to, stormwater retention and detention ponds and BMPs, which retain water for a period of time to control runoff and/or improve the quality (i.e., by reducing the concentration of nutrients, sediments, hazardous substances and other pollutants) of stormwater runoff.

Stream Bed: The substrate of the stream channel between the ordinary high water marks. The substrate may be bedrock or inorganic particles that range in size from clay to boulders. Wetlands contiguous to the stream bed, but outside of the ordinary high water marks, are not considered part of the stream bed.

Stream Channelization: The manipulation of a stream channel to increase the rate of water flow through the stream channel. Manipulation may include deepening, widening, straightening, armoring, or other activities that change the stream cross-section or other aspects of stream channel geometry to increase the rate of water flow through the stream channel. A channelized stream remains a water of the US, despite the modifications to increase the rate of water flow.

Tidal Wetland: A tidal wetland is a wetland (i.e., water of the US) that is inundated by tidal waters. The definitions of a wetland and tidal waters can be found at 33 CFR 328.3(b) and 33 CFR 328.3(f), respectively. Tidal waters rise and fall in a predictable and measurable rhythm or cycle due to the gravitational pulls of the moon and sun. Tidal waters end where the rise and fall of the water surface can no longer be practically measured in a predictable rhythm due to masking by other waters, wind, or other effects. Tidal wetlands are located channelward of the high tide line (i.e., spring high tide line) and are inundated by tidal waters two times per lunar month, during spring high tides.

Vegetated Buffer: A vegetated upland or wetland area next to rivers, streams, lakes, or other open waters which separates the open water from developed areas, including agricultural land. Vegetated buffers provide a variety of aquatic habitat functions and values (e.g., aquatic habitat for fish and other aquatic organisms, moderation of water temperature changes, and detritus for aquatic food webs) and help improve or maintain local water quality. A vegetated buffer can be established by maintaining an existing vegetated area or planting native trees, shrubs, and herbaceous plants on land next to open waters. Mowed lawns are not considered vegetated buffers because they provide little or no aquatic habitat functions and values. The establishment and maintenance of vegetated buffers is a method of compensatory mitigation that can be used in conjunction with the restoration, creation, enhancement, or preservation of aquatic habitats to ensure that activities authorized by NWPs result in minimal adverse effects to the aquatic environment. (See General Condition 19.)

Vegetated Shallows: Vegetated shallows are special aquatic sites under the 404(b)(1) Guidelines. They are areas that are permanently inundated and under normal circumstances have rooted aquatic vegetation, such as seagrasses in marine and estuarine systems and a variety of vascular rooted plants in freshwater systems.

Waterbody: A waterbody is any area that in a normal year has water flowing or standing above ground to the extent that evidence of an ordinary high water mark is established. Wetlands contiguous to the waterbody are considered part of the waterbody.

New Proposed Nationwide Permits

The Corps is proposing several modifications to the above Nationwide Permits. While not final at this writing, it is expected that many of the proposed revisions will take effect in March 2007. Practitioners are urged to check with their local Corps District for the final version.

NWP 3, "Maintenance," will be split, and new NWP A, "Emergency Repair Activities," will be created.

NWP 3 will authorize removal of accumulated sediments from existing structures and from canals associated with intake and outfall structures.

NWP 4, "Fish and Wildlife Harvesting, Enhancement, and Attraction Devices and Activities," will lose its authorization of shellfish seeding because that provision will move to new NWP D if undertaken in an existing aquaculture operation, or to NWP 27 if conducted for restoration activities.

NWP 5, "Scientific Measurement Devices," will lose the PCN requirement for discharges of 10 to 25 cubic yards for construction of small weirs and flumes, but will retain the 25-cubic-yard limitation.

NWP 6, "Survey Activities," will add "exploratory trenching" and a requirement to restore the trenched area if there are minimal adverse effects on the aquatic environment. Temporary pads for survey activities will now be authorized with a 25-cubic-yard limitation.

NWP 7, "Outfall Structures and Associated Intake Structures," will be simplified by placing the provisions regarding the removal of accumulated sediments from outfall and intake structures and associated canals in NWP 3.

NWP 8, "Oil and Gas Structures on the Outer Continental Shelf," will now require a PCN to allow district engineers to review potential effects on navigation and national security.

NWP 12, "Utility Line Activities," will be slightly reorganized and PCNs will be required only for projects that require a §10 permit or that result in a loss of greater than .1 acre.

NWP 13, "Bank Stabilization," will allow district engineers to waive fill limitations if there are minimal individual or cumulative adverse effects so long as there is a PCN.

NWP 14, "Linear Transportation Projects," NWP 16, "Return Water from Upland Contained Disposal Areas," and NWP 17, "Hydropower Projects" will be reorganized but substantively unchanged.

NWP 18, "Minor Discharges," will be modified by applying the .1-acre limit to all losses of waters of the U.S., not just special aquatic sites.

NWP 19, "Minor Dredging," will no longer state "as part of a single and complete project" because that phrase applies to all NWPs.

NWP 21, "Surface Coal Mining Operations," still lacks an acreage limit and the Corps is specifically seeking comment on this point.

NWP 22, "Removal of Vessels," will be rearranged and will require a PCN if the project involves discharges in special aquatic sites.

NWP 23, "Approved Categorical Exclusions," will be reorganized and will require review of RGLs to determine if a PCN is required.

NWP 24, "Indian Tribe or State Administered Section 404 Programs," will add Indian Tribes to the list of approved administrators, currently only Michigan and New Jersey.

NWP 27, "Aquatic Habitat Restoration, Establishment, and Enhancement Activities," will be modified to prohibit conversion of natural wetlands to another aquatic use but still permit relocation of non-tidal wetlands under certain conditions. Restoration documentation from other agencies must be submitted to the Corps. "Values" will be replaced by "services."

NWP 29, "Residential Developments," will be combined with NWP 39 to authorize residential developments while NWP 39 will authorize commercial and institutional developments, and both will require a PCN. There will be a .5-acre and 300-linear-foot limit. The limit may be waived for ephemeral streams.

NWP 30, "Moist Soil Management for Wildlife," will be modified to allow any landowner to use this NWP.

NWP 31, "Maintenance of Existing Flood Control Facilities," will now include levees.

NWP 32, "Completed Enforcement Actions," will be slightly modified to make its meaning more clear but there are no substantive changes.

NWP 33, "Temporary Construction, Access, and Dewatering,"will require a restoration plan in the PCN.

NWP 34, "Cranberry Production Activities," will require a PCN and apply to on-going operations provided the 10-acre limit is not exceeded.

NWP 36, "Boat Ramps," will allow waivers to the 50-cubic-yard and 20-foot wide limitations if the adverse effects will be minimal. A PCN will be required if these limits will be exceeded.

NWP 37, "Emergency Watershed Protection and Rehabilitation," and NWP 38, "Cleanup of Hazardous and Toxic Waste," will be rearranged but not substantively changed.

NWP 39, "Commercial and Institutional Developments," will no longer cover residential developments but will now require a PCN which may trigger imposition of special conditions.
NWP 40, "Agricultural Activities," will no longer require USDA program authorization but will require a PCN for all activities. Construction of farm ponds may now be authorized.

NWP 41, "Reshaping Existing Drainage Ditches," will allow reshaping only if the purpose is to improve water quality, i.e., by providing shallower side slopes. Maintenance without changing the configuration continues to be an exempt activity. Sidecasting from a reshaping operation will no longer be prohibited.

NWP 42, "Recreation Facilities," will allow construction with minimal individual and cumulative adverse effects regardless of pre-construction grades or natural contours. The 300-foot limit on loss of stream bed may be waived for intermittent or ephemeral streams.

NWP 43, "Stormwater Management Facilities," will require PCNs for expansion but not maintenance of stormwater facilities. The 300-foot limit may be waived for ephemeral streams.

NWP 44, "Mining Activities," will continue to authorize all mining except coal mining (NWP 21). The PCN must contain a reclamation plan.

New NWPs:

NWP A, "Emergency Repair Activities," authorizes repairs if submitted within 12 months of the damage.

NWP B, "Discharges into Ditches and Canals," allows discharges if the ditches or canals are constructed in uplands, receive water from another water of the U.S., and divert water into another water of the U.S., with a one-acre limit.

NWP C, "Pipeline Safety Program Designated Time Sensitive Inspections and Repairs," will allow repair of any currently serviceable pipeline if determined to be time-sensitive by the Pipeline Safety Program.

NWP D, "Commercial Shellfish Aquaculture Activities," will authorize structures as well as discharges for new shellfish operations but not for existing ones. A PCN is required for larger projects.

NWP E, "Coal Remining Activities," will authorize the restoration of mine sites that are causing impacts to waters of the U.S.

NWP F, "Underground Coal Mining Activities," will allow discharges for "face up" activities with a .5-acre limitation.

Exempt Activities

After considering the regulatory exemptions discussed above, there are still six more statutory exemptions to §404's coverage, all of them designed to exclude from jurisdiction routine, essentially commercial activities that have minor impacts on wetlands:[48]

1. For discharges of dredged and fill material into wetlands and minor drainage (but not a gradual conversion from wetland to nonwetland) which occur during normal farming, silviculture, and ranching activities (plowing, seeding, cultivating, minor drainage, harvesting for the production of food, fiber, and forest products, or upland soil and water conservation practices) so long as the discharge occurred only in an area which was, at the time of the discharge, part of a legitimate, continuously operated farming operation.[49] If the farm field has lain fallow long enough that it now requires modification of its evolved hydrologic regime to convert it back to farmland, then the exemption will be lost.[50]
2. For the purpose of maintenance of currently serviceable dikes, dams, levees, groins, riprap, breakwaters, causeways, bridge abutments or approaches, and transportation structures;[51]
3. For the purpose of construction or maintenance of farm or stock ponds or irrigation ditches;[52]

---

48. 33 U.S.C. §1344(f)(1); but see "Recapture Provision" below, if the impact of these exempt activities is more than minimal. See also *United States v. Akers*, 785 F.2d 814 (9th Cir. Cal. 1986), *cert. denied*, 479 U.S. 828, 93 L.Ed.2d 56, 107 S.Ct. 107 (1986); *United States v. Huebner*, 752 F.2d 1235 (7th Cir. Wisc. 1985), *cert. denied*, 474 U.S. 817, 88 L.Ed.2d 50, 106 S.Ct. 62 (1985).

49. See Regulatory Guidance Letter, *Clarification of the Phrase "Normal Circumstances" as it pertains to Cropped Wetlands, No. 90-7 (September 26, 1990).*

50. 33 U.S.C. §1344(f)(1)(A)33 U.S.C. §1344(f)(1)(A). See also *U.S. v. Larkins*, 852 F.2d 189 (6th Cir. Ky. 1988), *cert. denied*, 489 U.S. 1016, 103 L.Ed.2d 193, 109 S.Ct. 1131 (1989); *U.S. v. Cumberland Farms of Connecticut*, 647 F. Supp. 1166 (D.Mass.), *aff'd*, 826 F.2d 1151 (1st Cir. 1987), *cert. denied*, 489 U.S. 1061, 98 L.Ed.2d 981, 108 S.Ct. 1016 (1988); *U.S. v. Akers*, supra.; *U.S. v. Huebner*, supra.; *Memorandum for the Field, Clean Water Act Section 404 Regulatory Program and Agricultural Activities* (May 3, 1990) and the Environmental Protection Agency's regulations at 40 C.F.R. §232.3.

51. 33 U.S.C. §1344(f)(1)(B).

52. 33 U.S.C. §1344(f)(1)(C). See also Regulatory Guidance Letter, No. 87-7, *Section 404(f)(1)(C) Statutory Exemption for Drainage Ditch Maintenance* (August 17, 1987).

4. For the purpose of construction of temporary sedimentation basins on a construction site (but not the placement of fill material into navigable waters);[53]
5. For the purpose of construction or maintenance of farm, forest, or temporary mining roads, so long as these roads are constructed and maintained in such a way as to assure compliance with §404(f)(2);[54] and,
6. Certain state programs.[55]

These specifically enumerated exemptions are not subject to jurisdiction under §301(a) or §402 either.

The Recapture Provision

Even though there are six specific topics of exempt activities, these activities will lose their exempt status if the purpose of the activity is to bring "an area of navigable waters into a use to which it was not previously subject, where the flow or circulation of navigable waters may be impaired, or the reach of such waters is reduced."[56] The essential inquiry is whether the activity is "normal and ongoing" or whether it is truly a "new use," which the Corps concedes requires a "judgment call."[57] A "new use" can readily be found if the activity causes some significant alteration to the area's hydrology.

---

53. 33 U.S.C. §1344(f)(1)(D).
54. 33 U.S.C. §1344(f)(1)(E). *See also* Regulatory Guidance Letter, No. 86-3, *Section 404(f)(1) Exemption of Farm and Forest Roads (33 CFR Part 323.4(a)(6)),* April 4, 1986. *See also U.S. v. Sargent County Water Resource Dist.,* 876 F.Supp. 1090 (D.N.D. 1994); *U.S. v. Brace,* 41 F.3d 117 (3d Cir. 1994), *cert. denied,* 515 U.S. 1158, 115 S.Ct. 2610, 132 L.Ed.2d 854 (1995).
55. 33 U.S.C. §1344(f)(1)(F).
56. 33 U.S.C. §1344(f)(2)). This subsection is commonly referred to as the "recapture provision" because it "recaptures" certain apparently exempt activities and brings them back under the permit requirement. See also Regulatory Guidance Letter, No. 87-9, *Section 404(f)(1)(C) Exemption for Construction or Maintenance of Farm or Stock Ponds* (August 27, 1987); *Bayou Marcus Livestock & Agricultural Co. v. EPA,* 20 Envtl.L.Rep. (Envtl.L.Inst.) 20445 (N.D.Fla. 1989) (§403 of the Rivers and Harbors Act also prohibits unpermitted excavation or fill or alteration of the course, location, condition, and capacity of navigable waters).
57. Regulatory Guidance Letter, No. 87-9,

CHAPTER SIX

Permitting Procedures

Permit Applications in General

The regulations concerning the Corps's authority to issue permits for discharging dredged and fill material into wetlands under the Clean Water Act are found at 33 C.F.R. §§320.1(b)(5) and 320.2(f). Its procedures are set forth in great detail at 33 C.F.R. §325.1. The Corps is also required to follow certain *Guidelines* promulgated by the Environmental Protection Agency in deciding whether to issue or deny a permit.[1]

In addition to these national regulations, because the Corps has traditionally been "a highly decentralized organization,"[2] much of the permitting authority has been delegated to the thirty-six district engineers and eleven division engineers. Thus, if a district or division engineer makes a permit decision, if it was made in accordance with the regulations, the decision is final, but there is now an administrative appeal process for permit denials and jurisdictional determinations.[3]

Another manifestation of the Corps's traditional decentralization is that each district engineer should have established local procedures and policies to allow potential applicants to contact the office for preapplication consultation for major projects.[4] The district engineer should "endeavor, at this stage, to provide the potential applicant with all helpful information necessary in pursuing the application, including factors which the Corps must consider in its permit decision making process."[5]

Particularly in the case of potential permit applications that "may involve the preparation of an environmental document," the district engineer should advise the potential permit applicants of the requirements for the permit(s) and the "attendant public interest review."[6] Potential applicants should also be aware that even the basic permit application form may have regional variations, thus the potential applicant should obtain an application form from the office of the district in which the wetland lies.[7] There is a $100 filing fee for each permit application when the planned or ultimate purpose of the project is commercial or industrial in nature and is in support of operations that charge for the production, distribution, or sale of goods or services; the filing fee for noncommercial projects is ten dollars.[8]

The application form itself is surprisingly simple; its difficulty lies in supplying the information in the requisite degree of specificity and completeness to satisfy the Corps. First, the applicant must

---

1. 33 C.F.R. §320.2(f); See also "Environmental Protection Agency *Guidelines*," p. 90.
2. 33 C.F.R. §§320.1(a)(2) and 320.2(f).
3. 33 C.F.R. §331.
4. 33 C.F.R. §325.1(b).
5. *Id.*
6. *Id.*
7. 33 C.F.R. §325.1(c). A sample application form is reprinted as appendix A to 33 C.F.R. §325 but, since local variations are allowed, the better practice is to acquire an application form directly from the Corps district in which the subject property lies.
8. 33 C.F.R. §325.1(f).

include a complete description of the proposed activity including the necessary maps (including a vicinity map, bird's-eye view, and a cross-section), drawings, sketches, or plans sufficient for public notice.[9] Although generation of the public notice is a requirement laid on the Corps, since the information to be contained in the notice must come from the applicant, it is discussed here.

The district engineer has fifteen days to determine whether the application is complete.[10] If complete, the district engineer will issue a public notice of the pending application.

Public Notice and Comment

This regulation requires that the information included in the public notice be sufficient "to give a clear understanding of the magnitude of the activity to generate meaningful comment."[11] The "meaningful comment" contemplated by the regulation is an evaluation of the "probable impact on the public interest."[12] The Corps is required to state in the public notice fifteen separate items of information as they apply to a §404 permit:[13]

1. A statement of the applicable statutory authority(ies);
2. The name and address of the applicant;
3. The name or title, address, and telephone number of the Corps contact person from whom additional information concerning the application may be obtained;
4. The location of the proposed activity;
5. A brief description of the proposed activity, its purpose and intended use, including a description of the type of structures, if any, to be erected on fills or pile- or float-supported platforms;
6. A plan and elevation drawing showing the general and specific site location and character of all proposed activities,[14] including the size relationship of the proposed structures to the size of the impacted waterway and depth of water in the area;
7. A list of other government authorizations obtained or requested by the applicant, including required certifications relative to water quality, coastal zone management, or marine sanctuaries;
8. If appropriate, a statement that the activity is a categorical exclusion for purposes of the National Environmental Policy Act;
9. A statement of the district engineer's current knowledge on historic properties;
10. A statement of the district engineer's current knowledge on endangered species (if the district engineer finds that a proposed activity may affect an endangered or threatened species, he will initiate formal consultation procedures with the U.S. Fish and Wildlife Service or National Marine Fisheries Services[15]);
11. A statement on evaluation factors;[16]

---

9. 33 C.F.R. §325.1(d). See also *U.S. Army Corps of Engineers, Regulatory Program: Applicant Information.*
10. 33 C.F.R. §325.2.
11. 3 C.F.R. §325.3(a).
12. *Id.*
13. 33 C.F.R. §325.3(a) lists these topics as well as a handful of other notice requirements that do not apply to permit applications in wetlands.
14. See, e.g., *Save Our Sonoran v. Flowers*, 408 F.3d 1113 (9th Cir. 2005); *Wetlands Action Network v. U.S. Army Corps of Engineers*, 222 F.3d 1105 (9th Cir. 2000); *Pamlico-Tar River Foundation v. U.S. Army Corps of Engineers*, 329 F.Supp.2d 600 (E.D.N.C. 2004).
15. 33 C.F.R. §325.2(b)(5).
16. The exact wording of this statement, which is repeated in the regulations at 33 C.F.R. §320.4(a), is included in the regulations: "The decision whether to issue a permit will be based on an evaluation of the probable impact including cumulative impacts of the proposed activity on the public interest. That decision will reflect the national concern both for protection and utilization of important resources. The benefit which reasonably may be expected to accrue from the proposal must be balanced against its reasonably foreseeable detriments. All factors which may be relevant to the proposal will be considered including the cumulative effects thereof; among those are conservation, economics, aesthetics, general environmental concerns, wetlands, historic properties, fish and wildlife values, flood hazards, floodplain values, land use, navigation, shoreline erosion and accretion, recreation, water supply and conservation, water quality, energy needs, safety, food and fiber production, mineral needs, considerations of property ownership and, in general, the needs and welfare of the people." 33 C.F.R. §325.3(c)(1). Further, if the activity is to occur in a wetland, the statement must also include an application of the Environmental Protection Agency's *Guidelines.*

12. Any other available information that may assist interested parties in evaluating the likely impact of the proposed activity, if any, on factors affecting the public interest;
13. The comment period;[17]
14. A statement that any person may request, in writing, within the comment period specified in the notice, that a public hearing be held to consider the application provided that the request "state, with particularity, the reasons for holding a public hearing"; and
15. For private applications in states with an approved Coastal Zone Management Plan, a statement on compliance with the approved plan.

Once the Corps has collected the information and generated the public notice, it distributes the notice for posting to post offices or other appropriate public places in the vicinity of the proposed work.[18] Copies of the public notice are also sent to the applicant, appropriate city and county officials, adjoining property owners, appropriate state agencies, appropriate Indian tribes, concerned federal agencies, concerned business and conservation organizations, appropriate River Basin Commissions, appropriate state- and areawide clearing houses, local news media, and to any other interested party.[19] The Corps is required to keep a record of the list of addresses to whom the notice was sent.[20] In addition, if the Corps receives any interim information that would affect the public's view of the proposal, it must issue a "supplemental, revised, or corrected public notice."[21] The Corps "presumes" that all interested parties will wish to respond to public notices; therefore, a lack of response will be interpreted as no objection.[22]

Conflict Resolution

Having received a complete application and issued a public notice, the applicant then enters the "conflict resolution" stage of the permit procedure, which lasts for fifteen to thirty days but may be extended.[23] The Corps is required to acknowledge receipt of all comments and to "consider all comments received in response to the public notice."[24] The Corps must seek the advice and special expertise of other federal agencies if the comments received render such advice and expertise relevant.[25] Most important, the Corps is required to inform the applicant of any comments and to receive "the views of the applicant on a particular issue to make a public interest determination."[26] This step in the process is mandatory and a permit denial may be remanded to the Corps if a court finds that the Corps engaged in secret meetings with objectors to the proposed activity.[27] The applicant is given the option to contact the commentators directly to resolve their objections,[28] however, since the Corps is solely responsible to make a permit decision, it may convene a Corps-staffed mediation session between the

---

17. The public notice must be issued within fifteen days of receipt of all information required to be submitted. 33 C.F.R. §§325.2(a)(2) and 325.2(d)(2). The comment period runs from the date of the public notice and should be a "reasonable period of time within which interested parties may express their views," but no more than thirty nor less than fifteen days, determined by the Corps's consideration of (1) mail time and the need for comment from remote areas; (2) comments from similar proposals; and (3) the need for a site visit. 33 C.F.R. §325.2(d)(2). If the Corps believes that the comment period should be extended, it may do so for an additional thirty days.
18. 33 C.F.R. §325.3(d)(1).
19. *Id.*
20. 33 C.F.R. §325.3(d)(3).
21. 33 C.F.R. §325.2(a)(2).
22. 33 C.F.R. §325.3(d)(3).
23. 33 C.F.R. §325.2(d)(2).
24. 33 C.F.R. §325.2(a)(3).
25. *Id.*
26. *Id.*
27. *Mall Properties v. Marsh*, 672 F.Supp. 561 (D.Mass. 1987), rejecting remand as an appealable order, 841 F.2d 440 (1st Cir. 1988).
28. 33 C.F.R. §325.2(a)(3). In fact, the applicant is entitled to contact permit objectors. *Mall Properties, Inc. v. Marsh*, 672 F.Supp. 561 (D.Mass. 1987), *appeal dismissed*, 841 F.2d 440 (1st Cir. Mass. 1988), *cert. denied*, 488 U.S. 848, 102 L.Ed.2d 101, 109 S.Ct. 128 (1988).

applicant and the commentators.[29] This part of the permit procedure must be followed diligently by the Corps with delays not to exceed thirty days allowed only upon the request of the applicant.[30]

Unless the Corps determines that issues raised in the comments are "insubstantial" or there is "otherwise no valid interest to be served by a hearing," the Corps may decide that a public hearing is necessary.[31] The decision to hold a hearing or not must be made in writing, include the Corps's reasons for its decision; be communicated to all requesting parties; and give at least thirty days' notice of the hearing from the date of the public notice.[32] The Corps is required to hold a hearing "in case of doubt" or it may be ordered to hold one.[33] Parties may be represented by counsel and the presiding officer from the Corps may also have a "legal adviser" present.[34] "Any person" may present oral or written statements, call witnesses, and present "recommendations as to an appropriate decision."[35] Cross-examination of witnesses is not allowed.[36] Although the regulations are silent as to whether the rules of evidence apply, the presiding officer may exclude documentary evidence on the grounds of "redundancy."[37] The hearing must be transcribed verbatim.[38] Following the close of the hearing, an additional comment period of not less than ten days is required.[39] The transcript and all evidence introduced will be made part of the administrative record.[40] The Corps's decision must be in writing.[41]

Environmental Protection Agency *Guidelines*

As the Corps is proceeding in its permit decision, gathering all the information necessary, receiving comments after the public notice, and conducting any public hearing it considers necessary, the Corps is required to determine "the probable effect of the proposed work on the public interest" in conformity with the *Guidelines* established by the Environmental Protection Agency.[42] The Corps can override state and local government zoning or land-use decisions but must document the override[43] as well as other agencies' views.[44] Wetlands present a special case of permit decision for the Corps because of the multitude of expressions of policy against their alteration or destruction.[45] In fact, the Corps's regula-

29. 33 C.F.R. §325.2(a)(3).
30. *Id.*
31. 33 C.F.R. §§325.2(a)(5) and 327.4(b). The Corps is not required to hold a public hearing nor does due process require one. *AJA Associates v. U.S. Army Corps of Engineers,* 817 F.2d 1070 (3d Cir. 1987). Furthermore, these regulations do not require a full hearing under the federal Administrative Procedure Act. *Kreider Dairy Farms, Inc. v. Glickman,* 190 F.3d 113 (3d Cir. 1999); *Water Works & Sewer Bd. Of the City of Birmingham v. U.S. Army Corps of Engineers,* 983 F.Supp. 1052 (N.D.Ala. 1997); *Buttry v. United States,* 690 F.2d 1170 (5th Cir. 1982), *cert. denied,* 461 U.S. 927, 77 L.Ed.2d 298, 103 S.Ct. 2087 (1983); *Shoreline Assoc. v. Marsh,* 555 F.Supp. 169 (D.Md. 1983), *aff'd without op.,* 725 F.2d 677 (4th Cir. Md. 1984); *National Wildlife Federation v. Marsh,* 568 F.Supp. 985 (D.D.C. 1983); *Nofelco Realty Corp. v. United States,* 521 F.Supp. 458 (S.D.N.Y. 1981).
32. 33 C.F.R. §§327.4(b) and 327.11.
33. 33 C.F.R. §327.4(c).
34. 33 C.F.R. §§327.6 and 327.7.
35. 33 C.F.R. §327.8(b).
36. 33 C.F.R. §327.8(d).
37. 33 C.F.R. §327.8(f).
38. 33 C.F.R. §327.8(e).
39. 33 C.F.R. §327.8(g).
40. 33 C.F.R. §327.9.
41. 33 C.F.R. §325.2(a)(6).
42. 33 C.F.R. §325.2(a)(6).
43. 33 C.F.R. §§320.4(j)(2), 320.4(j)(4), and 325.2(a)(6).
44. 33 C.F.R. §§320.4(c) and 320.4(j)(4); *Sierra Club v. Alexander,* 484 F.Supp. 455 (N.D.N.Y.), *aff'd,* 633 F.2d 206 (2d Cir. N.Y. 1980); *Hart & Miller Islands Area Environmental Group, Inc. v. Corps of Engineers of United States Army,* 505 F.Supp. 732 (D.Md. 1980).
45. See, e.g., 33 C.F.R. §320.4(b)(1): "Most wetlands constitute a productive and valuable public resource, the unnecessary alteration or destruction of which should be discouraged as contrary to the public interest"; 33 C.F.R. §320.4(b)(4): "No permit will be granted which involves the alteration of wetlands . . . unless the (Corps) concludes . . . that the benefits of the proposed alteration outweigh the damage to the wetlands resource." The *Guidelines* themselves contain similar admonitions to the permit applicant: "Fundamental to the *Guidelines* is the precept that dredged or fill material should not be discharged into the aquatic ecosystem, unless it can be demonstrated that such a discharge will not have an unacceptable adverse impact either individually or in combination with known and/or probable impacts of other activities affecting the ecosystems of concern" (40 C.F.R. §230.1(c)) and "From a national perspective, the degradation or destruction of special aquatic sites, such as filling operations in wetlands, is considered to be among the most severe environmental impacts covered by these *Guidelines.* The guiding principle should be that degradation or destruction of special sites may represent an irreversible loss of valuable aquatic resources."(40 C.F.R. §230.1(d)).

tions require that a §404 permit be denied if the discharge would not comply with the EPA's *Guidelines*.[46]

The *Guidelines* are divided into eight subparts, two of which will be considered in this text: Subpart A, 40 C.F.R. §§230.1-230.7, which outlines general policy, definitions, and procedures to be followed; and Subpart B, 40 C.F.R. §§230.10-230.12, which outlines restrictions on discharge, factual determinations to be made, and findings of compliance or noncompliance with the general restrictions on discharge.

In applying the *Guidelines* to determine whether a potential discharge may be permitted, the Corps must follow a specific procedure. First, it reviews the restrictions on discharge set forth in 40 C.F.R. §§230.10(a) through (d), then the minimization actions in 40 C.F.R. §§230.70 through 230.77, and then the factual determinations required to be made in 40 C.F.R. §230.11.[47] Next the Corps must determine whether any general permits apply.[48] If no general permits apply, the Corps then must examine "practicable alternatives" to the proposed discharge, which are either to not allow the discharge at all or to permit the discharge but into an alternative aquatic site with potentially less damaging consequences after determining proposed alternative sites by applying certain specific factors listed in 40 C.F.R. §230.10(a).[49] If the Corps decides to permit the discharge, it must then "delineate the candidate disposal site" following the criteria and evaluations set forth in 40 C.F.R. §230.11(f).

Next, following Subpart C, the Corps must determine the potential impacts on the physical and chemical characteristics of the aquatic ecosystem by considering the effects on the substrate,[50] the suspended particulates,[51] the chemistry and physical characteristics of the receiving water,[52] current patterns and water circulation,[53] normal water fluctuations such as daily, seasonal, and annual tidal and flood fluctuations,[54] and existing salinity gradients.[55] The Corps then must evaluate any special or critical characteristics of the candidate disposal site and any surrounding areas that may be affected related to their living communities or human uses following the factors listed in Subparts D, E, and F: potential impacts upon biological characteristics including threatened and endangered species,[56] fish, crustaceans, mollusks, and other aquatic organisms in the food web,[57] and other wildlife;[58] potential impacts upon special aquatic sites including sanctuaries and refuges,[59] wetlands,[60] mud flats,[61] vegetated

---

46. 33 C.F.R. §§320.4(a) and 320.4(b)(4); 40 C.F.R. §230.1(c); See also *Bersani v. U.S. Environmental Protection Agency*, 850 F.2d 36 (2d Cir. N.Y. 1988), *cert. denied*, 489 U.S. 1089, 103 L.Ed.2d 859, 109 S.Ct. 1556 (1989).

47. 40 C.F.R. §230.5(a).

48. 40 C.F.R. §230.5(b). This regulation refers the Corps to 40 C.F.R. §230.7, "General Permits," which restates the familiar conditions for issuance of general permits, i.e., (1) that the Corps determine that the activities in the category of activities to be generally permitted are similar in nature and similar in their impact upon water quality and the aquatic environment; (2) that the activities in such category will have only minimal adverse effects when performed separately; and (3) that the activities will have only minimal cumulative adverse effects on water quality and the aquatic environment. Further, the Corps, in its evaluation of a potential general permit, must consider the four prohibitions listed in 40 C.F.R. §230.10(b), namely (1) that the discharge may not cause or contribute to violations of any applicable state water-quality standard; (2) that the discharge may not violate any applicable toxic effluent standard or prohibition; (3) that the discharge may not jeopardize the continued existence of endangered or threatened species or result in the likelihood of destruction or adverse modification of a critical habitat unless an exemption has been granted; and (4) that the discharge may not violate any requirement imposed to protect any designated marine sanctuary, and to 40 C.F.R. §230.10(c), which states the factors to be considered by the Corps in issuing a general permit, namely that there be no discharges which cause or contribute to significant degradation of waters of the United States. See "Significant Degradation of Water," p. 93.

49. 40 C.F.R. §230.5(c). See also "Practicable Alternatives," p. 93.

50. 40 C.F.R. §§230.5(e) and 230.20.

51. 40 C.F.R. §230.21.

52. 40 C.F.R. §230.22.

53. 40 C.F.R. §230.23.

54. 40 C.F.R. §230.24.

55. 40 C.F.R. §230.25.

56. 40 C.F.R. §§230.5(f) and 230.30.

57. 40 C.F.R. §230.31.

58. 40 C.F.R. §230.32.

59. 40 C.F.R. §230.40.

60. 40 C.F.R. §230.41.

61. 40 C.F.R. §230.42.

shallows,[62] coral reefs,[63] and riffle and pool complexes;[64] and potential impacts upon human use characteristics including municipal and private water supplies,[65] recreational and commercial fisheries,[66] water-related recreation,[67] aesthetics,[68] and parks, national and historical monuments, national seashores, wilderness areas, research sites, and other similar preserves.[69] Next the Corps will review its factual determinations to ensure that the information meets the requirements of 40 C.F.R. §230.11.[70] The Corps must also evaluate the material to be discharged to determine the possibility of chemical contamination or physical incompatibility using the procedures outlined in 40 C.F.R. §§230.60 and 230.61.[71] The Corps must also consider appropriate and practicable changes to the project plan to minimize the environmental impact of the discharge by changing the location of the discharge;[72] changing the material to be discharged;[73] controlling the material after its discharge;[74] changing the method of dispersion; [75] use of appropriate technology, design, and equipment;[76] minimizing the adverse effects on plant and animal populations;[77] minimizing adverse effects on human uses;[78] and other miscellaneous actions in special kinds of projects.[79]

All of these Corps factual determinations, findings of compliance, and minimization actions must be made in writing.[80] Even so, the regulations recognize that some projects may be so minor or routine that a full-blown determination with written findings is not necessary, that "different levels of effort . . . should be associated with varying degrees of impact and require or prepare commensurate documentation."[81]

Water Dependency

In the short history of the Clean Water Act, a few of the *Guidelines* have been applied more frequently and/or with more sweeping effect than others. One of the more notable *Guidelines* is a regulatory presumption that practicable alternatives that do not involve discharges into wetlands are available when the project "does not require access or proximity to or siting within" a wetland to fulfill the project's basic purpose, i.e., is not "water dependent,"[82] unless the applicant can clearly demonstrate otherwise.[83] In other words, if the project is not water-dependent, the Corps must presume that other practicable alternatives are available unless it receives compelling proof to the contrary.

---

62. 40 C.F.R. §230.43.
63. 40 C.F.R. §230.44.
64. 40 C.F.R. §230.45.
65. 40 C.F.R. §230.50.
66. 40 C.F.R. §230.51.
67. 40 C.F.R. §230.52.
68. 40 C.F.R. §230.53.
69. 40 C.F.R. §230.54.
70. 40 C.F.R. §230.5(g).
71. 40 C.F.R. §§230.5(h) and (i).
72. 40 C.F.R. §§230.5(j) and 230.70.
73. 40 C.F.R. §230.71.
74. 40 C.F.R. §230.72.
75. 40 C.F.R. §230.73.
76. 40 C.F.R. §230.74.
77. 40 C.F.R. §230.75.
78. 40 C.F.R. §230.76.
79. 40 C.F.R. §§230.77 and 230.5(j).
80. 40 C.F.R. §§230.5(k) and (l), 230.11, and 230.12(b).
81. 40 C.F.R. §230.6.
82. Lack of "water-dependency may be very broad. Proposed houses with their own boat slips are not water-dependent. *Korteweg v. U.S. Army Corps of Engineers*, 650 F.Supp. 603 (D.Conn. 1986). On the other hand, a county water supply reservoir was held to be "water-dependent" perhaps on the basis that the "alternatives" proposed by the EPA did not persuade the Court as "practicable." *James City County, Virginia, v. EPA*, 955 F.2d 254 (4th Cir. Va. 1992), *cert. denied*, 130 L.Ed.2d 39, 115 S.Ct. 87 (1994).
83. 40 C.F.R. §230.10(a)(3).

Practicable Alternatives

The regulations specifically state that no discharge of dredged or fill material will be permitted if there is a "practicable alternative" to the proposed discharge that would have less adverse impact on the aquatic ecosystem.[84] Practicable alternatives are presumed to exist for non-water-dependent projects unless clearly demonstrated otherwise.[85] "Practicable alternatives" include activities that do not involve a discharge at all or discharges at other locations.[86]

An "alternative" is "practicable" if it is "available and capable of being done after taking into consideration cost, existing technology, and logistics in light of the overall project purposes."[87] Even an area not presently owned by the applicant must be considered.[88] The Corps should accept the applicant's description of the project's purpose,[89] but does not have to accept the applicant's representation that there are no practicable alternatives;[90] it may conduct its own feasibility study of alternative sites and deny a permit if it finds such an alternative site.[91] The applicant is advised to seek the assistance of relevant, experienced professionals in preparing a practicable alternatives study for presentation to the Corps along with the permit application.

Significant Degradation of Water

Similar to the "recapture provision" applicable to Nationwide Permits, the regulations provide that even if the applicant can pass all of the factual determinations and minimization requirements, if the Corps still finds that the project's discharge would cause a "significant degradation of waters of the United States," the Corps may deny a permit.[92] The finding of a significant degradation must be based upon the factual determinations, evaluations, and tests described above, but it must also pay special heed to the "persistence and permanence" of the adverse effects and may be considered individually or collectively.[93]

Some of these catch-all adverse effects are the discharge of pollutants which affects human health or welfare (including municipal water supplies, plankton, fish, shellfish, wildlife, and special aquatic sites); on the life stages of aquatic life and other wildlife dependent on aquatic ecosystems (including the transfer, concentration, and spread of pollutants or their by-products outside of the disposal site through biological, physical, and chemical processes); on aquatic ecosystem diversity, productivity, and

---

84. 40 C.F.R. §230.10(a).

85. 40 C.F.R. §230.10(a)(3). "Practicable alternatives" are a moving target. For example, depending on the project purpose, unusual standards may apply. See, e.g., *Conservation Law Foundation v. FHA*, 827 F.Supp. 871 (D.R.I. 1993), *aff'd.*, 24 F.3d 1465 (1st Cir. P.R. 1994) in which the project purpose of separating through traffic from local traffic militated allowing the filling of wetlands upon a finding of "no practicable alternatives." Financial considerations may also limit practicable alternatives. *City of Shoreacres v. Waterworth*, 332 F.Supp. 992 (S.D.Tex. 2004); *Alliance for Legal Action v. U.S. Army Corps of Engineers*, 314 F.Supp.2d 534 (M.D.N.C. 2004); *Maryland Native Plant Society v. U.S. Army Corps of Engineers*, 332 F.Supp.2d 845 (D.Md. 2004).

86. 40 C.F.R. §230.10(a)(1).

87. 40 C.F.R. §230.10(a)(2).

88. In *Bersani v. U.S. Environmental Protection Agency, supra.*, the court found that other properties, development of which was less adverse to the environment, were available when the applicant first entered the market to purchase developable land and before it ever applied for a §404 permit. See also *Hough v. Marsh*, 557 F.Supp. 74 (D.Mass. 1982). But see *National Audubon Society v. Hartz Mountain Development Corp.*, 14 Envtl.L.Rep. (Envtl.L.Inst.) 20724 (D.N.J. 1983); *Louisiana Wildlife Federation, Inc. v. York*, 603 F.Supp. 518 (W.D.La.), *aff'd in part and vacated in part*, 761 F.2d 1044 (5th Cir. La. 1985); *Sylvester v. U.S. Army Corps of Engineers*, 882 F.2d 407 (9th Cir. Cal. 1989).

89. *Louisiana Wildlife Federation, Inc. v. York*, 761 F.2d 1044 (5th Cir. La. 1985).

90. *Shoreline Assocs. v. Marsh, supra*. See also *James City County v. EPA, supra*.

91. *Deltona Corporation v. Alexander*, 504 F.Supp. 1280 (M.D.Fla. 1981), *aff'd.*, 682 F.2d 888 (11th Cir. Fla. 1982).

92. 40 C.F.R. §230.10(c).

93. 40 C.F.R. §230.10(c).

stability (including loss of fish and wildlife habitat or the loss of the capacity of a wetland to assimilate nutrients, purify water, or reduce wave energy); and, on recreational, aesthetic, and economic values.

Other Considerations

NONWETLANDS ENVIRONMENTAL EFFECTS

The Corps may consider other factors than simply the direct effect of a discharge of dredged or fill material in a wetland when making its permit decision. As has been discussed above, there are many opportunities in the regulations for the Corps to accept advice and comments from other agencies, particularly the U.S. Fish and Wildlife Service.[94] State and local land-use and zoning decisions will not be considered.[95]

SOCIOECONOMIC EFFECTS

The Corps is permitted to consider to a limited extent socioeconomic effects of permit applications under §10 of the Rivers and Harbors Act but not under §404 of the Clean Water Act.[96] However, the Corps insists that it will continue to consider socioeconomic effects although district engineers are cautioned to "give less weight to impacts that are, at best, weakly related to the purpose of our permit action and statutory authority, and not let such impacts be the sole or most important basis for a permit denial."[97]

INDIRECT EFFECTS

The Corps has attempted to distinguish between attenuated and nonattenuated indirect impacts and tries to consider the attenuated indirect impacts less heavily. Some examples of indirect impacts are water withdrawals for hydroelectric power generation on downstream aquatic communities and spin-off development from a major project. The Corps considers the spin-off development to be attenuated and thus not entitled to "heavy" consideration. On the other hand, the effect on downstream aquatic communities, while also indirect, is not attenuated and thus must be considered "heavily."[98]

MITIGATION

The overriding principle of permit issuance is the avoidance of impacts such that no discharge will be permitted if there is a practicable alternative to the proposed discharge that would have a less adverse impact on the aquatic ecosystem, so long as the alternative does not have other significant adverse environmental consequences. Therefore, the first step for the Corps is to determine the least environmentally damaging practicable alternative. Compensatory mitigation is forbidden in this early determination as a method to reduce environmental impacts. The second step is for the Corps to require

---

94. 33 C.F.R. §320.4.
95. 33 C.F.R. §320.4(j)(2).
96. *Mall Properties, Inc. v. Marsh, supra.*
97. Regulatory Guidance Letter, 88-11, *Mall Properties, Inc. v. Marsh,* ¶4.
98. *Riverside Irrigation District v. Andrews,* 758 F.2d 508 (10th Cir. 1985).

appropriate and practicable project modifications and permit conditions in order to minimize the adverse impacts.[99]

Finally, appropriate and practicable compensatory mitigation is required for those impacts remaining after the foregoing avoidance and minimization steps have been satisfied, for the so-called "unavoidable" impacts.[100] Compensatory mitigation contemplates the restoration of existing degraded wetlands or the creation of man-made wetlands first of all on-site or in areas adjacent or contiguous to the discharge site, and only secondarily off-site in the same geographic area (defined as close physical proximity and, to the extent possible, the same watershed) if practicable. In addition to the preference for on-site compensatory mitigation over off-site, the Corps must consider the functional values lost by the resource impacted, with particular attention to be paid to the likelihood of success of the effort. Since wetland creation is an uncertain endeavor, restoration is the preferred method of compensatory mitigation.

In the March 28, 2006, Federal Register the Corps and Environmental Protection Agency issued new proposed mitigation rules. The proposed mitigation regulations are:

- "Intended to establish performance standards and criteria for the use of compensatory mitigation and mitigation banks, and to improve the quality and success of compensatory mitigation projects for activities authorized by [Corps] permits;
- Intended to account for regional variations in aquatic resource types, functions, and values, and apply equivalent standards to each type of compensatory mitigation to the maximum extent practicable;
- Includes a watershed approach to improve the quality and success of compensatory mitigation projects in replacing losses of aquatic resource functions, services, and values resulting from activities authorized by [Corps] permits require in-lieu fee programs, after a five-year transition period, to meet the same standards as mitigation banks."

Other Approvals

In addition to obtaining a §404 permit, applicants must always obtain a state water-quality certificate and frequently must obtain other approvals as well.[101] In fact, the Corps will cease processing a permit without these approvals but can process a §404 permit concurrently with the processing of these other approvals.[102] The Corps, too, is required to consult with other agencies with respect to permit review.[103]

STATE WATER-QUALITY CERTIFICATION

The Clean Water Act and the regulations require that any applicant for a §404 permit "that may result in a discharge of a pollutant into waters of the United States" also obtain a certification from the discharge-originating state or the interstate water pollution control agency that has jurisdiction over the

---

99. 40 C.F.R. §§230.70-230.77.
100. The mitigation requirement does not constitute a Fifth Amendment taking. *Norman v. U.S.*, 63 Fed.Cl. 231 (2004).
101. Regulatory Guidance Letter, *Regulatory Thresholds, 88-12* (September 9, 1988).
102. 33 C.F.R. §320.4(j)(1). *See also National Wildlife Federation v. Norton*, 332 F.Supp.2d 170 (D.D.C. 2004).
103. 33 U.S.C. §1344(q); *Memorandum of Agreement Between the Environmental Protection Agency and the Department of the Army Concerning Clean Water Act Section 404(q), (August 11, 1992)*, (August 11, 1992); *Memorandum of Agreement between the Department of Commerce and the Department of the Army Concerning Clean Water Act Section 404(q)*, (August 11, 1992); *Memorandum of Agreement between the Department of the Interior and the Department of the Army, Concerning Clean water Act Section 404(q)*, (December 21, 1992). If there is a dispute between the Corps and these agencies, these *Memoranda* require that the dispute be "elevated" to a higher level within the agency so as to avoid delay in individual permit decisions when there is policy dispute.

point source of the pollution that the discharge will comply with the "applicable effluent limitations and water quality standards."[104] Although technically no permit will be granted until the certification has been obtained, a waiver by the certifying agency may be deemed to have occurred if the agency fails to act within sixty days of the request.[105] The Corps has the authority to notify the agency that a shorter period of time than sixty days may be required, and, conversely, the Corps may determine that a longer period will be necessary based on information provided by the agency.[106] In no event will this time enlargement last longer than one year.[107]

Once the certification has been issued prior to the permit decision, any subsequent denial or modification of the certification will not affect ordinarily a §404 permit, but the Corps may consider the subsequent denial or modification as part of the public interest review and may respond accordingly.[108] However, if the Corps finds that there has been a "sufficient change" in the project, then the Corps may require that a new water-quality certification be applied for.[109] An exception to this process is when a state court voids a certification prior to the §404 permit issuance.[110] In that case, the Corps cannot issue the §404 permit until the certification is "legally revived," that is, by the appellate process, reissuance, or waiver.[111]

After the §404 permit has been issued, a subsequent denial or modification of a certification or the voiding of the certification by a court will not necessarily affect the terms of the §404 permit, but the Corps may consider modification, suspension, or revocation of the §404 permit.

COASTAL ZONE MANAGEMENT PROGRAM

Obviously not all states have a coastal zone management program, but among those that do, the Coastal Zone Management Act, 16 U.S.C. §1456(c), requires the applicant to furnish another certification that the proposed activity will comply with the state's coastal zone management program.[112] The procedure for obtaining the certificate is a little different from the water-quality certification. The applicant submits his "certification" directly to the Corps, which then sends a copy of the public notice, including the applicant's certification, to the National Oceanic and Atmospheric Administration (which administers the federal Coastal Zone Management Act,[113] and to the relevant state coastal zone management agency requesting its concurrence or objection.[114] If the state agency objects, the Corps cannot issue the §404 permit until the state agency concurs or is overruled by the Secretary of Commerce on the grounds that the proposed activity is consistent with the federal coastal zone management program or is "necessary in the interest of national security."[115] The state agency has only six months to concur or object, after which concurrence is conclusively presumed.

---

104. 33 U.S.C. §1341; 33 C.F.R. §§320.3(a), 320.4(d), and 325(b)(1).
105. 33 C.F.R. §325.2(b)(1)(ii).
106. *Id.*
107. *Id.*
108. Regulatory Guidance Letter, *Section 401 Water Quality Certification,* 87-3, ¶2.b.
109. *Id.*
110. There is no review of state water-quality certificates in federal court. *Roosevelt Campobello International Park Commission v. U.S. Environmental Protection Agency,* 684 F.2d 1041 (1st Cir. 1982).
111. Regulatory Guidance Letter, *Water Quality Consideration,* 90-4.
112. 33 C.F.R. §320.3(b).
113. 16 U.S.C. §§1451, *et seq.*; 33 C.F.R. §§320.3(b) and 320.4(h).
114. 33 C.F.R. §325.2(b)(2)(ii). The individual state may require a separate permit. Furthermore, the states may limit application of a Nationwide Permit in a coastal zone. See Regulatory Guidance Letter, *Section 401 Water Quality Certification and Coastal Zone Management Act Conditions for Nationwide Permits,* m 92-4 (September 14, 1992).
115. *Id.*

MARINE PROTECTION, RESEARCH, AND SANCTUARIES ACT

The applicant should determine whether his proposed activities will take place in an area that has been designated a marine sanctuary by the Secretary of Commerce under the Marine Protection, Research, and Sanctuaries Act, 16 U.S.C. §1432.[116] If so, then the proposed activities must also be certified by the Secretary as consistent with the purposes of the Act and consistent with the regulations under the Act. Generally these areas are in coastal areas.

ENVIRONMENTAL IMPACT STATEMENT

The regulations require that the provisions of the National Environmental Policy Act apply to the §404 permit process although generally only for small portions of larger federal projects.[117] For most §404 permit applications, the Corps will require only an Environmental Assessment, reserving the requirement of a full Environmental Impact Statement for large projects with considerable federal involvement.

NATIONAL HISTORIC PRESERVATION ACT

Under the National Historic Preservation Act, the Advisory Council on Historic Preservation is authorized to review and comment upon federally licensed activities that will have an effect upon properties listed (or eligible for listing) in the National Register of Historic Places.[118] Whenever a project "alters any terrain such that significant historical or archaeological data is threatened, the Secretary of the Interior may take action necessary to recover and preserve the data prior to the commencement of the project."[119] The Corps's regulations state that §404 permit application actions "should, insofar as possible, be consistent with, and avoid significant adverse effects on the values or purposes for which" a classification such as the National Register of Historic Places was established.[120] The Corps should attempt to reach an agreement with the Federal Advisory Council on Historic Preservation on how the project will be carried out, but if no agreement is possible, the Corps may proceed to permit issuance without it.[121]

INTERSTATE LAND SALES FULL DISCLOSURE ACT

The Interstate Land Sales Full Disclosure Act (15 U.S.C. §1701 *et seq.*) requires a developer, prior to selling or leasing any lot in a subdivision (defined in 15 U.S.C. §1701(3)), to provide a written report that states whether or not a §404 permit has been applied for, issued, or denied; and/or whether any enforcement action has been taken as a consequence of any nonapplication for or denial of a permit.[122]

---

116. 33 C.F.R. §320.3(c).
117. 33 C.F.R. §320.3(d).
118. 16 U.S.C. §470; 33 C.F.R. §§320.3(g) and 325.2(b)(3); 36 C.F.R §800.
119. 33 C.F.R. §320.3(g).
120. 33 C.F.R. §320.4(e). See also appendix C to 33 C.F.R. §§325.
121. 36 C.F.R. §800.5.
122. 33 C.F.R. §320.3(h).

ENDANGERED SPECIES ACT

The Endangered Species Act declares a dual intent to conserve threatened and endangered species as well as the ecosystems on which those species depend.[123] In conserving ecosystems, even those beyond the geographic area of the project in question, if the Corps finds that the activity will have a physical effect on off-site endangered species or if the project can be redesigned to avoid the effect on endangered species,[124] the Corps must consult with the U.S. Fish and Wildlife Service and the National Marine Fisheries Service to take any action necessary to insure that a §404 licensed project "is not likely to jeopardize the continued existence of such endangered or threatened species or result in the destruction or adverse modification of habitat of such species" that the Secretaries of Commerce or Interior have determined to be critical.[125]

ENVIRONMENTAL PROTECTION AGENCY VETO AUTHORITY

Section 404(c) of the Clean Water Act authorizes the Environmental Protection Agency to veto the issuance of a permit if it determines, "after notice and opportunity for public hearings, that the discharge . . . will have an unacceptable adverse effect on municipal water supplies, shellfish beds, and fishery areas (including spawning and breeding areas), wildlife, or recreational areas."[126] Thus, notwithstanding any of the foregoing, and although it has done so only very rarely, the Environmental Protection Agency can veto a permit issuance even though the proposed activities are within all of the *Guidelines* and other statutory authorities and regulations.

Administrative Appeals

Prior to the establishment of an administrative appeal procedure, property owners who were unhappy with their permit decisions were forced to violate the permit, draw an enforcement penalty, and then seek judicial review of the enforcement penalty.[127] In 1999, the Corps established policies and procedures to be used for the administrative appeal of permit applications denied with prejudice, and for the administrative appeals of declined individual permits. Affected parties may appeal permit denials or declined individual permits where the permit denial or the proffered individual permit occurs after March 9, 1999, but may not appeal permit denials or declined permits where the Corps took that action before March 9, 1999.

The appeal process will allow the affected party to pursue an administrative appeal of certain final Corps of Engineers decisions with which they disagree. It is the announced policy of the Corps "to promote and maintain an administrative appeal process that is independent, objective, fair, prompt, and efficient." No affected party, however, may file a legal action in the Federal courts based on a permit denial or declined individual permit until after a final Corps decision has been made and the appellant

---

123. 16 U.S.C. §§1531 *et seq.*

124. *Riverside Irrigation District v. Andrews*, 758 F.2d 508 (10th Cir. 1985); *Winnebago Tribe of Nebraska v. Ray*, 621 F.2d 269 (8th Cir. 1980), *cert. denied*, 449 U.S. 836, 66 L.Ed.2d 43, 101 S.Ct. 110 (1980); *Save the Bay, Inc. v. U.S. Army Corps of Engineers*, 610 F.2d 322 (5th Cir. 1980), *cert. denied*, 449 U.S. 900, 66 L.Ed.2d 130, 101 S.Ct. 269 (1980).

125. 33 C.F.R. §320.3(i).

126. 33 U.S.C. §1344(c).

127. *Southern Pines Associates v. United States*, 912 F.2d 713 (4th Cir. Va. 1990); *Hampton Venture No. One v. United States*, 768 F.Supp. 174 (E.D.Va. 1991); *Route 26 Land Development Association v. United States*, 753 F.Supp. 532 (D.Del. 1990), *aff'd.*, 961 F.2d 1568 (3d Cir. Del. 1992); 740 F.Supp. 736 (E.D.Mo. 1990).

has exhausted all applicable administrative remedies. The appellant is considered to have exhausted all administrative remedies when a final Corps decision is made in accordance with the administrative appeal procedures.

Under this new procedure, permit decisions made by a Division Engineer or higher authority may be appealed to an Army official at least one level higher than the decision maker. Affected parties will be notified in writing of a Corps decision on an appealable action. For permit denials, the notification must include a copy of the decision document for the permit application, a special "fact sheet," and a Request For Appeal (RFA) form. For proffered individual permits, when the initial proffered permit is sent to the applicant, the notification must include a fact sheet. For declined permits (i.e., proffered individual permits that the applicant refuses to accept and sends back to the Corps), the notification must include a fact sheet and an RFA form. Additionally, an affected party has the right to obtain a copy of the administrative record.

"Declined permit" means a proffered individual permit, including a letter of permission, that an applicant has refused to accept because he has objections to the terms and conditions therein. A declined permit can also be an individual permit that the applicant originally accepted but was subsequently modified by the District Engineer in such a manner that the resulting permit contains terms and conditions that lead the applicant to decline the modified permit, provided that the applicant has not started work in waters of the United States authorized by such permit. Where an applicant declines a permit (either initial or modified), the applicant does not have a valid permit to conduct regulated activities in waters of the United States, and must not begin construction of the work requiring a Corps permit unless and until the applicant receives and accepts a valid Corps permit. "Permit denial" means a written denial with prejudice of an individual permit application.

The Reviewing Officer will conduct an independent review of the administrative record to address the reasons for the appeal cited by the applicant in the Request For Appeal. In addition, to the extent that it is practicable and feasible, the Reviewing Officer will also conduct an independent review of the administrative record to verify that the record provides an adequate and reasonable basis supporting the District Engineer's decision, that facts or analysis essential to the District Engineer's decision have not been omitted from the administrative record, and that all relevant requirements of law, regulations, and officially promulgated Corps policy guidance have been satisfied. Should the Reviewing Officer require expert advice regarding any subject, he may seek such advice from any employee of the Corps or of another Federal or state agency, or from any recognized expert, so long as that person had not been previously involved in the action under review.

The reason(s) for requesting an appeal of a permit denial, or a declined individual permit, must be specifically stated in the Request For Appeal, and must be more than a simple request for appeal because the affected party did not like the permit decision, or the permit conditions. Examples of reasons for appeals include, but are not limited to, the following: a procedural error, an incorrect application of law, regulation or officially promulgated policy; omission of material fact; incorrect application of the Section 404(b)(1) *Guidelines*; or use of incorrect data.

An affected party appealing a permit denial or declined permit must submit an RFA that is received by the Division Engineer within sixty days of the date of the permit denial or permit rejection. In the case where an applicant objects to a proffered individual permit, the appeal process proceeds as follows: To initiate the appeal process regarding the terms and conditions of the permit, the applicant must write a letter to the District Engineer explaining his objections to the permit.

The District Engineer, upon evaluation of the applicant's objections, may: modify the permit to address all of the applicant's objections; or modify the permit to address some, but not all, of the applicant's objections; or not modify the permit, having determined that the permit should be issued as previously written. In the event that the District Engineer agrees to modify the proffered individual permit to address all of the applicant's objections, the District Engineer will issue such modified permit. Should the District Engineer modify the proffered individual permit to address some, but not all, of the applicant's objections, the District Engineer will send the applicant such modified permit and the decision document for the project.

If the District Engineer does not modify the proffered individual permit, the District Engineer will offer the unmodified permit to the applicant a second time, enclosing a copy of the decision document. If the applicant still has objections, the applicant may decline such modified or unmodified permit; this declined individual permit may be appealed to the Division Engineer upon submittal of a complete Request For Appeal form. The completed RFA must be received by the Division Engineer within 60 days of the notice from the Corps District Engineer.

Upon receipt of a Request For Appeal, the Corps shall review the Request and the administrative record to determine whether the Request meets the criteria for appeal. If the Request meets the criteria for appeal, the Reviewing Officer will so notify the appellant in writing within thirty days of the receipt of the Request. If the Reviewing Officer believes that the Request does not meet the criteria for appeal, the Reviewing Officer will make a recommendation on the Request to the Division Engineer. If the Division Engineer determines that the Request is not acceptable, the Division Engineer will notify the appellant of this determination by a certified letter detailing the reason(s) why the appeal failed to meet the criteria for appeal. No further administrative appeal is available, unless the appellant revises the Request to correct the deficiencies noted in the Division Engineer's letter. The revised Request must be received by the Division Engineer within 30 days of the date of the certified letter refusing the initial Request. If the Corps determines that the revised Request still fails to meet the criteria for appeal, the Division Engineer will notify the appellant of this determination by a certified letter within thirty days of the date of the receipt of the revised Request, and will advise the appellant that the matter is not eligible for appeal. No further Requests will be accepted after this point.

Within thirty days of receipt of a complete RFA, the Reviewing Officer should determine if a site investigation is needed to clarify the administrative record. The Reviewing Officer should conduct any such site investigation within sixty days of receipt of a complete Request. The Reviewing Officer may also conduct a site investigation at the request of the appellant, provided he or she has determined that such an investigation would be of benefit in interpreting the administrative record. The appellant and the appellant's authorized agent(s) must be provided an opportunity to participate in any site investigation, and will be given fifteen days notice of any site investigation. The Reviewing Officer, the appellant, the appellant's agent(s) and the Corps district staff are authorized participants at the site investigation. The Reviewing Officer may also invite any other party the Reviewing Officer has determined to be appropriate, such as any technical experts consulted by the Corps.

Conferences held in accordance with the appeal process will be informal, and will be chaired by the Reviewing Officer. The purpose of the appeal conference is to provide a forum that allows the participants to discuss freely all relevant issues and material facts associated with the appeal. An appeal conference will be held for every appeal of a permit denial or a declined individual permit, unless the Reviewing Officer and the appellant mutually agree to forego a conference. The conference will take place within 60 days of receipt of an acceptable Request For Appeal, unless the Reviewing Officer determines that unforeseen or unusual circumstances require scheduling the conference for a later date. Presentations by the appellant and the Corps district representatives may include interpretation, clarification, or explanation of the legal, policy, and factual bases for their positions.

The conference will be governed by the following guidelines: The Reviewing Officer will set a date, time, and location for the conference. The Reviewing Officer will notify the appellant and the Corps district office in writing within thirty days of receipt of the Request For Appeal, and not less than fifteen days before the date of the conference.

The purpose of the appeal conference will be to discuss the reasons for appeal contained in the RFA. Any material in the administrative record may be discussed during the conference, but the discussion should be focused on relevant issues needed to address the reasons for appeal contained in the RFA. Issues not identified in the administrative record by the date of the permit decision for the application may not be raised or discussed, because substantive new information or project modifications would be treated as a new permit application.

The appeal conference is an informal proceeding, intended to provide clarifications and explanations of the administrative record for the Reviewing Officer and the Division Engineer; it is not intended to supplement the administrative record. Consequently, the proceedings of the conference will not be recorded verbatim by the Corps or any other party attending the conference, and no verbatim transcripts of the conference will be made. However, after the conference, the Reviewing Officer will write a memorandum for the record (MFR) summarizing the presentations made at the conference, and will provide a copy of that MFR to the Division Engineer, the appellant, and the District Engineer.

Because a decision to deny or condition a permit depends on the facts, circumstances, and physical conditions particular to the specific project and site being evaluated, appeal decisions would be of little or no precedential utility. Therefore, an appeal decision of the Division Engineer is applicable only to the instant appeal, and has no other precedential effect. Such a decision may not be cited in any other administrative appeal, and may not be used as precedent for the evaluation of any other permit application. While administrative appeal decisions lack precedential value and may not be cited by an appellant or a District Engineer in any other appeal proceeding, the Corps goal is to have the Corps regulatory program operate as consistently as possible, particularly with respect to interpretations of law, regulation, an Executive Order, and officially promulgated policy. Therefore, a copy of each appeal decision will be forwarded to Corps headquarters; those decisions will be periodically reviewed at the headquarters level for consistency with law, Executive Orders, and policy. Additional official guidance will be issued as necessary to maintain or improve the consistency of the Corps's appellate and permit decisions.

The Division Engineer will disapprove the entirety of or any part of the District Engineer's decision only if he determines that the decision on some relevant matter was arbitrary, capricious, an abuse of discretion, not supported by substantial evidence in the administrative record, or plainly contrary to a requirement of law, regulation, an Executive Order, or officially promulgated Corps policy guidance. The Division Engineer will not attempt to substitute his judgment for that of the District Engineer regarding a matter of fact, so long as the District Engineer's determination was supported by substantial evidence in the administrative record, or regarding any other matter if the District Engineer's determination was reasonable and within the zone of discretion delegated to the District Engineer by Corps regulations. The Division Engineer may instruct the District Engineer on how to correct any procedural error that was prejudicial to the appellant (i.e., that was not a "harmless" procedural error), or to reconsider the decision where any essential part of the District Engineer's decision was not supported by accurate or sufficient information, or analysis, in the administrative record. The Division Engineer will document his decision on the merits of the appeal in writing, and provide a copy of this decision to the applicant (using certified mail) and the District Engineer. The final decision of the Division Engineer on the merits of the appeal will conclude the administrative appeal process, and this decision will be filed in the administrative record for the project.

After-the-fact permit denials and declined individual permits after the fact are appealable actions for the purposes of these regulations. If the Corps accepts an after-the-fact permit application, an administrative appeal of a permit denial or declined individual permit may be filed and processed in accordance with these regulations subject to the following special procedures: If the District Engineer determines that initial corrective measures are necessary, a Request For Appeal for an appealable action will not be accepted by the Corps until the initial corrective measures have been completed to the satisfaction of the District Engineer.

If an affected party requests an administrative appeal of an appealable action prior to the resolution of the unauthorized activity, and the Division Engineer determines that the appeal has no merit, the responsible party remains subject to any civil, criminal, and administrative penalties as provided by law.

Any person who applies for an after-the-fact permit, where the application is accepted and processed by the Corps, thereby agrees that the statute of limitations regarding any violation associated with that application is tolled until one year after the final Corps decision. Moreover, the applicant for an after-the-fact permit must also memorialize that agreement to toll the statute of limitations, by signing an agreement to that effect, in exchange for the Corps acceptance of the after-the-fact permit application and/or any administrative appeal. No after-the-fact permit application or administrative appeal will be accepted until such written tolling agreement is furnished to the District Engineer.

CHAPTER SEVEN

Administrative Penalties

The power to penalize the discharge of dredged or fill material into a wetland without a permit, or a violation of a condition of an existing permit, stems from two statutory sources: the Environmental Protection Agency's power to issue administrative orders for unpermitted fills under §309(a)(3),[1] and

---

1. "Whenever on the basis of any information available to him the Administrator [of the Environmental Protection Agency] finds that any person is in violation of section 1311 [which makes the discharge of pollutants illegal except in compliance with the law], 1312 [establishing water quality-related effluent limitations], 1316 [establishing standards of performance for the control of the discharge of pollutants], 1317 [establishing toxic and pretreatment effluent standards], 1318 [requiring owners and operators of point sources to keep records of effluents data, report such data, and allow entry to his or her premises and records], 1328 [allowing the discharge of specific pollutants under controlled conditions associated with an approved aquaculture project], or 1345 [governing the issuance of permits for the disposal of sewage sludge] of this title, or is in violation of any permit condition or limitation implementing any of such sections in a permit issued under section 1342 of this title by him or by a State or in a permit issued under section 1344 of this title by a State, he shall issue an order requiring such person to comply with such section or requirement, or he shall bring a civil action in accordance with subsection (b) of this section." 33 U.S.C. §1319(a)(3)33 U.S.C. §1319(a)(3).

(1) Whenever on the basis of any information available to him the Secretary [of the Army] finds that any person is in violation of any condition or limitation set forth in a permit issued by the Secretary under this section, the Secretary shall issue an order requiring such person to comply with such condition or limitation, or the Secretary shall bring a civil action in accordance with paragraph (3) of this subsection.

(2) A copy of any order issued under this subsection shall be sent immediately by the Secretary to the State in which the violation occurs and other affected States. Any order issued under this subsection shall be by personal service and shall state with reasonable specificity the nature of the violation, specify a time for compliance, not to exceed thirty days, which the Secretary determines is reasonable, taking into account the seriousness of the violation and any good faith efforts to comply with applicable requirements. In any case in which an order under this subsection is issued to a corporation, a copy of such order shall be served on any appropriate corporate officers.

(3) The Secretary is authorized to commence a civil action for appropriate relief, including a permanent or temporary injunction for any violation for which he is authorized to issue a compliance order under paragraph (1) of this subsection. Any action under this paragraph may be brought in the district court of the United States for the district in which the defendant is located or resides or is doing business, and such court shall have jurisdiction to restrain such violation and to require compliance. Notice of the commencement of such action shall be given immediately to the appropriate State.

(4) Any person who violates any condition or limitation in a permit issued by the Secretary under this section, and any person who violates any order issued by the Secretary under paragraph (1) of this subsection, shall be subject to a civil penalty not to exceed $25,000 per day for each violation. In determining the amount of a civil penalty the court shall consider the seriousness of the violation or violations, the economic benefit (if any) resulting from the violation, any history of such violations, any good faith efforts to comply with applicable requirements, the economic impact of the penalty on the violator, and such other matters as justice may require. 33 U.S.C. §1344(s).

the Corps's power to issue "cease and desist" orders in the form of letters to permit violators under §404(s).[2]

Administrative Monetary Penalties

In addition to issuing administrative orders, the Corps and Environmental Protection Agency can assess two kinds of administrative monetary penalties: "Class I" for lesser violations, and "Class II" for serious violations,[3] which will take the form of an administrative complaint, including a calculation of the amount of the administrative penalty.[4] The Corps assesses penalties for permit violations and EPA assesses penalties for unpermitted discharges.

CLASS I VIOLATIONS—CORPS REGULATIONS

Alleged violators who wish to contest the Corps's administrative monetary penalty for a permit violation may request a hearing.[5] The Corps must also give public notice of the proposed penalty and allow public comment.[6] In the case of a Class I penalty, the alleged violator must request a hearing within

---

2. *See also* Regulatory Guidance Letter 90-09, "Wetlands Enforcement Initiative," for additional guidance on judicial civil and criminal enforcement priorities. Regulatory Guidance Letter 05-06 contains a list of still-current Regulatory Guidance Letters, including 90-09.

(g) Administrative penalties
(1) Violations
Whenever on the basis of any information available—
(A) the Administrator finds that any person has violated section 1311, 1312, 1316, 1317, 1318, 1328, or 1345 of this title, or has violated any permit condition or limitation implementing any of such sections in a permit issued under section 1342 of this title by the Administrator or by a State, or in a permit issued under section 1344 of this title by a State, or
(B) the Secretary of the Army (hereinafter in this subsection referred to as the "Secretary") finds that any person has violated any permit condition or limitation in a permit issued under section 1344 of this title by the Secretary, the Administrator or Secretary, as the case may be, may, after consultation with the State in which the violation occurs, assess a class I civil penalty or a class II civil penalty under this subsection.

(2) Classes of penalties
(A) Class I
The amount of a class I civil penalty under paragraph (1) may not exceed $10,000 per violation, except that the maximum amount of any class I civil penalty under this subparagraph shall not exceed $25,000. Before issuing an order assessing a civil penalty under this subparagraph, the Administrator or the Secretary, as the case may be, shall give to the person to be assessed such penalty written notice of the Administrator's or Secretary's proposal to issue such order and the opportunity to request, within 30 days of the date the notice is received by such person, a hearing on the proposed order. Such hearing shall not be subject to section 554 or 556 of Title 5, but shall provide a reasonable opportunity to be heard and to present evidence.

(B) Class II
The amount of a class II civil penalty under paragraph (1) may not exceed $10,000 per day for each day during which the violation continues; except that the maximum amount of any class II civil penalty under this subparagraph shall not exceed $125,000. Except as otherwise provided in this subsection, a class II civil penalty shall be assessed and collected in the same manner, and subject to the same provisions, as in the case of civil penalties assessed and collected after notice and opportunity for a hearing on the record in accordance with section 554 of Title 5. The Administrator and the Secretary may issue rules for discovery procedures for hearings under this subparagraph.

(3) Determining amount
In determining the amount of any penalty assessed under this subsection, the Administrator or the Secretary, as the case may be, shall take into account the nature, circumstances, extent and gravity of the violation, or violations, and, with respect to the violator, ability to pay, any prior history of such violations, the degree of culpability, economic benefit or savings (if any) resulting from the violation, and such other matters as justice may require. For purposes of this subsection, a single operational upset which leads to simultaneous violations of more than one pollutant parameter shall be treated as a single violation. 33 CFR §326.6.

3. 40 C.F.R. §22.14(a)(4).
4. 33 C.F.R. §326.6.
5. 33 C.F.R. §326.6(b).
6. 33 U.S.C. §1319(g)(2).

thirty days of receipt of the notice of the penalty.[7] The Corps must also give notice of the hearing to all who filed comments on the proposed penalty.[8] Class I hearings are relatively informal, but there must be at least an opportunity to present evidence.[9]

If still not satisfied with the result, the next level of appeal, which must also be filed within thirty days of the date the penalty order is issued, is to the United States District Court for the District of Columbia or in the district in which the violation occurred.[10] A copy of the notice of appeal must also be sent by certified mail to the Administrator, if the Environmental Protection Agency is assessing the penalty, or to the Secretary of the Army, if the Corps is assessing the penalty.

These appeals are difficult for the alleged violator to win as the Clean Water Act expressly states that "[s]uch court shall not set aside or remand such order unless there is *not substantial evidence* in the record, taken as a whole, to support the finding of a violation or unless the Administrator's or Secretary's assessment of the penalty constitutes an abuse of discretion."[11] The court cannot impose any additional penalties for the same violation unless the Administrator's or Secretary's assessment constitutes an abuse of discretion.[12]

CLASS II VIOLATIONS

In the case of a Class II penalty, violators are entitled to a full adjudicatory hearing following rules set forth in the federal Administrative Procedure Act and the Environmental Protection Agency's regulations.[13] An alleged violator has twenty days to answer the administrative complaint and request a hearing.[14] If he or she does not answer, once the Environmental Protection Agency has made out a prima facie case, a default may be entered sixty days after service of the complaint, whereupon the assessed penalty becomes immediately payable without any further proceeding.[15]

Assuming that the violator requested a hearing, there are regulations governing the conduct of the hearing,[16] at the end of which the hearing officer will issue an "initial decision."[17] A motion to reopen the hearing to present additional evidence may be filed within twenty days of the issuance of the initial decision.[18] There may be interlocutory appeals brought before the hearing has concluded, and there

---

7. 33 C.F.R. §326.6(c).
8. 33 C.F.R. §326.6(h)–(j).
9. Judicial review:

Any person against whom a civil penalty is assessed under this subsection or who commented on the proposed assessment of such penalty in accordance with paragraph (4) may obtain review of such assessment—
    (A) in the case of assessment of a class I civil penalty, in the United States District Court for the District of Columbia or in the district in which the violation is alleged to have occurred, or
    (B) in the case of assessment of a class II civil penalty, in United States Court of Appeals for the District of Columbia Circuit or for any other circuit in which such person resides or transacts business,
    by filing a notice of appeal in such court within the 30-day period beginning on the date the civil penalty order is issued and by simultaneously sending a copy of such notice by certified mail to the Administrator or the Secretary, as the case may be, and the Attorney General. The Administrator or the Secretary shall promptly file in such court a certified copy of the record on which the order was issued. Such court shall not set aside or remand such order unless there is not substantial evidence in the record, taken as a whole, to support the finding of a violation or unless the Administrator's or Secretary's assessment of the penalty constitutes an abuse of discretion and shall not impose additional civil penalties for the same violation unless the Administrator's or Secretary's assessment of the penalty constitutes an abuse of discretion. 33 U.S.C. §1319(g)(8).

10. *Id.* (emphasis added).
11. *Id.* Logically this could only occur if the abuse of discretion found by the court is that the penalty amount was ridiculously low.
12. 33 U.S.C. §1319(g)(2)(B); 5 U.S.C. §554; 40 C.F.R. §22.
13. 40 C.F.R. §22.15(a).
14. 40 C.F.R. §22.17(a).
15. 40 C.F.R. §§22.21 through 22.26.
16. 40 C.F.R. §22.27.
17. 40 C.F.R. §22.28.
18. 40 C.F.R. §§22.29(a), 22.29(b), 22.30.

may be an appeal of the initial decision directly to the Environmental Protection Agency Administrator within twenty days of the initial decision.[19] Intervention is permitted in this appellate process as well as *amicus curiae* participation.[20]

A violator may also seek judicial review of a Class II penalty in the United States Court of Appeals for the District of Columbia Circuit or any other federal circuit court of appeals in which the violator resides or does business so long as the appeal is brought within thirty days of final issuance of the penalty order.[21]

Failure to Pay

Failure to pay the penalty after all appeals have failed allows the Administrator or Secretary to request the Attorney General to bring a civil action to recover the amount assessed.[22] The validity, amount, and appropriateness of the penalty may not be relitigated in this proceeding, but there may be a motion to reconsider filed within ten days after service of the final order.[23] In addition to the penalty, the Attorney General is also required to ask for interest, attorneys' fees, and costs for the collection proceeding, as well as a "quarterly nonpayment penalty" equal to 20 percent of the aggregate of the original penalty plus any other nonpayment penalties that are unpaid as of the beginning of the quarter in which the proceedings commenced.

---

19. 40 C.F.R. §§22.11 and 22.30(a)(2).
20. If any person fails to pay an assessment of a civil penalty—

(A) after the order making the assessment has become final, or
(B) after a court in an action brought under paragraph (8) has entered a final judgment in favor of the Administrator or the Secretary, as the case may be,
the Administrator or the Secretary shall request the Attorney General to bring a civil action in an appropriate district court to recover the amount assessed (plus interest at currently prevailing rates from the date of the final order or the date of the final judgment, as the case may be). In such an action, the validity, amount, and appropriateness of such penalty shall not be subject to review. Any person who fails to pay on a timely basis the amount of an assessment of a civil penalty as described in the first sentence of this paragraph shall be required to pay, in addition to such amount and interest, attorneys' fees and costs for collection proceedings and a quarterly nonpayment penalty for each quarter during which such failure to pay persists. Such nonpayment penalty shall be in an amount equal to 20 percent of the aggregate amount of such person's penalties and nonpayment penalties which are unpaid as of the beginning of such quarter. 33 U.S.C. §1319(g)(9).

21. 33 U.S.C. §1319(g)(9); 40 C.F.R. §22.31(b).
22. 40 C.F.R. §22.31(b).
23. 33 U.S.C. §1319(g)(9).

CHAPTER EIGHT

Enforcement Procedures

Government Investigation

As a practical matter, because the Corps has more field personnel, it will conduct the initial investigation.[1] However, the Enforcement MOA establishes a concept called the "lead enforcement agency" and proceeds to allocate responsibility between the Corps and the Environmental Protection Agency, depending upon the type of violation.[2] In the case of simple unpermitted discharges, the Corps is the lead enforcement agency subject to four exceptions:

1. if the unpermitted activity involves repeat violator(s);
2. if the violation is "flagrant";
3. if the Environmental Protection Agency requests a class of cases or a particular case; or
4. if the Corps recommends that an Environmental Protection Agency administrative penalty may be warranted.[3]

The Corps is the lead enforcement agency in (1) cases involving permit condition violations; (2) cases in which the EPA has notified the Corps that it will not take the case; and (3) if the EPA asks the Corps to take action on a permit condition violation.[4] In any of these possible lead enforcement selections, if the Corps determines that there is no violation of a permit condition, that is the end of the inquiry for the governmental enforcement.[5]

Although the Corps and the EPA are the only two authorized enforcement agencies,[6] the Enforcement MOA requires them to seek and accept assistance from the U.S. Fish and Wildlife Service; the National Marine Fisheries Service; and any other federal, state, tribal, or local agency "when appropriate."[7] Obviously the U.S. Fish and Wildlife Service is in the best position to detect and report violations because of its tremendous number of field personnel stationed in areas likely to contain wetlands. Nonetheless, the Corps has identified "surveillance" as an appropriate method using Corps employees;

1. *Memorandum of Agreement Between The Department of the Army and the Environmental Protection Agency Concerning Federal Enforcement for the Section 404 Program of the Clean Water Act,* ¶II.A (January 19, 1989) (hereinafter the "Enforcement MOA").
2. Enforcement MOA, ¶II.D and ¶III.D.
3. Enforcement MOA, ¶III.D.1.
4. Enforcement MOA, ¶III.D.2-4.
5. Enforcement MOA, ¶III.D.4.
6. 33 U.S.C. §§1319(a)(5) and 1344(s); 33 C.F.R. §326.3(d).
7. Enforcement MOA, ¶II.A.

members of the public; and representatives of state, local, and other federal agencies,[8] and "inspections" of permitted activities by Corps personnel; members of the public; and interested state, local, and other federal agency representatives "encouraging" them to report suspected violations.[9]

Civil Enforcement

The Enforcement MOA requires the Corps and the Environmental Protection Agency to follow five predetermined procedural steps once an unpermitted violation is discovered.[10] First, in the initial investigatory stage, the Corps's field investigation report is prepared after it has checked with the EPA to make sure that it has not already begun an investigation.[11]

Once a violation is found, the field investigation report shall include at least a detailed description of the illegal activity, the existing environmental setting, an initial description of potential impacts, and a recommendation of the need for corrective measures.[12] Second, after preparation of the report, the investigating agency must notify the violator to inform them to cease their illegal activity pending further federal action.[13] The input from other agencies may be considered at this early stage if time permits.[14] In addition, the investigating agency will notify the other agency of its violation letters and request the other agency's views and recommendations on the case.[15]

The third step, selection of the lead enforcement agency, has already been discussed above. Briefly repeated, the EPA will take the unpermitted activity cases involving repeat violators, flagrant violations, requests by the EPA, or referral from the Corps. The Corps will take the remaining unpermitted activity cases as well as the permit-condition violation cases.[16]

The lead enforcement agency then determines the appropriate enforcement response, which may include an administrative order, administrative penalty complaint, a civil or criminal referral to the Department of Justice, or any other appropriate formal enforcement response.[17]

Having made up its mind on the appropriate enforcement response, the lead enforcement agency arranges for monitoring if it required corrective measures or removal, makes its final determination that the violation is resolved, and so notifies the other agency unless the decision has been made to refer the violation to the Department of Justice.[18] If the case will involve further administrative enforcement actions or further remedial measures, the failure to comply with which will later result in legal action, the Corps's regulations require that it keep its case open.[19]

---

8. 33 C.F.R. §326.3(a).

9. 33 C.F.R. §326.4(a).

10. Enforcement MOA, ¶III.A. Attached to the Enforcement MOA is a flowchart of procedures which, the text states, may be "combined in an effort to expedite the enforcement process." The only exception to the procedure is when the unpermitted activity occurs in a specially defined geographic area over which the Environmental Protection Agency has already asserted exclusive jurisdiction under the *Memorandum of Agreement Between the Department of the Army and the Environmental Protection Agency Concerning the Determination of the Geographic Jurisdiction of the Section 404 Program and the Application of the Exemption Under Section 404(f) of the Clean Water Act* (January 19, 1989), ¶V.A.

11. 33 C.F.R. §326.3(g).

12. Enforcement MOA, ¶III.B. 33 C.F.R. §326.3(b) also requires the Corps to "confirm whether a violation exists, and if so, . . . identify the extent of the violation and the parties responsible."

13. Enforcement MOA, ¶III.C. The Corps can issue a cease and desist order at this stage for uncompleted projects. 33 C.F.R. §326.3(c)(1)33 C.F.R. §326.3(c)(1). In other appropriate cases, the Corps may "allow the work to continue, subject to appropriate limitations and conditions." *Id.*

14. *Id.*; Further, the Corps and the Environmental Protection Agency are "encouraged to enter into interagency agreements with other federal, state, tribal and local agencies which will provide assistance to the Corps and EPA in pursuit of Section 404 enforcement activities." Enforcement MOA, ¶IV.A.

15. *Id.*

16. Enforcement MOA, ¶III.D.

17. Enforcement MOA, ¶III.E; In addition, the Corps is specifically prohibited from accepting application for "after-the-fact" permits until the lead enforcement agency has "resolved" the violation. Enforcement MOA, ¶III.G and 33 C.F.R. §326.3(e).

18. Enforcement MOA, ¶III.F.

19. 33 C.F.R. §326.5(a).

JUSTICE DEPARTMENT REFERRALS

Referrals to the Department of Justice are made when "appropriate," which the Corps's regulations define as violations that are "willful, repeated, flagrant, or of substantial impact."[20] If the Department of Justice declines to take the case, the local district engineer may close the enforcement case, or if the case warrants special attention, then the district engineer is "encouraged" to forward a litigation report to the Office, Chief of Engineers.[21]

If the Department of Justice does decide to take the case, it may seek a number of different remedies in the federal district court in which the defendant resides, is located, or does business, including injunctive relief, commanding the alleged violator to cease his or her violation or to restore the wetland to its previolation condition.[22] In addition, courts are permitted to assess civil penalties of their own.[23]

There is no specific statute of limitations under the Clean Water Act, but the courts apply the five-year limitations period for civil penalty actions.[24] Defendants have a right to a jury trial on the issue of liability, although the court will decide the amount of civil penalty and the terms of an injunction.[25]

Criminal Enforcement

In addition to civil penalties, under §309(c)[26] of the Clean Water Act, the Environmental Protection Agency has pursued criminal sanctions against violators in cases involving extreme conduct, such as refusing to obey cease and desist orders or drastic harm to wetlands. Some cases have involved a combination of civil penalties and criminal sanctions.[27] The criminal penalty for negligent violations is a fine

---

20. 33 C.F.R. §326.5(a). There is no requirement that the Corps or EPA follow either the administrative penalty process (chapter 7, or proceed directly to judicial enforcement. *United States v. Earth Sciences, Inc.*, 599 F.2d 368 (10th Cir. Colo. 1979).

21. 33 C.F.R. §326.5(e).

22. See, e.g., *United States v. Bayshore Associates, Inc.*, 934 F.2d 1391 (6th Cir. Mich. 1991); *United States v. Rivera Torres*, 656 F.Supp. 251 (D.P.R. 1986), *aff'd*, 826 F.2d 151 (1st Cir. P.R. 1987);*United States v. Tilton*, 705 F.2d 429 (11th Cir. Fla. 1983); *United States v. Leuzen*, 816 F.Supp. 1171 (S.D.Tex. 1993); *United States v. Malibu Beach, Inc.*, 711 F.Supp. 1301 (D.N.J. 1989)*United*; *United States v. Larkins*, 657 F.Supp. 76 (W.D.Ky. 1987), *aff'd*, 852 F.2d 189 (6th Cir. Ky. 1988), *cert. denied*, 489 U.S. 1016, 101 L.Ed.2d 193, 109 S.Ct. 1131 (1989); *United States v. Lambert*, 589 F.Supp. 366 (M.D.Fla. 1984); *United States v. Robinson*, 570 F.Supp. 1157 (M.D.Fla. 1983); *United States v. Bradshaw*, 541 F.Supp. 884 (D.Md. 1982); *United States v. Weisman*, 489 F.Supp. 1331 (M.D.Fla. 1980); *United States v. D'Annolfo*, 474 F.Supp. 220 (D.Mass. 1979). But see *United States v. Huebner*, 752 F.2d 1235 (7th Cir.), *cert. denied*, 474 U.S. 817, 88 L.Ed.2d 50, 106 S.Ct. 62 (1985); *United States v. Sexton Cove Estates, Inc.*, 526 F.2d 1293 (5th Cir. 1976).

23. 33 U.S.C. §1319(d). The court's maximum penalty is $25,000 per day for each violation. Each day a violation is in place has been held to be a separate violation. *United States v. Cumberland Farms of Connecticut, Inc.*, *supra* (civil penalty forgiven if restoration project is completed); *United States v. Tull*, 615 F.Supp. 610 (E.D.Va. 1983), *aff'd*, 769 F.2d 182 (4th Cir. 1985), *rev'd on other grounds sub nom. Tull v. United States*, 481 U.S. 412, 95 L.Ed.2d 365, 107 S.Ct. 1831 (1987) (in *Tull*, the defendant admitted that he had placed fill in four locations but denied that the properties were wetlands; the government sought the maximum penalty of $22,890,000; the trial court found that the properties were wetlands, ordered Mr. Tull to restore those properties that he had not yet sold, awarded the government $75,000 in outright civil penalties, and ordered a suspended additional civil penalty of $250,000 on the condition that one of the properties be restored to its former navigable condition, which Mr. Tull discovered would require him to purchase additional property that cost $700,000); *United States v. Ciampitti*, 669 F.Supp. 684 (D.N.J. 1987), *aff'd*, 772 F.2d 893 (3d Cir. N.J. 1985), *cert. denied sub nom. Ciampitti v. United States*, 475 U.S. 1014, 89 L.Ed.2d 307, 106 S.Ct. 1192 (1986).

24. 28 U.S.C. §2462. *Sasser v. EPA*, 990 F.2d 127 (4th Cir. 1993); *United States v. Windward Properties, Inc.*, 821 F.Supp. 690 N.D.Ga.1993); *United States v. Hobbs*, 736 F.Supp. 1406 (E.D.Va. 1990), *aff'd* 947 F.2d 941 (1991), *cert. denied*, 112 S.Ct. 2274 (1992); *Public Interest Research Group of New Jersey v. Powell Duffryn Terminals, Inc.*, 913 F.2d 64 (3d Cir. N.J. 1990), *cert. denied*, 498 U.S. 1109, 112 L.Ed.2d 1100, 111 S.Ct. 1018 (1991); *Atlantic States Legal Foundation, Inc. v. Al Tech Specialty Steel Corp.*, 635 F.Supp. 284 (N.D.N.Y. 1986).

25. *United States v. M.C.C. of Florida, Inc.* 848 F.2d 1133 (11th Cir. 1988), *reh'g granted*, 863 F.2d 802 (11th Cir. Fla. 1989), *appeal after remand*, 967 F.2d 1559 (11 Cir. Fla. 1992); *United States v. Key West Towers, Inc.*, 720 F.Supp. 963 (S.D.Fla. 1989).

26. 33 U.S.C. §1319 (c).

27. "Any person who violates section 1311, 1312, 1316, 1317, 1318, 1328, or 1345 of this title, or any permit condition or limitation implementing any of such sections in a permit issued under section 1342 of this title by the Administrator, or by a State, … or in a permit issued under section 1344 of this title by a State, or any requirement imposed in a pretreatment program approved under section 1342(a)(3) or 1342(b)(8) of this title, and any person who violates any order issued by the Administrator under subsection (a) of this section, shall be subject to a civil penalty not to exceed $25,000 per day for each violation. In determining the amount of a civil penalty the court shall consider the seriousness of the violation or violations, the economic benefit (if any) resulting from the violation, any history of such violations, any good-faith efforts to comply with the applicable requirements, the economic impact of the penalty on the violator, and such other matters as justice may require. For purposes of this subsection, a single operational upset which leads to simultaneous violations of more than one pollutant parameter shall be treated as a single violation." 33 U.S.C. §1319(d).

of not less than $2,500 nor more than $25,000 per day of violation, or by imprisonment for not more than one year, or both.[28] A second violation draws a doubled fine and sentence. Knowing violations are punishable by a fine of not less than $5,000 nor more than $50,000 per day of violation, or by imprisonment for not more than three years, or both.[29] False statements on permit applications and tampering with monitoring devices may draw a fine of not more than $10,000, or imprisonment for not more than two years, or both.[30]

The courts have ordered some fairly severe fines and sentences.[31] For example, in *United States v. Pozgai*,[32] despite many warnings and entry of a temporary restraining order of which he had already been held in contempt, Mr. Pozgai was finally sentenced to three years in prison. In *United States v. Ellen*,[33] the project manager was sentenced to six months in jail. Violators and potential violators should be advised that criminal sanctions are a real possibility and have been applied with increasing frequency in recent years.

Citizen Suits

Although private citizens cannot sue for damages under either the Rivers and Harbors Act of 1899 or the Clean Water Act because there is no general private right of action,[34] they can sue the United States, the EPA, and/or the Corps for an unpermitted discharge of fill material in a wetland, a wrongful permit issuance, and erroneous determinations of wetlands jurisdiction,[35] and can seek equitable relief in the form of an injunction directly against violators. Jurisdiction in the federal courts is authorized by the general federal question statute[36] and, under the Clean Water Act only, a special citizens' suit provision.[37] Venue is proper only in the district in which the "source is located," that is, usually but not necessarily where the wetland is located.[38] If the citizen suit seeks monetary penalties, the statute of limitations is five years from the date on which knowledge of the violation was first obtained, rather than the date of the violation itself.[39] If, however, the suit seeks equitable relief, there is no statute of limitations, although there is some authority that the citizen suit cannot be maintained for "wholly-past" violations.[40] Of course, the citizen suit must be an actual case or controversy under Article III of the U.S. Constitution, meaning that plaintiff must have standing to bring the action by showing individualized harm.[41]

Prior to actually filing a citizen suit, plaintiff is required to give a notice of intent to sue to the violator, the Administrator of the EPA (and, although not specifically mentioned, to the Secretary of the

---

28. 33 U.S.C. §1319(c)(1). If the defendant has one or more Clean Water Act convictions on his or her record already, the maximum amount of the fine and the jail term are both doubled.

29. 33 U.S.C. §1319(c)(2). For persons with one or more previous convictions, the fine may not exceed $100,000 per day of violation, and the jail term is not more than six years, or both.

30. 33 U.S.C. §1319(c)(4). Multiple prior convictions double the fine and jail term.

31. See, e.g., *U.S. v. Perez*, 366 F.3d 1178 (11th Cir. 2004).

32. *United States v. Pozgai*, m 88-00450 (E.D.Pa. December 30, 1988), *aff'd*, 897 F.2d 524 (3d Cir.), *cert. denied*, 498 U.S. 812, 112 L.Ed.2d 24, 111 S.Ct. 48 (1990).

33. *United States v. Ellen*, 961 F.2d 462 (4th Cir. Md. 1992), *cert. denied*, 121 L.Ed.2d 155 (1992).

34. *Middlesex County Sewerage Authority v. National Sea Clammers Association*, 453 U.S. 1 (1981) (no private right of action under the Clean Water Act); *California v. Sierra Club*, 451 U.S. 287 (1981) (no private right of action under the Rivers and Harbors Act of 1899).

35. 33 U.S.C. §§1365(a)(1) and 1365(f); *Vieux Carre Property Owners, Residents & Assocs. v. Brown*, 875 F.2d 453 (5th Cir. La. 1989), *cert. denied*, 493 U.S. 1020, 107 L.Ed.2d 739, 110 S.Ct. 720 (1990); *Orleans Audubon Society v. Lee*, 742 F.2d 901 (5th Cir.), *reh'g denied*, 750 F.2d 69 (5th Cir. 1984); *Hough v. Marsh*, 557 F.Supp. 74 (D.Mass. 1982).

36. 28 U.S.C. §1331.

37. 33 U.S.C. §1365.

38. 33 U.S.C. §1365(c).

39. 28 U.S.C. §246228 U.S.C. §2462; *United States v. Hobbs*, 736 F.Supp. 1406 (E.D.Va. 1990).

40. *Gwaltney of Smithfield v. Chesapeake Bay Foundation*, 484 U.S. 49 (1987). In wetland cases, a continuing violation can be found from the continued existence of the fill in the wetland, as opposed to some historic single-event discharge of a pollutant.

41. *Cane Creek Conservation Authority v. Orange Water Authority*, 590 F.Supp. 1123 (M.D.N.C. 1984).

Army as well), and to the state in which the wetland is located.[42] This notice is mandatory and, therefore, jurisdictional.[43] The purpose of the notice is to provide the government an opportunity to bring its own enforcement action[44] as citizen suits were never intended to take the place of government enforcement actions,[45] but only as an aid in the protection of the environment.[46] If, however, the government declines to take action within the sixty-day notice period, then the citizen must also serve a copy of his or her complaint on the government to allow it to monitor the citizen suit for potential abuse.[47] Another limitation on the availability of citizen suits is that they cannot be used to force the government to take enforcement action, which has been held repeatedly to be a "discretionary," as opposed to a "mandatory," duty of the government.[48]

A final problem in maintaining a citizen suit is what to do with the monetary penalties once the suit has been successful. Obviously it would do little to advance the cause of protecting the environment if private citizens could keep the penalty award. Generally, the funds should be used for environmental improvement projects, either directly or indirectly related to the violation.[49]

---

42. 33 U.S.C. §1365(b).

43. See 40 C.F.R. §§135.1, 135.2, and 135.3 for the service and content requirements of the notice. See also *National Environmental Foundation v. ABC Rail Corporation*, 926 F.2d 1096 (11th Cir. Ala. 1991); *Canada Community Improvement Society v. City of Michigan City, Indiana*, 742 F.Supp. 1025 (N.D.Ind. 1991).

44. 33 U.S.C. §1365(b)(1)(B), which prohibits the maintenance of a citizen suit if the federal or state government "has commenced and is diligently prosecuting a civil or criminal action." Citizens still maintain a right to intervene in the government action. For discussion of the meaning of "diligently prosecuting," see *Atlantic States Legal Foundation v. Universal Tool & Stamping Company*, 735 F.Supp. 1404 (N.D.Ind. 1990); *New York Public Interest Research Group v. Limco Manufacturing Corporation*, 697 F.Supp. 608 (E.D.N.Y. 1987); *Connecticut Fund for the Environment v. Job Plating Company*, 623 F.Supp. 207 (D.Conn. 1985).

45. *Save Our Sound Fisheries Association v. Callaway*, 429 F.Supp. 1136 (D.R.I. 1977).

46. *Pennsylvania Environmental Defense Foundation v. Bellefonte Borough*, 718 F.Supp. 431 (M.D.Pa. 1989).

47. 40 C.F.R. §135.

48. *Harmon Cove Condominium Association, Inc. v. Marsh*, 815 F.2d 949 (3d Cir. 1987); *Sierra Club v. Train*, 557 F.2d 485 (5th Cir. 1977); *National Wildlife Federation v. Laubscher*, 662 F.Supp. 548 (S.D.Tex. 1987). See also the Federal Administrative Procedure Act, 5 U.S.C. §500 *et seq.* for distinction between maintenance of suits by private individuals to compel the government's performance of mandatory, as opposed to discretionary, duties.

49. *Sierra Club v. Electronic Controls Design, Inc.*, 703 F.Supp. 875 (D.Or. 1989), *rev'd. on other grounds and remanded.*

CHAPTER NINE

Litigation and Defenses

Litigation under the Clean Water Act will arise in one of three ways: (1) the Corps or Environmental Protection Agency may refer their enforcement case to the Department of Justice; or (2) a private citizen (an individual person, a corporation, or an environmental group) may bring an enforcement action against either the Corps or the Environmental Protection Agency, or both, and the alleged violator; or (3) a permit applicant may be somehow unhappy with the outcome of the permit application, alleging either that its denial was unlawful or the conditions imposed upon its grant work too great a hardship. Section 505 of the Clean Water Act allows private citizen suits against the EPA for failure to perform "non-discretionary acts."[1] The Corps may be joined as a party defendant under a number of theories despite the fact that suits against it are not specifically authorized by §505.[2]

Although there is generally no judicial review of a governmental agency's refusal to pursue enforcement measures,[3] one case permitted a private suit for monetary damages under the Federal Tort Claims Act.[4] In *Hurst* the plaintiff became aware of permit violations in a project upstream from his property. He notified the Corps which investigated and conceded that violations were occurring. Nonetheless the Corps took no enforcement action and, as a consequence of the violations, plaintiff's property was flooded. In that case the court was persuaded that once the Corps becomes aware of a permit violation, enforcement is no longer considered "discretionary," at least as far as after-the-fact damage caused by the violation.

In a private citizen suit for enforcement there are two additional factual thresholds for plaintiff to cross: (1) it must have standing to sue, that is, be an "aggrieved person"; and (2) the violation must be ongoing in the present. "Standing" is a concept that basically requires that the proper person bring the lawsuit. In the context of Clean Water Act litigation, "standing" requires that only those persons who actually use the affected area, will be significantly affected, or will suffer a particular individualized harm from the government action may sue.[5] The limitation in which citizen suits cannot be heard for wholly past violations is weak and easily overcome.[6]

---

1. 33 U.S.C. §136533.
2. See *National Wildlife Federation v. Hanson*, 859 F.2d 313 (4th Cir. 1988) (Corps may be joined when it fails to make a reasonable wetlands determination); *Golden Gate Audubon Society, Inc. v. U.S. Army Corps of Engineers*, 18 Envtl.L.Rep. 21401 (N.D.Cal. 1988) (Corps may be sued under the Administrative Procedure Act, 5 U.S.C. §500 *et seq.*).
3. See chapter 8.
4. *Hurst v. United States*, 882 F.2d 306 (8th Cir. 1989).
5. *Cane Creek Conservation Authority v. Orange Water Authority*, 590 F.Supp. 1123, 1127 (M.D.N.C. 1984)
6. See chapter 8.

Procedural Issues

RIPENESS

Private persons may sue in federal court. Jurisdiction is proper in federal court because a claim under the Clean Water Act presents a federal question.[7] However, the case must be "ripe" prior to filing such a suit.

"Ripeness" is a doctrine applied by the courts to prevent premature lawsuits. In other words, the controversy must have reached a certain stage of disagreement such that there is something for the court to adjudicate, that is, a so-called justiciable actual controversy under Article III of the U.S. Constitution. Before that stage is reached, courts say that a case is not "ripe," and that the court therefore lacks jurisdiction to decide it.

The issue of ripeness arises frequently in cases involving judicial review of administrative decisions. In Clean Water Act litigation, the doctrine of ripeness requires first of all that the regulation is question must actually be applied against the landowner rather than merely enacted as a potential regulation in a hypothetical set of circumstances. The Corps must have actually determined that the property is a wetland or have taken some action toward the landowner based upon that determination, usually either a permit denial or an enforcement action, or the reverse in a citizen suit. The landowner would then seek either a declaratory judgment that the wetlands determination is improper or incorrect, or an injunction to prohibit an enforcement action, or the private citizen would allege that the wetlands determination was erroneous and, consequently, a permit should have been denied or conditioned.

In considering whether a case is "ripe" or not, these administrative determinations must be complete and final. If they are not, the case is not ripe. Particularly in cases in which the private landowner complains that his land has been "taken" by the government by virtue of a denial of a permit, the landowner must first show that he properly applied for the permit and that it was in fact denied.[8] The court is then relieved of the potential responsibility of making a wetland determination itself and can concentrate instead on the legal propriety of the permit grant or denial or enforcement action.

JUDICIAL REVIEW OF ADMINISTRATIVE DECISIONS

Another threshold procedural issue, sometimes stated separately but in reality a corollary of the concept of ripeness, is the general prohibition against judicial review of administrative decisions until the administrative decision is complete and final, including the requirement that the person complaining about the administrative decision must have availed himself of every avenue of remedy within the administrative agency before coming to court (called "exhaustion of administrative remedies"). Even then, the judicial review must be limited to the record generated in the administrative proceeding.[9] An administrative agency such as the Corps possesses specialized knowledge and is considered to be in the best position to make an accurate administrative decision based upon the facts before it—more so, at least, than the reviewing court. The court's role is supposed to be limited to reviewing the administrative

---

7. 28 U.S.C. §1331.

8. *United States v. Riverside Bayview Homes*, 474 U.S. 121 (1985); *Williamson County Regional Planning Commission v. Hamilton Bank*, 473 U.S. 172, 87 L.Ed.2d 126, 105 S.Ct. 3108 (1985); *Hodel v. Virginia Surface Mining Reclamation Ass'n.*, 452 U.S. 264, 69 L.Ed.2d 1, 101 S.Ct. 2352 (1981). As the Supreme Court stated in *Williamson*, "a claim that the application of government regulations effects a taking of a property interest is not ripe until the government entity charged with implementing the regulations has reached a final decision regarding application of the regulations to the property at issue." *Hamilton*, 473 U.S. at 186.

9. *Avoyelles Sportmen's League, Inc. v. Marsh*, 715 F.2d 897 (5th Cir. 1983).

record to determine whether the administrative agency's determination or enforcement action was "arbitrary and capricious."[10]

This concept of exhaustion of administrative remedies coupled with the limitation of review to the administrative record may be more honored in the breach since it embraces two components, both of which *should* be satisfied prior to judicial review: completeness and finality. Whether the administrative decision was based upon a complete record can be difficult to determine. At this stage in the development of the case law it is difficult to derive a hard and fast rule with respect to the Clean Water Act because litigation concerning it frequently involves the application of other, additional statutes that skew the judicial results.

If one starts with the basic rule that the court is limited in its review to the administrative record before it,[11] in cases involving wetlands determinations under the Clean Water Act an immediate problem arises: the "record" may be virtually nonexistent because the wetland determination and consequent assertion of jurisdiction may have been based only upon an informal site visit at which very little documentation was produced. In litigation concerning an improper grant of a permit, in addition to application of the Clean Water Act, the National Environmental Policy Act may apply, which under certain circumstances requires the production of an environmental assessment or an environmental impact statement that may itself be inadequate or nonexistent.

In this situation the courts have two options: they may either remand the case back to the Corps with instructions to generate an adequate record for the court to review or they may proceed to review that case anyway under the National Environmental Policy Act to determine the adequacy of the environmental assessment or environmental impact statement if one was required to be prepared. Which option the court will select has, at least historically, been dependent upon whether the underlying dispute involves merely a wetlands determination or a final grant or denial of a permit.

If the case involves merely a wetlands determination, in the majority of cases so far, the courts limit their consideration to the administrative record.[12] If the record is inadequate, the courts remand the case back to the Corps to generate a better record.[13] Nonetheless, one lower court has received new evidence beyond the scope of the administrative record in a wetlands determination case.[14]

If the case involves the grant of a permit, the majority of courts still limit their review to the administrative record. In this situation there is more likely to be an adequate administrative record generated by the procedures outlined above. However, if the case *also* involves an allegation that an environmental assessment or environmental impact statement should have been prepared under the National Environmental Policy Act, or that the environmental assessment or environmental impact statement that was prepared is somehow inadequate, then the courts *may* allow additional evidence, though even this additional evidence is limited to the scope of the administrative record.[15]

If the case involves the denial of a permit and the private landowner alleges that the effect of a permit denial is a taking of his property such that the Fifth Amendment of the U.S. Constitution requires that he or she be paid just compensation,[16] these procedural thresholds take on additional significance. Exhaustion of administrative remedies becomes more important because in order to show a taking, the landowner must show not only that his or her first plan drew a permit denial, but that all plans he or

---

10. 5 U.S.C. §706(2)(a).

11. *Avoyelles Sportsmen's League, Inc. v. Marsh, supra.; Bailey v. United States,* 647 F.Supp. 44 (D.Idaho (1986); *Shoreline Associates v. Marsh,* 555 F.Supp. 169 (D.Md. 1983), *aff'd,* 725 F.2d 677 (4th Cir. 1984).

12. *Avoyelles Sportsmen's League, Inc. v. Marsh, supra.*

13. *National Wildlife Federation v. Hanson,* 859 F.2d 313 (4th Cir. 1988).

14. *Leslie Salt Co. v. U.S.,* 700 F.Supp. 476 (N.D.Cal. 1988), *reversed on other grounds.,* 20 Envtl.L.Rep. 20477 (9th Cir. 1990), *Leslie Salt Co. v. U.S.,* 700 F.Supp. 476 (N.D.Cal. 1988), *reversed on other grounds.,* 20 Envtl.L.Rep. 20477 (9th Cir. 1990).

15. *Louisiana Wildlife Federation v. York,* 603 F.Supp. 518 (W.D.La. 1984), *aff'd in part, vacated in part and remanded,* 761 F.2d 1044 (5th Cir. 1985).

16. See "The Fifth Amendment Taking Defense," below.

she might submit would also draw a permit denial thus there is no economically viable use left in the property[17] and that all administrative procedures to obtain compensation have been exhausted.[18]

Whether the landowner has exhausted his or her administrative remedies and whether the Corps's decision is complete and final can be a difficult threshold to cross. For example, how many plans must the developer submit? Has he or she submitted every conceivable development plan such that denial of all of them deprives the landowner of all economically viable use? Certainly this procedural threshold would require the submission of at least two plans, the first which was denied and a second attempt.[19] The reason for this "final and authoritative" determination requirement is that the court cannot figure out if a regulation goes "too far" without knowing to what extent the regulation will be applied. To make that determination, the court has to know with some specificity the nature of the activity being limited or prohibited by the permit denial. In addition, the potential plaintiff must have applied for every other permit that might conceivably be applicable so that the court can determine which permit denial was the culprit causing the taking if one occurred.[20] There is also an issue of how long the potential plaintiff should spend submitting these additional development plans. Temporary takings are recognized[21] during the period of time the administrative process was ongoing, but the courts have been fairly generous in allowing time for the permit application process.[22]

STATUTE OF LIMITATIONS

The courts have applied the general six-year statute of limitations[23] to suits against the Corps and the Environmental Protection Agency arising out of their permit decisions. This limitation period should be distinguished from the five-year limitations period for civil enforcement suits brought by the Corps or EPA against permit violators or for unpermitted discharges.

LIABILITY

In enforcement actions brought by the government, §404 of the Clean Water Act and §10 of the Rivers and Harbors Act of 1899 provide for strict liability even to the extent of piercing the corporate veil and holding officers liable if they participated in the violation.[24] In addition to enforcement actions against the property owner, other persons who assisted in the violation may also be held liable.[25]

---

17. *MacDonald, Sommer & Frates v. Yolo County*, 477 U.S. 340 (1986); *Williamson County Regional Planning Commission v. Hamilton Bank*, 473 U.S. 172 (1985); *Ruckelshaus v. Monsanto*, 467 U.S. 986, 81 L.Ed.2d 815, 104 S.Ct. 2862 (1984); *Hodel v. Virginia Surface Mining & Reclamation Association*, 452 U.S. 264, 69 L.Ed.2d 1, 101 S.Ct. 2352 (1981); *Agins v. City of Tiburon*, 447 U.S. 255, 65 L.Ed.2d 106, 100 S.Ct. 2138 (1980); *Penn Central Transportation Co. v. New York City*, 438 U.S. 104, 57 L.Ed.2d 631, 98 S.Ct. 2646 (1978), *reh'g. denied*, 439 U.S. 883, 58 L.Ed.2d 198, 99 S.Ct. 226 (1978).

18. *Williamson County Regional Planning Commission v. Hamilton Bank*, 473 U.S. 172 (1985).

19. *MacDonald, Sommer & Frates v. Yolo County, supra*; *Williamson County Regional Planning Commission v. Hamilton Bank*, 473 U.S. 172 (1985); *Agins v. City of Tiburon*, 447 U.S. 255 (1980); *Penn Central Transportation Co. v. New York City*, 438 U.S. 104 (1978).

20. There is a futility exception espoused by a few lower courts in which, under certain facts, the requirement of submitting a second plan or applying for other required permits may be waived if, under an extreme set of facts, it would be futile to do so.

21. *First English Evangelical Lutheran Church of Glendale v. County of Los Angeles*, 493 U.S. 1056, 107 L.Ed.2d 950, 110 S.Ct. 866 (1990), in which an ordinance barred reconstruction in a flood zone. The Supreme Court held that assuming that the ordinance worked a taking, compensation should be paid during the time the ordinance was in effect.

22. In one case the plaintiffs wished to develop a 112-acre parcel but it took the Corps sixteen months to decide which 70 acres of the parcel was the wetland. *Dufau v. United States*, 22 Cl.Ct. 156 (1990). While the plaintiffs were waiting for their wetland determination and permit, the bottom fell out of the real estate market to the extent that when they finally did get their permit, there was no one to buy the lots. They claimed a temporary taking during the permit application process. The court rejected their claim. Perhaps compelling to the court was a finding that some of the delay had been caused by the plaintiffs themselves. *Dufau* teaches that not only must the potential plaintiff submit additional proposals, he or she must be diligent and timely about these additional efforts as well. See also *1902 Atlantic, Ltd.* v. Hudson, 574 F.Supp. 1381 (E.D.Va. 1983).

23. 28 U.S.C. §2401(a).

24. *United States v. Pollution Abatement Services of Oswego*, 763 F. 2d 133 (2d Cir. N.Y. 1985), *cert. denied sub nom. Miller v. U.S.*, 474 U.S. 1037, 88 L.Ed.2d 583, 106 S.Ct. 605 (1985).

25. *United States v. Pollution Abatement Services of Oswego, Inc., supra.*; *United States v. Board of Trustees of Florida Keys Community College*, 531 F.Supp. 267 (S.D.Fla. 1981). But see *United States v. Sexton Cove Estates, Inc.*, 526 F.2d 1293 (5th Cir. Fla. 1976); *United States v. Joseph G. Moretti, Inc.*, 526 F.2d 1306 (5th Cir. Fla. 1976).

ATTORNEYS' FEES

Attorneys fees and expert witness fees are allowed for any prevailing or substantially prevailing party under §505(d) of the Clean Water Act.[26]

The Fifth Amendment Taking Defense

The Fifth Amendment taking defense has met with only varying success. It is not precisely a defense since its successful outcome against the government does not alter the Corps's wetland determination or permit denial or conditioning. Instead, the plaintiff will receive money but lose his or her property. Of the remaining defenses asserted, so few have been successful, and among the successful ones, their application is so limited to the special facts of each individual case that it may be fairly said that liability under the Clean Water Act is truly strict liability, with only a Fifth Amendment claim available to ameliorate the effects of what the Corps intended to do in the first place—make a wetlands determination and/or deny a permit.

Before tackling the issue of regulatory takings, however, it is important to understand that not all property is capable of private ownership. An ancient concept of sovereignty allows a government to limit the uses to which certain land may be put in the public interest by controlling the natural resources found on the land. This concept is now called the public trust doctrine. Under this concept of sovereignty, which may have its roots as far back in time as the first organized society, there is recognized the notion that some natural resources are so important to all of society that no individual private citizen should be able to exclude others from their use. Even though one of the essential elements of private property ownership is the right to exclude others, nonetheless, some "things common to mankind by the law of nature"[27] are so universally important to the survival and prosperity of all that they should remain in common usage and there should be no exclusion of anyone. There is even a modern argument that there is no right of property ownership in the orthodox sense in these natural resources, that they simply cannot be owned by human beings.

Under Roman law these natural resources were held in trust for the public by the sovereign. The English went further, saying that the crown actually owned, as opposed to held in trust, tidal navigable waterways.[28] In the United States the doctrine was adopted by the thirteen colonies with each colony holding its individual navigable waterways in trust[29]. With the westward expansion away from the coastline, as the new states were added to the Union, they, too, acquired control over navigable waterways in trust for the public. However, since not all of the navigable waterways in the interior portions of the United States are tidal, the United States included nontidal navigable waterways[30] in its public trust doctrine.[31] In the case of inland, nontidal navigable waterways, the upper reach of the waterway held in public trust was the ordinary high-water line.[32] Recently, some courts have been willing to extend the reach of the lands held in public trust to include the nonnavigable tributaries of navigable waterways if the activity in the tributary affects the public trust value in the navigable portion.[33]

---

26. 33 U.S.C. §1365(d).

27. This is the Roman law definition, from the Institutes of Justinian, which included air, running water, the sea, and the seashore below high-tide line.

28. Stevens, "The Public Trust: Sovereign's Ancient Prerogative Becomes the People's Environmental Right," 14 U.C. Davis L.Rev. 195 (1980).

29. Except for some grants in the Commonwealth of Massachusetts which extend private property ownership down to low tide line instead of high tide line for particular uses.

30. *Martin v. Waddell,* 41 U.S. 367 (1842).

31. *Pollard's Lessee v. Hagan,* 44 U.S. 212, 229 (1845).

32. *Barney v. Keokuk,* 94 U.S. 324 (1876).

33. *National Audubon Society v. Superior Court,* 33 Cal.3d 419, 434-38, 658 P.2d 709, 719-21, 189 Cal. Rptr. 346, 356-57, *cert. den.,* 464 U.S. 977 (1983).

Under Roman and English law, the public trust doctrine protected commercial shipping and fishing. In the United States these activities as well as recreational activities, fowling, and drinking and irrigation water needs have been included.[34] As the uses to which water is put have increased, the courts have similarly expanded the interest protected under the public trust doctrine. For example, California now includes lands in their natural state, which may serve as ecological study areas, provide food and habitat for birds and marine life, or simply serve to "favorably affect the scenery and climate of the area."[35] Perhaps the most modern expression of the public trust doctrine is that whereas in the past the sovereign held certain lands in trust for certain uses, now there is some discussion that the resources themselves, independent of their human use, may be entitled to protection in their own right.[36]

The public trust doctrine would appear to grant authority to the government to take almost any action with respect to private property so long as it could be justified as a measure to protect an essential public resource. Governmental limitations on the use of property under the authority of the Clean Water Act would seem to be a particularly appropriate application of the public trust doctrine in light of the special purpose of the statute, to restore and maintain clean water. Apart from the discussion of whether water itself would have a right to protection, certainly the public's interest in a continued supply of clean water should outweigh an individual's use that fouls it. Indeed some conservationists have taken this middle position, between the water having its own right to protection and the individual's right to do anything he or she chooses with the water present on private property. To some extent the argument was successful until a constitutional principle, the Fifth Amendment "taking clause," was applied to limit the unfettered application of the public trust doctrine.[37]

Another limitation on regulatory takings is the concept of nuisance, under which some uses of property can be legitimately abated by government regulation if those uses are injurious to the public.[38]

As a written legal principle the taking clause is nearly 800 years old. Chapter 28 of the Magna Carta contains a similar limitation on the unfettered application of sovereignty, perhaps in reaction to King John's abuse of the public trust doctrine to take for himself all the best hunting grounds. Chapter 28 says, directly enough, "No constable or other bailiff of ours shall take anyone's corn or other chattels unless he pays on the spot in cash for them or can delay payment by arrangement with the seller."[39] Two other chapters also require the "agreement" of the property owner before the crown could take property. Chapter 30 promised that "[n]o sheriff, or bailiff of ours, or anyone else shall take the horses or carts of any free man for transport work save with the agreement of that free man." And chapter 31 promises "[n]either we nor our bailiffs will take, for castles or other works of ours, timber which is not ours, except with the agreement of him whose timber it is."[40] Obviously the "agreement" contemplated in chapters 30 and 31 would be forthcoming upon the payment of compensation.

Chapters 28, 30, and 31 did not forbid the crown from ever taking property—the ancient concept of the public trust was preserved—they only require the payment of money or the consent of the owner. Similarly it is important to remember that the taking clause does not forbid the government from taking property for public use; it, too, only requires that just compensation be paid.

---

34. *Lamprey v. Metcalf*, 52 Minn. 181, 53 N.W. 1139 (1893).

35. *Marks v. Whitney*, 6 Cal.3d 251, 259-60, 491 P.2d 374, 380, 98 Cal.Rptr. 790, 796 (1971).

36. See Christopher D. Stone, *Should Trees Have Standing? Toward Legal Rights For Natural Objects* (Palo Alto, CA: William Kaufmann, Inc., 1974), p. 9. Stone's essay proposes "that we give legal rights to forests, oceans, rivers and other so-called 'natural objects' in the environment—indeed, to the natural environment as a whole." See also Aldo Leopold, *A Sand County Almanac and Sketches Here and There*, American Museum of Natural History Special Members' Edition, 1968 (New York: Oxford University Press, 1949), pp. 201–26 ("The Land Ethic").

37. See, e.g., *Nollan v. California Coastal Commission*, 483 U.S. 825 (1987).

38. *Sweet v. Rechel*, 159 U.S. 380 (1895); *Mugler v. Kansas*, 123 U.S. 623 (1887); *Miller v. Schoene*, 276 U.S. 272 (1928); *Lucas v. South Carolina Coastal Council*, 505 U.S. 1003 (1992).

39. *Encyclopaedia Britannica*, 15th ed. 1990, vol. 7, p. 675.

40. *Id.*

In order for there to be a "taking" of property by the government[41] triggering the constitutionally required payment of just compensation, it would seem axiomatic that there must be (a) "property" of some kind, and (b) some form of governmental activity that has the effect of denying property rights. Under the taking clause, "property" means more than fee-simple ownership of real estate. "Property" as the term is used in taking clause cases means "the group of rights inhering in the citizen's relation to the physical thing, as the right to possess, use, and dispose of it."[42] In wetlands cases, the "property" will almost always be an interest in real property, such as fee-simple ownership, but it can also include possessory interests such as easements,[43] leaseholds,[44] liens,[45] mineral estates,[46] air space,[47] and water rights.[48] In addition to these traditional ownership or possessory interests in land, it is at least logically possible that some aspects of personal property might be taken in a wetland case, such as the interest of a limited partner in a real estate development partnership that was denied a permit by the Corps.

A "taking" of property will always occur when there is an interference with a property right that amounts to an actual physical invasion of the property. Not so obvious are cases in which takings have been found when there was less than a physical invasion. These cases are called "regulatory takings" or "inverse condemnations." The allegation is that the regulation has gone "too far" and so limited the use to which property may be put that the government might as well have condemned the property outright and taken all the badges of ownership including fee-simple title.[49] These cases are called "inverse condemnations" because the plaintiff is the landowner, whereas in ordinary condemnation cases the plaintiff is the government. The denial of a permit to develop a wetland has become a fertile ground for alleging a regulatory taking.

Assuming there is a property right that the law recognizes as protectable, the next step is to focus on the character of the governmental activity to determine whether a regulatory taking has occurred. The first and most obvious is when the government actually invades the land, such as by building new roads, widening streets, erecting utility poles, and the like. The government will institute an action to force the landowner to sell his land for "just compensation." A middle type of case is when the governmental invasion is intermittent or less than continuous. In these cases the issue is the proper measure of

---

41. The taking clause applies to the states as well as the federal government by operation of the due process clause in the Fourteenth Amendment. *MacDonald, Sommer & Frates v. County of Yolo, supra,* reaffirming *Chicago, Burlington and Quincy Railroad Co. v. Chicago,* 166 U.S. 226, 41 L.Ed.2d 979, 17 S.Ct. 581 (1897). Further, many state constitutions contain provisions similar to the Taking Clause thus those states' interpretations of their constitutions may also be instructive.

42. *Ruckelshaus v. Monsanto Co.,* 467 U.S. 986 (1984). In *Ruckelshaus* the property interests alleged to have been taken were trade secrets that the plaintiff was required to disclose to the EPA in support of an application for a pesticide registration. For a period of time while the application was pending, the EPA had a duty to keep the information confidential. Instead, it revealed the information. The court found that during the confidentiality-guaranteed period, the government had taken the trade secret.

43. *United States v. Welch,* 217 U.S. 333 (1910); *United States v. 8.41 Acres of Land,* 680 F.2d 388 (5th Cir. Tex. 1982), *cert. denied,* 479 U.S. 820, 93 L.Ed.2d 38, 107 S.Ct. 85 (1986); *United States v. 2979.72 Acres of Land,* 237 F.2d 165 (4th Cir. Va. 1956); *Redevelopment Agency v. Tobriner,* 153 Cal.App.3d 367, 200 Cal.Rptr. 364, *cert. denied,* 469 U.S. 882, 83 L.Ed.2d 187, 105 S.Ct. 250 (1984).

44. *Alamo Land & Cattle Co. v. Arizona,* 424 U.S. 295 (1976); *Almota Farmers Elevator & Warehouse Co. v. United States,* 409 U.S. 470, 35 L.Ed.2d 1, 93 S.Ct. 791 (1973); *United States v. Pewee Coal Co.,* 341 U.S. 114, 95 L.Ed.2d 809, 71 S.Ct. 670 (1951); *United States v. Westinghouse Electric & Mfg. Co.,* 339 U.S. 261, 94 L.Ed.2d 816, 70 S.Ct. 644 (1950); *United States v. Petty Motor Co.,* 327 U.S. 372, 90 L.Ed.2d 729, 66 S.Ct. 596 (1946), *reh'g. denied,* 327 U.S. 818, 90 L.Ed. 1040, 66 S.Ct. 813 (1946); *United States v. General Motors,* 323 U.S. 373, 89 L.Ed. 311, 65 S.Ct. 357 (1945); *United States v. Right To Use And Occupy 3.38 Acres Of Land,* 484 F.2d 1140 (4th Cir. 1973); *Sun Oil Co. v. United States,* 572 F.2d 786 (Ct.Cl. 1978).

45. *Louisville Joint Stock Land Bank v. Radford,* 295 U.S. 555 (1935).

46. *Keystone Bituminous Coal Association v. De Benedictis,* 480 U.S. 470 (1987); *Pennsylvania Coal Co. v. Mahon,* 260 U.S. 393, 67 L.Ed. 322, 43 S.Ct. 158 (1922).

47. *Griggs v. Allegheny County,* 369 U.S. 84, 7 L.Ed.2d 585, 82 S.Ct. 531, *reh'g. denied,* 369 U.S. 857, 8 L.Ed.2d 16, 82 S.Ct. 931 (1962); *United States v. Causby,* 328 U.S. 256, 90 L.Ed. 1206, 66 S.Ct. 1062 (1946) (which holds that a landowner, in this case a chicken farmer, "owns at least as much of the space above the ground as he can occupy or use in connection with the land," thus when government aircraft flew over the chicken barn, causing the chickens to panic and fly against the inside of the barn, killing themselves, the court found that the government had taken the air space (and presumably the chickens as well) by its direct and immediate interference with the use and enjoyment of the land). See also W. Blackstone, 2 *Commentaries,* §18W, for the Latin legal maxim *Cujus est solum, ejus est usque ad coelum et ad infernos* or "To whomsoever the soil belongs, he owns also to the sky and to the depths."

48. *United States v. Gerlach Livestock Co.,* 339 U.S. 725, 94 L.Ed. 1231, 70 S.Ct. 955 (1950); *Ball v. United States,* 1 Ct.Cl. 180 (1982).

49. *Deltona Corporation v. United States,* 657 F.2d 1184 (1981).

damages.[50] The third and last type of governmental activity is when there is no physical invasion but a regulation is applied to limit the uses to which the property may be put. The essential inquiry in these "regulatory taking" cases will be whether it is fair to force a few private individuals to bear a burden alone (by not receiving any compensation for the limitation on the use of their property) or whether it is fair that the burden should be spread over all of society (by requiring the government to pay compensation out of the public fisc).[51]

The complaining landowner cannot stop a regulatory taking because the taking clause only prohibits uncompensated takings, not all takings.[52] There is no action available for injunction or declaratory relief when plaintiff alleges a taking. Instead, the landowner can only sue the government for adequate compensation.[53]

In making a plaintiff's case, landowners should be aware that "there is no set formula to determine where a regulation ends and taking begins."[54] Concepts of fairness, justice, and judgment rule the day.[55] The Supreme Court has struggled to devise a system of analysis by which regulatory takings could be distinguished from abatements of nuisances (which have always been permissible under the police power of the government), minor intrusions on property ownership rights (without which government could not function), and major intrusions that amount to takings. Prior to 1922, the police power had been used to justify even some major intrusions.[56] The law changed in 1922 with the *Pennsylvania Coal* case.[57] In that case a homeowner held an 1877 deed from a coal company that reserved the right of the coal company to remove coal from under the land. In 1921, Pennsylvania passed the Kohler Act which made mining coal illegal if it caused surface subsidence. The coal company argued that its coal had been taken by the passage of the Kohler Act and the majority of the Supreme Court agreed. *Pennsylvania Coal* stated a new test: the "diminution in value" test. Under this test, if a regulation goes "too far" and the diminution in value is consequently too great, there will be a taking. The dissent in *Pennsylvania Coal* was just as vigorous in arguing that mining coal that causes surface subsidence is a nuisance and can be legitimately eliminated by the police power. It may simply be that the two opinions can be explained by their differing view of the facts: The majority believed that the subsidence would only affect the individual landowner; thus if there was a nuisance, it was not a public nuisance; the dissent believed that the mining subsidence would affect the entire city of Scranton, and thus it was a public nuisance.

Another distinction between the majority and the dissent in *Pennsylvania Coal* centers on how to arithmetically determine the diminution in value, whether to value the property including both surface and mining rights, or to value the mining rights and surface rights separately. If valued together, even after forbidding mining, the land would retain some value, that is, its surface value. If valued separately, the forbidding of mining would completely destroy the value of those property rights. If there is residual value, there is less diminution in value, but if there is no residual value, a greater diminution in value can be found. This debate continues today with wetland-permit-denied plaintiffs arguing that if they

---

50. See, e.g., *Ruckelshaus v. Monsanto*, 467 U.S. 986 (1984).

51. The 9 1/2-year period of time during which an erroneous cease and desist order was pending was held not to be a taking. *Sartori v. U.S.*, 67 Fed.Cl. 263 (2005).

52. *First English Evangelical Lutheran Church v. County of Los Angeles, supra*; *Williamson County Planning Commission v. Hamilton Bank, supra*.

53. The Tucker Act, 28 U.S.C. §1491, vests exclusive jurisdiction over taking cases in excess of $10,000 in the United States Claims Court. *Johnson v. City of Shorewood*, 360 F.3d 810 (8th Cir. 2004). However, even before going to the Claims Court, plaintiff must have exhausted all of his or her other administrative or state court avenues to compensation. *Williamson County Planning Commission v. Hamilton Bank, supra*.

54. *Goldblatt v. Town of Hempstead*, 369 U.S. 590 (1962).

55. *Andrus v. Allard*, 444 U.S. 51, 62 L.Ed.2d 210, 100 S.Ct. 318 (1979); *Penn Central Transportation Co. v. New York City*, 438 U.S. 104, 57 L.Ed.2d 631, 98 S.Ct. 2646 (1978).

56. See e.g., *Mugler v. Kansas*, 123 U.S. 623, 31 L.Ed. 205, 8 S.Ct. 273 (1887) (holding that there is no taking if the government action involved preventing a detriment to the public, but there would be a taking if the government used the land to secure a benefit to the public); *Hadacheck v. Sebastien*, 239 U.S. 394, 60 L.Ed. 348, 36 S.Ct. 143 (1915) (holding that an ordinance outlawing brickyards, which utterly eliminated the value of Hadacheck's brickyard, was a legitimate exercise of the police power, even though the brickyard was not a nuisance).

57. *Pennsylvania Coal Co. v. Mahon*, 260 U.S. 393, 67 L.Ed. 322, 43 S.Ct. 158 (1922).

cannot develop their wetlands, then no value is left to them, while others say that even if the permit to develop is denied, the land may still be put to other uses thus retaining some value, which prevents there being a taking.

After *Pennsylvania Coal* there was a fifty-year hiatus in major taking cases until *Penn Central Transportation*[58] and *Agins*.[59] *Penn Central* refined taking case analysis beyond the diminution in value test to include an examination of three factors: (1) the economic impact of the government action, (2) the extent to which there is interference with the distinct investment-backed expectations, and (3) the character of the government action. Two years later another refinement came in *Agins*, which was to be applied in land-use cases: (1) does the regulation deny all economically viable use? and (2) does the regulation substantially advance a legitimate government interest? Wetland regulation is considered a land-use question; thus the *Agins* two-part analysis has been applied, but the *Penn Central* three-part test is subsumed into the economic viability inquiry in the *Agins* test.

Under the substantial advancement test, the old concept of abating a nuisance arises as the court first looks to see whether the intended but now regulated use was a nuisance. If the court finds a nuisance, the case ends and there is no taking.[60] But if the court cannot find a nuisance, it must find some public benefit (a legitimate government interest) and then weigh the benefit against the burden to the landowner. In examining the burden to the landowner, the court moves to the three issues in *Penn Central*. A remaining economically viable use does not mean the property's highest and best use and is calculated including the value of the property as a whole.[61] Interference with investment-backed expectations analysis has been less than clear. Sometimes the courts have found no interference when one would seem obvious.[62] The character of the governmental action inquiry distinguishes actual physical invasions from regulations on uses and weighs the private burden against the public benefit or prevention of nuisances as previously discussed. Where there is a physical invasion, the diminution in value or interference with investment-backed expectations is irrelevant no matter how minor the invasion or how great the public benefit obtained thereby.[63]

In wetlands cases, arguments in favor of finding a taking by a permit denial center on the government's elimination of what has been viewed as the only use of otherwise useless land, that is, development in a wetland. To accept this outcome, wetlands have to be conceived of as useless in their natural state and capable of economic viability only if they are developed. From a scientific outlook, such a concept is simply outdated. Wetlands do in fact have economic uses apart from their susceptibility to development.

Since the Clean Water Act is now over thirty years old, few real estate developers could reasonably hold an investment-backed expectation of profit from developing a wetland given the publicity and common knowledge attained by the §404 permit requirement. Certainly landowners hope they will get their §404 permit and make a profit, but they must also recognize that there is a reasonable chance that their permit application will be denied. A hope is not a reasonable expectation.

---

58. *Penn Central Transportation Co. v. New York City, supra.*

59. *Agins v. City of Tiburon, supra.*

60. *John R. Sand & Gravel Company v. U.S.*, 60 Fed.Cl. 230 (2004).

61. *Keystone Bituminous Coal Association v. DeBenedictis, supra.* (holding that a regulation requiring a coal company to leave half of its coal in place in order to support the surface was not a taking because the company could still sell the other half of its coal); *Penn Central Transportation Co. v. New York City, supra.* (holding that the denial of the use of the air space above Grand Central Station to build an office building was not a taking because the owner could still use the existing building); *Florida Rock Industries, Inc. v. United States*, 45 Cl.Ct. 38 (1999); *Palazzolo v. Rhode Island*, 533 U.S. 606, 121 S.Ct. 2448, 150 L.Ed.2d 592 (2001).

62. If the property was purchased after the enactment of the Clean Water Act, there is not an automatic taking when a permit is denied to the developer. *Walcek v. U.S.*, 49 Cl.Ct. 248 (2001).

63. *Loretto v. Teleprompter Manhattan CATV Corp.*, 458 U.S. 419, 73 L.Ed.2d 868, 102 S.Ct. 3164 (1982) (holding that requiring a building owner to permit the attachment of cable television was a taking, albeit minor).

If it was purchased after the enactment of the Clean Water Act, then very careful inquiry should be made into the owner's actual expectations. To allow developers to purchase land, knowing there is a chance that a development permit will be denied, and then claim a Fifth Amendment taking when their permit application is denied, opens the door to collusive practices in which developers could guarantee themselves a profit, paid by the government, for any project plan, no matter how irrational, which would never receive a permit. At the same time, mitigation banking and wetlands-creation science and design continue to expand to ensure that a now recognized vital resource is not needlessly destroyed to the detriment of a public resource, or excessively protected to the detriment of the public fisc.

CHAPTER TEN

Commerce Clause Jurisdiction after *Rapanos*[1]

Under the U.S. Constitution, the Congress has only certain defined, enumerated powers,[2] while the States retain "numerous and indefinite" powers.[3] One of Congress's powers is the power to "regulate Commerce with foreign Nations and among the several States, and with the Indian Tribes."[4] As early as 1824, the Supreme Court noted that "[c]omprehensive as the word 'among' is, it may very properly be restricted to that commerce which concerns more States than one."[5]

For a hundred years the commerce clause languished on the sidelines, more often mentioned for its limitations than its powers, until the 1887 enactment of the Interstate Commerce Act[6] and the 1890 enactment of the Sherman Antitrust Act.[7] The Supreme Court soon recognized, however, that its prior refusal to regulate traditional intrastate means and instrumentalities of commerce such as "production," "manufacturing,"[8] or "mining"[9] would no longer stand. Instead, it became apparent that, in a more modern economy, the intrastate and interstate aspects of commerce had become so commingled that full regulation of interstate commerce would necessitate incidental regulation of intrastate commerce.[10] The Court shifted to a "direct" versus "indirect" effect on interstate commerce analysis but still warned that the power had limits.[11] In probably the apogee of this analysis, *Wickard v. Filburn*, the Court allowed that an "activity," even if purely local and even if it could not be construed as "commerce,"

> may still, whatever its nature, be reached by Congress if it exerts a substantial economic effect on interstate commerce, and this irrespective of whether such effect is what might at some earlier time have been defined as "direct" or "indirect."[12]

The Court further noted that although Filburn's "[o]wn contribution to the demand for wheat may be trivial by itself is not enough to remove him from the scope of federal regulation where, as here, his contribution, taken together with that of many others similarly situated, is far from trivial."[13] In more modern times, the Court reaffirmed its position that "where a general regulatory scheme bears a substantial

---

1. Originally published in the Washington State Bar Association Environmental and Land Use Law Section newsletter.
2. U.S. Constitution, Article I, §8.
3. The Federalist Papers, no. 45.
4. U.S. Constitution, article I, §8, clause 3 (the "commerce clause").
5. *Gibbons v. Ogden*, 9 Wheat. 1, 6 L.Ed. 23 (1824).
6. 49 U.S.C. §1, *et seq.*
7. 15 U.S.C. §1, *et seq.*
8. *U.S. v. E.C. Knight Co.*, 156 U.S. 1 (1895).
9. *Carter v. Carter Coal Co.*, 298 U.S. 238 (1936).
10. *Shreveport Rate Cases*, 234 U.S. 342 (1914).
11. *NLRB v. Jones & Laughlin Steel Corp.*, 301 U.S. 81 (1937)
12. *Wickard v. Filburn*, 317 U.S. at 125. See also *U.S. v. Lopez*, 514 U.S. 549 (1995).
13. *Id.*

relation to commerce, the *de minimis* character of individual instances arising under that statute is of no consequence."[14]

The commerce clause has become the battleground of Clean Water Act jurisdiction in recent years particularly with respect to whether commerce clause jurisdiction extends to isolated wetlands.[15] The fight began in earnest in 1990 with the Leslie Salt litigation. After five years of litigation, the Ninth Circuit squarely concluded that the presence of migratory birds was a sufficient basis for commerce clause jurisdiction over otherwise isolated wetlands.[16]

Meanwhile, in 1986, a Corps employee had detected that Hoffman Homes, Inc., had, without a permit, filled a one-acre clay-lined basin that frequently collected rain water and snow melt but was not connected to any body of water either on the surface or by groundwater.[17] Hoffman was fined $50,000 for this violation. The penalty was vacated upon the Seventh Circuit's rejection of EPA's argument that there was Clean Water Act jurisdiction because the area "could be used by migratory birds," requiring instead that there had to be evidence of actual use by migratory birds in order to support commerce clause jurisdiction.[18]

Shortly thereafter, the Fourth Circuit ordered a new trial in a criminal case, finding that the district court's instructions to the jury, that jurisdiction extended to wetlands that had no direct or indirect surface water connection to other waters of the United States, "intolerably stretches the ordinary meaning of the word 'adjacent' and the phrase 'waters of the United States' to include wetlands remote from any interstate or navigable waters."[19] The Seventh Circuit promptly disagreed, citing *Wickard v. Filburn*, and held that the commerce clause "authorizes the federal government to regulate activities whose effect on interstate commerce is substantial only in the aggregate."[20]

Then, in 2001, the U.S. Supreme Court ruled that the presence of migratory birds was not a sufficient basis for commerce clause jurisdiction.[21] The EPA's and the Corps's response was to issue a joint memorandum proposing that neither agency would assert jurisdiction over isolated wetlands that are both intrastate and nonnavigable where the sole basis for asserting jurisdiction would be the presence or potential presence of migratory birds.[22] The Corps and EPA subsequently did not amend their own regulations, although, in one case, the Corps withdrew its claim of jurisdiction over vernal pools because they are isolated wetlands.[23] Nonetheless a number of courts have maintained jurisdiction over nonadjacent wetlands where there is at least some arguable connection to navigable waters.[24]

In 2006, the U.S. Supreme Court decided two consolidated cases dealing with isolated wetlands that were not visited by migratory birds. *Rapanos v. U.S.*[25] involved a civil enforcement action for filling wetlands in the face of multiple cease and desist orders. *Carabell v. Army Corps of Engineers*[26] in-

14. *Maryland v. Wirtz*, 392 U.S. 183, 197 (1968).

15. The Corps's regulations define an isolated wetland as nontidal waters that lack a surface connection to navigable waters. 33 C.F.R. §330.2(e).

16. 55 F.3d 1388 (9th Cir. 1995). See also 51 Fed.Reg. 41217 (1986).

17. *Hoffman Homes, Inc. v. U.S. Environmental Protection Agency*, 999 F.2d 256 (7th Cir. 1993).

18. *Cf. Utah v. Marsh*, 740 F.2d 799 (9th Cir. 1984). (Commerce clause jurisdiction is proper because the wholly intrastate lake was "on the flyway of several species of migratory waterfowl which are protected under international treaties.")

19. *U.S. v. Wilson*, 133 F.3d 251 (4th Cir. 1997).

20. *Solid Waste Agency of Northern Cook County v. U.S. Army Corps of Engineers*, 191 F.3d 845 (7th Cir. 1998).

21. *Solid Waste Agency of Northern Cook County v. U.S. Army Corps of Engineers*, 531 U.S. 159 (2001). ("Permitting respondents to claim federal jurisdiction over ponds and mudflats falling within the 'Migratory Bird Rule' would result in a significant impingement of the States' traditional and primary power over land and water use.")

22. 68 Fed.Reg. 1991 (Jan. 15, 2003).

23. *Borden Ranch Partnership v. U.S. Army Corps of Engineers*, 261 F.3d 810 (9th Cir. 2001).

24. See, e.g., *Baccarat Fremont Developers, LLC v. Army Corps of Engineers*, 425 F.3d 1150, 1152, 1157 (9th Cir. 2005); *Save Our Sonoran, Inc. v. Flowers*, 408 F.3d 1113, 1118 (9th Cir. 2005); *Treacy v. Newdunn Associates, LLP*, 344 F.3d 407 (4th Cir. 2003); *U.S. v. Deaton*, 332 F.3d 698 (4th Cir. 2003); *Community Assn. for Restoration of Environment v. Henry Bosma Dairy*, 305 F.3d 943, 954-955 (9th Cir. 2002); *Headwaters, Inc. v. Talent Irrigation Dist.*, 243 F.3d 526, 534 (9th Cir. 2001).

25. *Rapanos v. U.S.*, __ U.S. __, 126 S.Ct. 2208 (2006).

26. 391 F.3d 704 (6th Cir. 2004).

volved the denial of a permit to fill a wetland separated from a ditch by a man-made berm that prevented water from flowing from the wetland to the ditch. The ditch itself ultimately connected to a navigable water.

Justices Antonia Scalia, John Roberts, Clarence Thomas, and Samuel Alito wrote a "plurality opinion," but Justice Anthony Kennedy delivered the controlling opinion. Although agreeing with the plurality that the case should be remanded, Justice Kennedy disagreed with the plurality's definition of "waters" as requiring a continuous surface-water connection to navigable waters. Justice Kennedy is satisfied that

> Consistent with SWANCC [Solid Waste Agency of Northern Cook County] and Riverside Bayview and with the need to give the term "navigable" some meaning, the Corps' jurisdiction over wetlands depends upon the existence of a significant nexus between the wetlands in question and navigable waters in the traditional sense. The required nexus must be assessed in terms of the statute's goals and purposes. Congress enacted the law to "restore and maintain the chemical, physical, and biological integrity of the Nation's waters," 33 U.S.C. § 1251(a), and it pursued that objective by restricting dumping and filling in "navigable waters," §§ 1311(a), 1362(12). With respect to wetlands, the rationale for Clean Water Act regulation is, as the Corps has recognized, that wetlands can perform critical functions related to the integrity of other waters-functions such as pollutant trapping, flood control, and runoff storage, 33 CFR § 320.4(b)(2). Accordingly, wetlands possess the requisite nexus, and thus come within the statutory phrase "navigable waters," if the wetlands, either alone or in combination with similarly situated lands in the region, significantly affect the chemical, physical, and biological integrity of other covered waters more readily understood as "navigable." When, in contrast, wetlands' effects on water quality are speculative or insubstantial, they fall outside the zone fairly encompassed by the statutory term "navigable waters."

The "continuous surface water connection" has already been rejected by the Ninth Circuit.[27] Northern California River Watch alleged that the City of Healdsburg was discharging sewage from its waste treatment plant without an NPDES permit into "Basalt Pond," an old rock quarry pit containing wetlands and open water that is separated from the Russian River by a man-made berm. There is no surface water connection between the Russian River and Basalt Pond, but water containing unnaturally high concentrations of chloride from the pond still seeped into the Russian River, a navigable-in-fact water.

Citing *Baccarat Fremont Developers, LLC v. U.S. Army Corps of Engineers*,[28] the Ninth Circuit first reiterated its holding that SWANCC did not overrule *United States v. Riverside Bayview Homes*,[29] with respect to jurisdiction over wetlands adjacent to navigable waters. The Ninth Circuit did find the "significant nexus" from the contaminated seepage out of the pond into the river. In other words, while a mere hydrologic connection may not be enough after *Rapanos*, assessing the seepage in terms of the Clean Water Act's goals and purposes to "restore and maintain the chemical, physical, and biological integrity of the Nation's waters," the Ninth Circuit reasoned that when pollution is actually transported to a navigable waterway, there will be jurisdiction under the Clean Water Act.

Similarly, in a criminal case before a District Court in Florida the defendants sought to suppress evidence obtained during a search of their property on the grounds that there was no jurisdiction under the Clean Water Act. In support of its request for search warrants, the EPA alleged that raw sewage was

---

27. *California River Watch v. City of Healdsburg*, 457 F.3d 1023 (9th Cir. 2006).
28. 425 F.3d 1150 (9th Cir. 2005).
29. 474 U.S. 121 (1985).

being knowingly discharged into a creek running behind the defendants' labor camp. The District Court had to determine whether the affidavits in support of the search warrant applications provided a sufficient basis for the magistrate to conclude that there was probable cause to believe that evidence of a violation of the Clean Water Act would be present at the defendants' labor camp. The EPA identified the creek running behind the labor camp as the headwaters of Cow Creek, which flows directly into the St. Johns River, a navigable-in-fact river.

The District Court found jurisdiction, noting that the plurality opinion in *Rapanos* still conceded that the discharge of any pollutant that naturally washes downstream likely violates the Clean Water Act even if the pollutants discharged from a point source do not emit "directly into" covered waters, but pass "through conveyances" in between, citing *United States v. Velsicol Chemical Corp.*[30] and *Sierra Club v. El Paso Gold Mines, Inc.*[31]

But when oil pollution never reached a navigable water because there was no flow at all in an intermittent stream, a district court in Texas found that there was no jurisdiction and refused to apply either the plurality's "continuous surface connection" or Justice Kennedy's "nexus requirement" and, instead, relied on prior Fifth Circuit case law requiring at a minimum the presence of water in a Clean Water Act case.[32]

In this case, Chevron operated a pipeline in a Texas oil field. The pipeline failed and 3,000 barrels of crude oil were discharged into an unnamed intermittent streambed. The government alleged jurisdiction over the streambed because, during times of flow, there was an unbroken surface water connection from the streambed into the Brazos River, a navigable waterway. However, there was no rain that summer, so there was no water flow in the streambed, and the oil did not travel beyond the original spill site. On that basis, the Court rejected jurisdiction under the Clean Water Act.

In yet a third variant approach, the First Circuit remanded *U.S. v. Johnson*[33] to allow the parties to develop additional evidence of a connection, or lack thereof, between cranberry bogs and the Weweantic River in Massachusetts. Similarly, the Seventh Circuit remanded *U.S. v. Gerke Excavating, Inc.*, to determine whether the requisite nexus existed.

The battle is far from over on this important issue. One thing is clear, however: In requiring the Corps to make individual jurisdictional determinations of allegedly isolated wetlands on a case-by-case basis, the time to obtain a permit will be significantly lengthened. And the courts have been left with no guidance on making jurisdictional determinations; consequently their results will be as inconsistent as has already been demonstrated by the handful of post-*Rapanos* decisions. It would appear, however, from the nearly two-hundred-year history of commerce clause cases, that a "cumulative effect" test may be the proper one, namely, will the elimination of this isolated wetland substantially impair the purposes of the Clean Water Act to restore and maintain the integrity of the Nation's waters?

30. 438 F.Supp. 945, 946-47 (W.D.Tenn.1976).
31. 421 F.3d 1133, 1137, 1141 (10th Cir. 2005).
32. *U.S. v. Chevron Pipe Line Company*, 437 F.Supp.2d 605 (N.D. Tex. 2006).
33. __ F.3d __, 2006 WL 3072145 (1st Cir. October 31, 2006).

Bibliography

Brinson, M. M. 1993. *A Hydrogeomorphic Classification for Wetlands.* Waterways Experiment Station Technical Report WRP-DE-4. Vicksburg, MS: U.S. Army Corps of Engineers. http://libweb.wes.army.mil/uhtbin/hyperion/TR-WRP-DE-4.pdf (accessed January 4, 2006).

Briuer, Elke. 1993. *Young Scientist's Introduction to Wetlands.* Wetlands Research and Technology Center, United States Army Corps of Engineers Waterways Experiment Station. http://el.erdc.usace.army.mil/wetlands/ysi.html (accessed July 14, 2005).

Clairain, E. J., Jr. 2002. "Hydrogeomorphic Approach to Assessing Wetland Functions: Guidelines for Developing Regional Guidebooks." Chapter 1 in *Introduction and Overview of the Hydrogeomorphic Approach.* Research and Development Center Report ERDC/EL TR-02-3. Vicksburg, MS: U.S. Army Corps of Engineers.

Cowardin, L. M., V. Carter, F. C. Golet, and E. T. LaRoe. 1979. *Classification of Wetlands and Deepwater Habitats of the United States.* Report FWS/OBS-79/31. Washington, DC: U.S. Department of the Interior, Fish and Wildlife Service.

Creature from the Black Lagoon. 1954. Hollywood, CA: Universal Studios.

Dahl, T. E. 1990. *Wetland Losses in the United States, 1780s to 1980s.* Washington, DC: U.S. Department of the Interior, Fish and Wildlife Service.

Dahl, T. E., and C. E. Johnson. 1991. *Status and Trends of Wetlands in the Conterminous United States Mid-1970s to Mid-1980s.* Washington DC: U.S. Department of the Interior, Fish and Wildlife Service.

Dunne, T., and L. B. Leopold. 1978. *Water in Environmental Planning.* New York: W. H. Freeman and Company.

Environmental Laboratory. 1987. *1987 Corps of Engineers Wetlands Delineation Manual.* Waterways Experiment Station Technical Report Y-87-1. Vicksburg, MS: US Army Corps of Engineers.

Helfgott, T. B., M. W. Lefor, and W. C. Kennard. 1973. *Proceedings: First Wetland Conference, June 20, 1973, at Storrs, Connecticut.* Report 21. Storrs, CT: University of Connecticut Institute of Water Resources. http://digitalcollections.uconn.edu/iwr/0021WETL.PDF (accessed November 3, 2005).

Institute for Wetland & Environmental Education & Research. n.d. *Wetland Primer.* www.wetlanded.com/database/Primer.cfm?OrderID=344 (accessed November 3, 2005).

Kent, D. M., ed. 1994. *Applied Wetlands Science and Technology.* Boca Raton, FL: Lewis Publishers.

Kollmorgen Corporation. 1988. *Munsell Soil Color Charts.* Baltimore, MD: Macbeth Division of Kollmorgen Corporation.

Lefor, M. W., and W. C. Kennard. 1977. *Inland Wetland Definitions.* Report 28. Storrs, CT: University of Connecticut Institute of Water Resources. http://digitalcollections.uconn.edu/iwr/0028INLA.PDF (accessed November 3, 2005).

Liebowitz, S. G. 2003. "Isolated Wetlands and Their Functions: and Ecological Perspective." *Wetlands* 23:3.

Mitsch, W. J., and J. G. Gosselink. *Wetlands*. 2nd ed. New York: Van Nostrand Reinhold Co., 1993.

National Audubon Society. 1993. *Saving Wetlands: A Citizens Guide for Action in the Mid-Atlantic Region*. Camp Hill, PA: National Audubon Society.

National Research Council Committee on Characterization of Wetlands. 1995. *Wetlands: Characteristics and Boundaries*. Washington, DC: National Academy Press.

Natureserve.org. 2005. *Biodiversity Values of Geographically Isolated Wetlands in the United States*. http://nature serve.org/publicaitns/isolatedwetlands.jsp (accessed April 18, 2006).

Ramsar Convention on Wetlands. 2002. *Wetlands: Water, Life, and Culture*. Eighth Meeting of the Conference of the Contracting Parties to the Convention on Wetlands, Valencia, Spain, 18–26 November 2002. Gland, Switzerland: Ramsar Convention Bureau. www.ramsar.org/cop8/cop8_conf_rpt_e.htm (accessed November 3, 2005).

———. 1971. Article 1.1. Gland, Switzerland: Ramsar Convention Bureau. http://www.ramsar.org/index_very_key_docs.htm (accessed November 3, 2005).

Reed, P. B., Jr. 1988 and 1993. *National List of Plant Species that Occur in Wetlands: Northwest (Region 9)*. Biological Report 88, and Supplement. Washington, DC: U.S. Department of the Interior, Fish and Wildlife Service.

Reppert, R. T., W. Siglio, E. Stakhiv, L. Messman, and C. Meyers. 1979. *Wetland Values: Concepts and Methods for Wetlands Evaluation*. Research Report 70-R-1. Fort Belvoir, VA: U.S. Army Corps of Engineers Institute for Water Resources.

Schot, P. P. 1999. "Wetlands." In *Environmental Management in Practice*. Vol. 3, ed. B. Nath, et al., 62–85. London & New York: Routledge, 1999.

Shaw, S. P., and C. G. Fredine. 1956. *Wetlands of the United States, Their Extent, and Their Value for Waterfowl and Other Wildlife*. Circular 39. Washington, DC: U.S. Department of the Interior, Fish and Wildlife Service.

Smardon, R. C. 1988. "Aesthetic, Recreational, Landscape Values of Urban Wetlands." In *Urban Wetlands: Proceedings of the National Wetland Symposium, June 26–29, 1988, Oakland, California*, ed. J. A. Kusler, S. Daly, and G. Brooks, 92–103. Berne, NY: Association of Wetland Managers.

Tarnocai, C. 1980. "Canadian Wetland Registry." In *Proceedings: Workshop on Canadian Wetlands*, ed. C. D. A. Rubec and F. C. Pollett, 9–30. Ottawa: Environment Canada Ecological Land Classification Series No. 12.

Tiner, R. W. 1989. "Wetlands of Rhode Island" In *National Wetlands Inventory*, appendix. Newton Corner, MA: U.S. Fish and Wildlife Service.

Tiner, R. W., H. C. Bergquist, G. P. DeAlessio, and M. J. Starr. 2002. *Geographically Isolated Wetlands: A Preliminary Assessment of Their Characteristics and Status in Selected Areas of the United States*. Hadley, MA: U.S. Department of the Interior, Fish and Wildlife Service, Northeast Region.

United States Army Corps of Engineers. 1998. *Recognizing Wetlands: An Informational Pamphlet*. www.usace .army.mil/inet/functions/cw/cecwo/reg/rw-bro.htm (accessed July 14, 2005, and October 31, 2005).

United States Department of Agriculture National Resources Conservation Service. 1996. Keys to Soil Taxonomy, Seventh Edition, US Government Printing Office, Washington, D.C.

United States Department of Agriculture Natural Resources Conservation Service. 2005. *Living in Harmony with Wetlands*. www.nrcs.usda.gov/feature/highlights/wetlands/ (accessed October 31, 2005).

United States Department of Agriculture National Resources Conservation Service. 2006. *The PLANTS Database, Version 3.5*. Data compiled from various sources by Mark W. Skinner. Baton Rouge, LA: National Plant Data Center. http://plants.usda.gov (accessed January 6, 2006).

United States Environmental Protection Agency. N.d. *America's Wetlands: Our Vital Link between Land and Water*. Washington, DC: U.S. Environmental Protection Agency Office of Wetlands, Oceans and Watersheds & Wetlands Division. www.epa.gov/owow/wetlands/ (accessed September 6, 2005).

United States Fish and Wildlife Service. 1976. *Existing State and Local Wetland Surveys (1965–1975), Volume II, Narrative*. Washington, DC: U.S. Fish and Wildlife Service Office of Biological Services Report.

Wakeley, James W. 2004. *Identifying Wetlands: A Tutorial.* Vicksburg MS: U.S. Army Corps of Engineers Research and Development Center. http://el.erdc.usace.army.mil/wrap/tools.html (accessed July 14, 2005).

Whigham, D. F., C. Chitterling, and B. Palmer. 1988. "Impacts of Freshwater Wetlands on Water Quality: A Landscape Perspective." *Environmental Management* 12, no. 5 (September): 663–71.

Index

About the Authors

Theda Braddock works for Westervelt Ecological Services, LLC, on natural resource damage restoration projects. She is admitted to practice in California, Maryland, Massachusetts, and Washington. She is also admitted before the United States District Courts for the Northern District of California, District of Maryland, and District of Massachusetts as well as the Fourth and Ninth Circuit Courts of Appeals, the United States Court of Federal Claims, and the United States Supreme Court.

Ms. Braddock is the author of the *Washington Environmental Law Handbook* (2005), *Wetlands Regulation: Case Law, Interpretation & Commentary* (2003), and *Wetlands: An Introduction to Ecology, the Law, and Permitting* (1995). She also writes the wetland law update for the California Bar's Environmental Law Section newsletter and for the Washington Bar's Environmental and Land Use Law newsletter.

Ms. Braddock attended the Great Books Program at St. Johns College in Annapolis, Maryland, and received her B.A. from Mills College in Oakland, California. She received her Juris Doctor from Golden Gate University in San Francisco, California.

When not practicing law, Ms. Braddock is a sailor. She has taught sailing for the Command, Seamanship, and Navigation Training Squadron at the U.S. Naval Academy and is qualified as an Offshore Skipper by the U.S. Naval Sailing Squadron.

Lisa Berntsen is a certified professional wetland scientist and has performed wetland delineations, mitigation plans, and Corps of Engineers fill and restoration permits throughout the Pacific Northwest and Alaska. She focuses on complex projects that involve natural resources investigations and permitting. She is a principal at Geo-Engineers, Inc., a national earth science and technology firm.